"THERE BEFORE YOU"

THE TRAVELLER'S
HISTORY OF BURMA

GERRY ABBOTT

Orchid Press
Bangkok

"THERE BEFORE YOU"
THE TRAVELLER'S HISTORY OF BURMA
Gerry Abbott
Hon. Fellow, School of Education
University of Manchester

First Published 1998
Reprinted 1999
Copyright © 1998 Orchid Press
Design & Layout: Win Tun (RBG)

"THERE BEFORE YOU" is a collection of books about what
you can see *there before you* as seen and experienced by
travellers who were *there before you* ...

For the peoples of Burma

Arrangements have been made for the royalties
on all sales of this book to be credited to
PROSPECT BURMA, a non-political educational
trust for the support of displaced Burmese
students.

Orchid Press
98/13, Soi Apha Phirom, Ratchada Road,
Chatuchak, Bangkok 10900 Thailand
Tel: (662)930-0149
Fax: (662)930-5646
http://redfrog.norconnect.no/~wop

ISBN: 974-8299-28-7

Acknowledgements

For much of the information relayed by this book, I am indebted to the staff and facilities of John Rylands Library (University of Manchester) and to the Oriental and India Office Collections (The British Library). In the latter case, I also owe much to the encouragement of Patricia Herbert, whose bibliography (World Bibliographical Series, Vol.132, Oxford: Clio Press) was always by my side.

For illustrations I relied partly upon those appearing in nineteenth-century books on Burma; partly upon the resources of the Oriental and India Office Collections, London, and the Chester Beatty Library, Dublin; partly upon the personal library of Hallvard Kuløy; and partly upon my own photographs. For technical help, I am grateful to David Griffiths of the Faculty of Education, University of Manchester.

My book has been four years in the making. For their moral support during that time, and for their very helpful comments on and corrections to the original typescript, I must thank Colleen Beresford and my wife Khin Thant Han. It goes without saying that I am responsible for any remaining mistakes.

A note on spellings

Western travellers to Burma have always found that the language presented great difficulties, not least in the representation of Burmese words in Roman characters. The Italians spelt the words in accordance with the conventions of their own language, the English in accordance with theirs, and so on. Where I think a traveller's spelling might puzzle the reader, I draw attention to the matter. As for my own practice, I have departed from *convention* where *common sense* and *phonetic considerations* seemed to demand.

1 *Convention*

There is a convention by which syllables that sound like JEE and CHEE are written as g*yi(gyee)* and k*yi(kyee)*. I do not depart from this. Similarly, although the current regime wishes the country to be known abroad as *Myanmar* I retain *Burma,* and place-names are spelt as they were before the introduction of the regime's new and cumbersome system of transliteration.

2 *Common sense*

The town of *Yangon* was not *Rangoon* until the British spelt it in that way. I therefore retain the original form up to that point in history. Secondly, since the reader meeting a personal or place name for the first time in print is often unsure of how to say it, I have used hyphens in such names where they first appear; for example, *Ba-gyi-daw* shows, if nothing else, that the name is *not* pronounced as *Bag-yid-aw*.

3 *Phonetic considerations*

I have used an accent where it seemed advisable to indicate stress. The accents in *Pegú* and *Pagán*, for instance, show that these places are not pronounced as PEAgoo or like the English adjective 'pagan'. The use of initial *hp, hs, ht* simply indicates aspiration: *hpaya* and *hsaya* have the same initial sounds as *pepper* and *salt* respectively and *hti* is pronounced exactly like the English word *tea*.

Sources

In the following pages I always provide the source of a single quoted passage, but do not supply page numbers; also, where there is a *series* of quotations from the same work I show the source only after the first of the series. This is to avoid cluttering the page with brackets, numbers, *op.cits* and so on — features which would look too formal for my purposes. The bibliographies give full details of all works quoted or consulted.

Contents

List of Illustrations and Maps

Plates:

Roof of Arakan Pagoda
© Gerry Abbott

The Mahamuni Image; the daily bathing, 1982
© C. Leslie

A Burmese Lady, mid-19ᵗʰ century
(A. Fytche : Burma past and present London, 1878)

The ruins of Ayuthaya
© Gerry Abbott

Arrival of British flotilla 1824
(Joseph Moore : *Eighteen Views taken at and near Rangoon.* London, 1825.)

Breaching a Stockade (Moore)

Approach to Shwe Dagon (Moore)

British Officers at Shwe Dagon (Moore)

The Palace at Amarapura
Watercolour by Colesworthy Grant © The British Library

Burmans on U Bein Bridge
Watercolour by Colesworthy Grant © The British Library

King Mindon
(Henry Yule : *Narrative of a Mission...to the Court of Ava in 1855* London)

Image of Mahagiri Nat, Pagan, c. 1826
(R.C. Temple : *The Thirty-Seven Nats* London. 1906)

`The Centre of the Universe` 1886
© The British Library

A corner of the Palace, 1886
© The British Library

Thibaw leaves Mandalay : A Burmese view
© Chester Beatty Library

The Shwe Dagon : Pyramid of Fire
© Gerry Abbott

In a Burmese Monastery
(Fytche)

The Ava Bridge
© Gerry Abbott

Boat on the Irrawaddy

PREFACE

In the Prefaces of two old books about Burma I found the following remarks:

The story is told of a Member of Parliament who did not know Burma from Bermuda.

(Winston, 1892)

.. finding how little was known at home of the beautiful country and interesting people of Burma,
I undertook the task of writing a book on the subject.

(Hart, 1897)

Returning from Burma almost a century after those books were published, I asked an English antiquarian bookseller if he had any books about that country. He ran his fingers along a shelf, shook his head and said, "Sorry". The shelf was labelled 'West Indies'. It is not only Burma's geographical position that many British people are uncertain about; finding that most of my acquaintances knew almost nothing about its history before the Second World War - more justifiably so in this case, because for many years no history of Burma has been published - I decided, like Mrs. Hart, to undertake the task of writing a book on the subject.

History books can make heavy reading--sometimes literally so; traditional guidebooks are lighter but tend to be superficial, so that we have difficulty in conjuring the past to life; and travel books, though more lively, offer only one person's view of a place at one given time, and we may learn more about that person than about the place and its inhabitants. I tried to avoid these drawbacks as far as possible by selecting a large number of short eyewitness accounts that span almost six centuries, and linking these 'first-person' sequences with a minimum of 'third-person' historical narrative. By using this anthological method I ran the risk of being partial in both senses of the word, in that the result might be *incomplete* or *biased* or both; so I must stress firstly that I did not attempt to write an exhaustive history and secondly that I have tried to counter the cultural prejudice found in many of the British sources I have used. I have also included, in various 'boxes' some cultural information which I hope will contribute to a better understanding of Burma and its peoples.

This book is addressed to anyone interested in travelling to Burma. I have assumed that the experience of seeing what is *there before you* will be enriched by the views of those who have been *there before you*. I have several reasons for closing the book with the coming of Independence in 1948, not least among which is the great complexity of events since then - a complexity which I hope will be faithfully recorded by a Burmese citizen, rather than by a British Burmophile.

G.W.A.
Manchester.

INTRODUCTION
BURMA BEFORE AVA

In difficult terrain - whether mountainous, jungle-covered or swampy - rivers have always been relied upon as major channels for communication and cooperation, for exploration and trade, for attack and retreat, and for migration. Southeast Asia's chief waterways all flow down from the vast Himalayan snows of Tibet into Yunnan. Just to the east of Burma's northern tip their courses converge into a corridor less than sixty miles wide where, along four roughly parallel gorges, an incredible volume of water rumbles southward.

The easternmost river, the Jinsha Jiang, then zigzags eastwards across China to complete a journey of 3,430 miles to the East China Sea, and is better known in the West as the Yangtze. Through the neighbouring gorge flows the Lancang Jiang. It skirts Burma and goes on to encounter Laos, Thailand, Cambodia and Vietnam, ending its 2,600 mile course in the South China Sea not far from Saigon; this river we know as the Mekong. The third gorge carries the Nu Jiang, much shorter but still in the top dozen of the world's longest rivers. It rushes south for a few hundred miles before cutting into Burmese territory and reaches the Gulf of Martaban after a trip of 1,800 miles all told; this is the Salween.

The fourth river is the longer of the Irrawaddy's two main tributaries. Slicing westwards into Burma, it becomes known as the Nmai Hka ('Bad River') because of its turbulent waters; the other tributary, Mali Hka ('Big River'), flows from a glacier where Burma borders with India, a little south of Tibet. What makes the Irrawaddy remarkable is the fact that, although it is only half as long as the Mekong, sizeable vessels can steam inland for a thousand miles up to Bhamo, not far from the Chinese border, whereas even the mighty Yangtze is only navigable for 580 miles. These rivers are important not only because they were used by modern explorers and traders but also because it was down these and other such routes that, more than two thousand years ago, successive waves of migrant peoples began to move south.

The original inhabitants of what we now call Burma* were probably a negrito people similar to the Andaman islanders, but they have left no trace. The first immigrant group to arrive seems to have been the Pyu; then came

---

* The official name is currently Myanmar, but this name is still not widely used. It is a romanised version of what the Burmese have traditionally called their own country; but the final letter is extraneous and (for Americans especially) is misleading as a guide to the pronunciation of the word, which does not end with a r- *sound.*

the Mon, or Talaing, who still cling precariously to their culture and language; the Shan, ethnically very numerous and widespread - *Shan, Siam* and *Assam* being at root the same word; the Karen; and various Tibeto-Burman tribes which included the Myanma, or Burmans, who had been so tyrannised by the people of Yunnan that they fled south to the hot malarial lowlands. Some groups - the Chin, Kachin, Wa, Palaung and others - remained hill peoples, perhaps because the fertile plains were already occupied.

The Irrawaddy basin separates two mountainous ranges that branch southwards from the Himalayan heights, the range to the west dividing the narrow coastal strip of Arakan from central Burma. Unlike their Burman neighbours, the Arakanese were of necessity builders and users of seagoing craft, and their kingdom was open to communication by sea as well as by land with India and Ceylon. It was almost certainly through Arakan that Buddhism came to central Burma, bringing with it certain Brahminical beliefs and practices that were adopted by the Burmese Court and have not yet been totally discarded. Also through Arakan - but a millennium later - came Islam, creating in Burma a large minority group which from time to time has been a focus of Burman resentment. Almost another millennium was to pass before the first Christian missionaries appeared. Unable to make significant inroads into Buddhism and Islam, Christianity took root mainly among the hill peoples, especially the Karen, in the eastern mountain range that formed a natural border between Burma and Siam.

Up to the arrival of the Burmans well over a thousand years ago the dominant group seems to have been the Pyu, whose capital was near Pyé (Prome) - at that time much nearer to the sea than now because the Irrawaddy had not yet formed such an extensive delta. In 832 the Pyu were dealt a heavy blow by the forces of a Nanchao chieftain who took three thousand captives back to Yunnan. Although their language survived until the thirteenth century other aspects of Pyu culture merged into that of the Burmans, who were by now the most organised and powerful of the lowland peoples. Some way upriver there was a rapidly-developing cluster of villages that grew into the city of Pagán, which became not only an extensive and architecturally magnificent centre for the Burmans themselves, but also the international capital of Theravada Buddhism.

It is tempting to dwell on the wonders of Pagán, whose pagoda-building programmes over three centuries were so massive that, according to some authorities, the deforestation necessary for the firing of the brick kilns may have helped create Burma's 'dry zone'. But we must pass on to the time when this, the most illustrious period in Burma's history was brought to a shameful close by enemies from the north. By this time the Nanchao kingdom in Yunnan had been conquered by the Mongols, who were sweeping all before them. In 1273 Kublai Khan, emperor of all the territories between the Danube and the East China Sea, sent an ambassador to Pagán, whose self-indulgent and self-important king Nara-thiha-paté took offence at the envoy's failure to defer sufficiently and ordered the execution of the whole party. The Mongol emperor showed some forbearance; but when his grandson finally brought an army over the northern passes and descended on Pagán, the king fled downriver to Pyé. The sacking of the city in 1287 meant that, although Pagán continued as a principality owing tribute to the emperor until 1555, it would no longer play an important part in Burma's history.

To escape the attentions of the Mongols, considerable numbers of Shans had already started moving south and entering Burma, and even before the fall of Pagán there was a sizeable Shan population at Myint-saing further upstream. Here, fleeing from a dangerous family dispute, a Shan princeling arrived and prospered. Each of his three sons became powerful and each governed a district, and an unsettled period ensued when the king nominally reigning in Pagán was disposed of, one of the brothers died and the youngest, Thiha-thu, then murdered the other. Needing now to establish his own city and knowing that the fertile delta to the south was controlled by a hostile chieftain, Thihathu could have chosen the obvious site: the spot where the river Myit-nge flowed into the great Irrawaddy, bringing cargoes of rice from the rich paddy-fields of Kyaukse. But the court Brahmins found the omens for this site inauspicious, and instead a city called Pinya was built a few miles north of Myint-saing. One of Thihathu's two sons was an adopted child and the two inevitably quarrelled over their inheritance, so each was given a province to rule; but the natural son eventually set up an independent throne at Sagaing in 1315. His unstable dynasty lasted only until 1364, when a member of the family called Thado-min-bya had all possible contenders for the throne, whether in Sagaing or Pinya, murdered. This time (the omens by now being auspicious) the obvious site was selected and Thadominbya established Ava* as his capital city on the southern edge of a lake created by the Irrawaddy when it is in full spate.

For this brief and unsettled period, then, Sagaing actually preceded Ava as a capital; but four centuries were to pass before it once again became a Burmese capital, and even then it would remain so for only three years. Its significance is, as we shall see, more spiritual than temporal, more aesthetic than strategic. It was Ava which came to represent the Burman nation - so much so, in fact, that even when the court moved to Amarapura and Mandalay it was still known as the Court of Ava, and early western visitors called the Irrawaddy itself the Ava River.

Although much of the early part of this book concentrates on the area around Ava it must be remembered that there were other kingdoms nearby and that bloody conflicts, both within and between them, were frequent. Arakan to the west has already been mentioned; to the south-east, Toungoo was a restless and sometimes treacherous neighbour; and Martaban, guarding the mouth of the Salween, was often mentioned in early western accounts. But the most powerful of these kingdoms after the fall of Pagán was Pegú, whose Mon king was often in conflict with his Burman cousins to the north. He controlled the Irrawaddy delta region, and the state of conflict made it difficult (to put it mildly) to travel up the river to Ava - the most

---

* Ava *is a westernised form of the Burmese name, which means 'entrance to the lake'.* In-wa *would be a more accurate transcription.*

convenient route. From the fifteenth century onwards many a merchant venturer - Italian, Portuguese, Dutch and English - set out for the Burman capital but failed to reach it; yet the very first European account on record is the story of one who succeeded, probably because he did *not* use the obvious route. We shall see what he had to say and then look at the accounts of some of the many who managed to get no farther than Pegú, before concentrating upon those few miles of history-drenched riverbank where, curving like a giant aorta through the Burman heartland, the Irrawaddy successively passes Mingun, Mandalay, Amarapura, Sagaing and Ava. Of these, only Sagaing and Ava were in existence when the first Europeans came to Burma.

Pagoda at Pagan

CHAPTER 1
Roofs of Gold
Pegú versus Ava, 1364 - 1752

> *Which pillage they with merry march bring home*
> *To the tent-royal of their emperor:*
> *Who, busied in his majesty, surveys*
> *The singing masons building roofs of gold...*
> William Shakespeare, *King Henry V, ii. III.*

The geographers of ancient Greece and the merchants of Rome knew of the existence of what we call Burma, yet from the end of the Roman Empire all knowledge of the country seems to have been lost to Europeans for a thousand years. We know that a Moslem merchant called Soliman was trading along its coast at the beginning of the ninth century, but not until 1435 A.D. do we find any record of a European setting foot on Burmese soil. The Venetian merchant Marco Polo had, it is true, reported on a battle in which the Burmese were defeated by Mongol forces in 1277, but there is no evidence that he actually entered Burma. As far as we know, then, the first European on the scene was another merchant of Venice called Nicolo di Conti, who in 1435 sailed into the mouth of a large river on the Arakan coast, worked his way upstream for six days and came to 'a very large city'.

Nicolo's account was recorded in Latin and in the 'third person' for the following reason. When he returned to Venice after many years abroad, he went to seek absolution from the Pope because at one point in his travels he had renounced his faith in order to save his own life; and his petition was granted only on condition that he narrate his adventures to the Pope's secretary. His story is therefore to all intents and purposes a 'first person' account. In this extract from the English translation, we find Nicolo leaving the large Arakanese city and heading eastwards. (The Victorian editor, evidently considering the subject of the second paragraph unsuitable for anyone lacking a classical education, left it in Latin. I am assured that my translation is acceptable.)

Quitting this city he travelled through mountains void of all habitations for the space of seventeen days, and then through open plains for fifteen days more, at the end of which time he arrived at a river larger than the Ganges, which is called by the inhabitants Dava (Ava). Having sailed up this river for the space of a month he arrived at a city more noble than all the others, called Ava, and the circumference of which is fifteen miles.

(Nicolo) says that in this one city there are numerous shops... He says that in these, and sold only by women, there are things called sonalia *- named, I suppose, from their sound - made of gold, silver or bronze in the shape of a small nut; it is to these women that a man goes before he takes a wife, otherwise he is rejected from marriage. The skin of the male organ (the story continues) is cut and raised a little, and between the skin and the flesh are inserted some of these* sonalia, *as many as twelve or more according to local preference. The skin is then sewn up, and in a few days it is healed. This is done to satisfy the women's lust because, from these 'nuts' and from the swelling of the organ, women achieve the utmost pleasure. The members of many men as they walk along tinkle loudly enough to be heard as they get bumped by their legs. Nicolo was continually urged to undergo this by women who ridiculed him over the smallness of his member, but he was unwilling that pain for him should be a source of pleasure to others.*

(Major, 1857)

The Pope's secretary may have considered this mariner's tale to be a tall story, but Nicolo's details are accurate enough when he goes on to describe how wild elephants were captured and tamed in that part of the world. So is his description of some of the region's fauna:

This country produces frightful serpents without feet, as thick as a man, and six cubits in length. The inhabitants eat them roasted, and hold them in great esteem as food. They also eat a kind of red ant, of the size of a small crab, which they consider a great delicacy seasoned with pepper.

There is here also an animal which has a head resembling that of a pig, a tail like that of an ox, and on his forehead a horn similar to that of the unicorn, but shorter, being about a cubit in length. It resembles the elephant in size and colour, with which it is constantly at war. It is said that its horn is an antidote against poisons, and is on that account much esteemed.

Pythons in modern Burma have certainly been known to swallow a man whole and to reach a length of about ten metres - even longer than 'six cubits'; there is also a species of large red ant called *hka-chin-nee* that is still eaten in Burma, mainly as a digestive; and it is known that the Greater one-horned rhinoceros was once common in the area. We have no reason therefore to doubt Nicolo's story about the *sonalia* or to suppose that he was pulling the devout secretary's leg. Besides, later travellers corroborate what he says on that subject. *(See box on p. 3)*

(See box on p. 3)

༄༅༄༅༄༅

Since no European had yet discovered the sea-route around Africa, mariners as well as other travellers bound for the east journeyed through the Middle East and then circumnavigated India. Tucked up in the Bay of Bengal, Burma lay outside the main shipping routes to the East; and tucked

'Sonalia'

It seems unlikely that Nicolo di Conti was merely pulling the Papal Secretary's leg, for his account is supported by other travellers. More than a hundred and fifty years after Nicolo's stay in Ava, Ralph Fitch reported a similar practice in Pegú and noted that among others Antonio Galvão, a Portuguese governor in the Moluccas, east of Borneo, had recorded the same custom. Moreover, a few years after Fitch's visit to Pegú, a Florentine merchant passing through Indo-China also came across the practice and on his return to Tuscany reported it in detail. Francesco Carletti's original manuscript *Ragionamento del mio viaggio intorno al mondo* is lost, the most accurate surviving version probably being a manuscript copy, *Codice 1331 (T.3.22)*, in the Biblioteca Angelica, Rome.

Nevertheless, there is just enough similarity between the accounts, especially between those of di Conti and Carletti, to make one suspicious. We have seen di Conti's description; here is what Fitch had to say about the custom as practised in what are now Burma, Laos and Siam:

> *They cut the skinne and so put them in, one into one side and another into the other side; which they doe when they bee five and twentie or thirtie yeeres old, and at their pleasure they take one or more of them out as they thinke good. When they be married the Husband is for every Child which his Wife hath, to put in one untill hee come to three, and then no more: for they say the women doe desire them. (...) The bunches aforesaid bee of divers sorts: the least be as bigge as a little Walnut, and very round: the greatest are as bigge as a little Hens egge: some are of Brasse, and some of Silver: but those of silver bee for the King and his Noblemen. These are gilded and made with great cunning, and ring like a little bell. There are some made of Lead, which they call Selwy, because they ring but little: and these be of lesser price for the poorer sort. The King sometimes taketh his out, and giveth them to his Noblemen as a great gift: and because hee hath used them, they esteeme them greatly. They will put one in and heale up the place in seven or eight dayes.*
>
> *(Purchas, X)*

And here is Carletti, describing a custom that the Siamese 'have taken from the people of Pegú, a kingdom now destroyed by the King of Siam':

> *Those people, using an ancient invention designed by a queen to rule out and render impossible the practicing of venery in illicit parts of the body even with men, ordered that each man must have stitched between the skin and the flesh of his member two or three rattles as large as large hazelnuts, these made in round or oval shape. And in these rattles - which I have seen made of gold - there is a pellet of iron. When these rattles are moved, they give off a dull sound because they are without holes, being like two shells fastened together delicately and masterfully. (...)*
>
> *And these rattles, placed, as I have said, under the skin, which is then sewn together and allowed to heal, have the result of enlarging the member, as anyone can imagine. And the women desire them for these reasons and others that are to be thought of rather than spoken, as being helpful to pleasure. (...) And this is confirmed by Nicolò de' Conti, who, during his voyages, which he described in the year 1444 by command of Pope Eugenius IV, says.....*
>
> *But I brought some of these rattles as proof, and they have also been taken to Holland by those who travel in those regions. And it is a certain thing and absolutely true that this diabolic invention was made and is used by the women of that country.*
>
> *(Carletti, 1965)*

These samples, however, would surely have been accepted 'as proof' only if they had still been *in situ*!

also inside a horseshoe of high ridges, it remained less visited by western traders than many more distant places. Not all of these merchants were from western Europe, however. In 1470 or very soon thereafter a Russian called Nikitin went down the Volga to the Caspian, across Persia to the Gulf, and then on to India by sea. From Ceylon he sailed north and east across the Bay of Bengal to Burma. At about this time Queen Shin-saw-bu, having retired to Dagon from her Mon capital Pegú, was erecting a splendid gilded pagoda to encase an old stupa that enshrined some relics of the Gaudama Buddha; but Nikitin makes no mention of the Shwe Dagon, tells us only that Pegú was 'no inconsiderable port', and does not mention Ava at all.

Setting out twenty-five years later, however, a Genoese merchant named Hieronimo di Santo Stefano reached Burma and left a much more substantial account. Travelling via the Nile, the Red Sea and Aden, he sailed round India and from Burdwan in Bengal and made the crossing to the Burmese coast. Like many other foreign visitors of that period and for a long time to come, Hieronimo and his companions fell foul of what today might be called an institutionalised system of obstruction and bribery, as he now explains.

We find him leaving Burdwan:

We departed thence ... and after twenty days reached a great city called Pegú. This part is called Lower India. Here is a great lord, who possesses more than ten thousand elephants, and every year he breeds five hundred of them. This country is distant fifteen days' journey by land from another, called Ava, in which grow rubies and many other precious stones. Our wish was to go to this place, but at that time the two princes were at war, so that no one was allowed to go from the one place to the other. Thus we were compelled to sell the merchandise which we had in the said city of Pegú, which were of such a sort that only the lord of the city could purchase them. He is an idolater, like the before-mentioned. To him, therefore, we sold them.The price amounted to two thousand ducats, and as we wished to be paid we were compelled, by reason of the troubles and intrigues occasioned by the aforesaid war, to remain there a year and a half, all which time we had daily to solicit at the house of the said lord....

Four years before Hieronimo's arrival in Burma a fellow Genoese, thinking the earth was much smaller than it is, had set out across the Atlantic and reached what he thought was Southeast Asia - 'the Indies'; and it was only two years after Hieronimo's arrival that Vasco da Gama discovered the sea route to the real (not the West) Indies by rounding the Cape of Good Hope in 1498. Soon, eastbound voyagers were confirming much of what Marco Polo had said two centuries earlier, the truth of which had been doubted by many. From now on, Burma's contact with Europeans would increase as first Portuguese then Dutch and English merchantmen arrived in search of a fortune, and that contact would continue to be dominated by the profit motive. Though this meeting of cultures did not lead to slaughter on the scale of that inflicted by the Spaniards upon native Americans there was nonetheless an uneasy meeting of two world views each of which was arrogant in its assumption of inherent superiority, and eventually the presence of growing numbers of merchant venturers and mercenaries, many of them Portuguese, did lead to violence on one or two occasions.

The Portuguese did not crowd out the merchants of Venice, however; three of these - Varthema, Fedrici and Balbi - provide useful descriptions of Pegú and Lower Burma, but not of Ava. If we bear in mind the red tape and extortionate Customs practices in the ports; if we add to this the fact that it took six weeks, sometimes two months, to sail upstream as far as Ava; and if we remember that the various kingdoms were in an almost continuous state of war; then it is not surprising that the Kingdom of Ava, the City of Gems, remained insulated from the outside world.

Ludovico di Varthema arrived in Burma ten years after Hieronimo and tried to sail upriver to Ava. Giving up after only three days because the interior was in such turmoil, he too was obliged to do his trading in Pegú, where he met King Bin-nya-ran and sold him some coral. Of the king he says:

> ..he wears more rubies on him than the value of a very large city, and he wears them all on his toes. And on his legs he wears certain great rings of gold, all full of the most beautiful rubies; also his arms and his fingers are full. His ears hang down half a palm, through the great weight of the many jewels he wears there, so that seeing the person of the king by a light at night, he shines so much that he appears to be a sun.
>
> (Badger, 1863)

That last touch smacks of sycophancy, and Ludovico may have been reflecting the conventional Court flattery rather than simply describing what he saw. The turmoil upcountry was part of a two-year-old war with Ava. Although King Binnyaran professed to be very short of cash because of it, he paid Ludovico with several handfuls of rubies from the mines of 'Capelan' that lay to the north of Ava. Of the city of Pegú Ludovico tells us little other than that it was walled and had 'good houses and Palaces built of stone with lime'.

Not long after King Binnyaran died, the city found itself under attack by the new young king of Toungoo, Tabin-shwe-hti. The Portuguese, who had established a 'factory' (trading-post) at the Pegúan port of Martaban, summoned a galleon from Goa; but even with the help of these allies the Pegúans could not save their city. In 1540 Tabinshwehti, now King of Pegú, began a process of empire-building that was continued by his successor Bayin-naung until the borders of Burma stood within what we now know as India, China, Laos and Thailand. Ava had become subject to Pegú, which flourished as never before and attracted more and more trade. The best extant description of this thriving capital is provided by yet another merchant of Venice called Cesare Fedrici (spelt *Caesar Fredericke* by

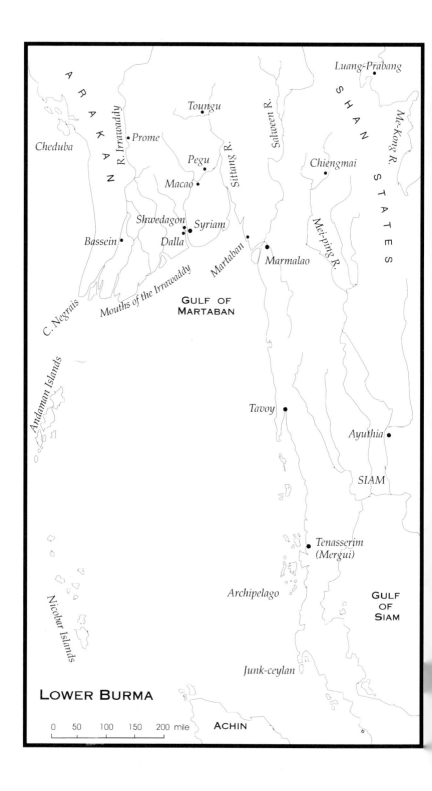

LOWER BURMA

0   50   100   150   200 mile

English translators). Cesare describes a system of town planning that was already traditional (*See "The Asian Walled City" p. 22*): a palace standing within a walled and moated fortress that is surrounded by extensive suburbs. The year is 1567.

> By the helpe of God we came safe to Pegú, which are two Cities, the old and the new, in the old Citie are the Merchant strangers, and Merchants of the Countrie, for there are the greatest doings and the greatest trade. This Citie is not very great, but it hath very great Suburbs. Their houses be made with canes, and covered with leaves, or with straw, but the Merchants have all one house or Magason, which they call Godon*, which is made of brickes, and there they put all their goods of any value, to save them from the often mischances that there happen to houses made of such stuffe. In the new Citie is the Palace of the King, and his abiding place with all his Barons and Nobles, and other Gentlemen; and in the time that I was there, they finished the building of the new Citie: it is a great Citie, very plaine and flat, and four square, walled round about, and with Ditches that compasse the Walls about with water, in which Ditches are many Crocodiles. It hath no Draw-bridges, yet it hath twenty Gates, five for every square on the Walls, there are many places made for Centinels to watch, made of Wood and covered or gilt with Gold, the streets thereof are the fairest that I have seene, they are as streight as a line from one Gate to another, and standing at the one Gate you may discover to the other, and they are as broad as ten or twelve men may ride a-breast in them: and those streets that be thwart are faire and large, these streets, both on the one side and the other, are planted at the doores of the Houses with Nut trees of India, which make a very commodious shadow, the Houses be made of wood, and covered with a kind of tiles in form of Cups, very necessary for their use: the Kings Palace is in the middle of the Citie, made in form of a walled Castle, with ditches full of water round about it, the Lodgings within are made of wood all over gilded, with fine pinacles, and very costly worke, covered with plates of gold. Truly it may be a Kings house: within the gate there is a fair large Court, from the one side to the other, wherein there are made places for the strongest and stoutest Elephants...

At this point, Cesare notes the Pegúans' extraordinary reverence for the white elephant, a long-standing tradition which died out only with the demise of the Burmese monarchy in 1885 (*See box on p. 10*):

> ... hee hath foure that be white, a thing so rare, that a man shall hardly finde another King that hath any such, as if this King knowe any other that hath white Elephants, he sendeth for them as for a gift. The time that I was there, there were two brought out of a farre Countrie, and that cost me something the sight of them, for that they command the Merchants to goe and see them, and then they must give somewhat to the men that bring

---

* i.e. a warehouse, or godown (from Malay godong).

them: the Brokers of the Merchants give for every man halfe a Ducket. which they call a Tansa, which amounteth to a great summe, for the number of Merchants that are in that Citie; and when they have payd the aforesaid Tansa, they may chuse whether they will see them at that time or no. because that when they are in the Kings stall, every man may see them that will: but at that time they must goe and see them, for it is the kings pleasure it should be so.

This King amongst all other his Titles, is called The King of the white Elephants, and it is reported, that if this King knew any other King that had any of these white Elephants, and would not send them unto him, that he would hazard his whole Kingdome to conquere them. He esteemeth these white Elephants very deerely, and they are had in great regard, and kept with very meet service, every one of them is in a house, all gilded over, and they have their meate given them in vessels of silver and old.

(Purchas 1625, Vol.X)

Cesare goes on to describe the pagoda-studded landscape. Wrongly assuming Buddhism to be a form of idolatry, he considers pagoda-building to be a vanity of vanities; but what breaks his commercial heart is the apparent waste of two highly marketable commodities:

The Mercandizes that goe out of Pegú, are Gold, Silver, Rubies, Saphires, Spinelles, great store of Benjamin, long Pepper, Lead, Lacca, Rice, Wine, some Sugar, yet there might be great store of Sugar made in the Countrey, for that they have abundance of Canes, but they give them to Eliphants to eate, and the people consume great store of them for food, and many more doe they consume in vaine things, as these following. In that Kingdome they spend many of these Sugar-canes in making of Houses and Tents which they call Varely for their Idols, which they call Pagodes, whereof there are great abundance, great and small, and these houses are made in forme of little Hils, like to Sugar-loaves or to Bels, and some of these houses are as high as a reasonable Steeple, at the foot they are verie large, some of them be in circuit a quarter of a mile. The said houses within are full of earth, and walled about with Brickes and dirt in stead of lime, and without forme, from the top to the foot they make a covering for them with Sugar-canes, and plaister it with lime all over, for otherwise they would bee spoyled, by the great abundance of Raine that falleth in those Countries. Also they consume about these Varely or Idol-houses great store of leafe-gold, for that they overlay all the tops of the houses with Gold, and some of them are covered with gold from the top to the foot: in covering whereof there is great store of Gold spent, for that every ten yeeres they new overlay them with gold, from the top to the foot, so that with this vanitie they spend great abundance of Gold. For every ten yeeres the rain doth consume the gold from these houses. And by this meanes they make gold dearer in Pegú then it would bee.....

But King Bayin-naung had so stretched his frontiers and so exhausted

Roof of Arakan Pagoda

The Mahamuni Image; the daily bathing, 1982

his manpower that the centre could not hold. When on his death his son Nanda-bayin succeeded him, the Court would have snorted with derision at the suggestion that within twenty years the splendour of Pegú would be no more. His Court had proceeded in its usual pomp and ceremony for two years or so when Nandabayin had occasion to snort at an equally preposterous idea. In 1583 he gave audience to another Venetian merchant called Gasparo Balbi. Gasparo gives an interesting account of the rituals for abasing oneself before the king, as well as an amusing picture of the incredulity of this absolute monarch when presented with the concept of a republic:

> *..the noise of Trumpets was heard, which signified wee should see the King and have audience of him, wee entered within the second gate, whereby they goe into the Court-yard, and the Interpreter and I cast ourselves upon our knees on the ground, and with our hands elevated in humble wise, and making a shew three times before we rose of kissing the ground; and three other times we did thus before wee came neere to the place where the King sate with his Semini, prostrate on the earth (for no Christian, how neere soever to the King, nor Moorish Captaines, except of his Semini, come in that place so neere the King) I heard all his Speach, but understood it not: I gave the Emeralds to the Interpreter, who lifted them up over his head, and again made reverence, of them called Rombee: and as soone as the King saw it, a Nagiran, that is to say, the Lord of his words, or Interpreter, making the like Rombee, tooke the Emeralds, and gave them into the Kings hand, and then went out of his presence, who a little while after called him, commanding him as Lord of his words, that he should aske mee what Countriman I was, how many yeeres it was since I left my Countrie, and what was my name, and from what place I had brought those Emeralds, and I with the accustomed Rombee (for at very word they speake they must make such obeisance) answered that my name was Gaspar Balbi, that I had beene in my Voyage foure yeeres, and that I brought the Emeralds from Venice to give his Majestie, the fame of whose bountie,courtesie and greatnesse was spread over the world, and especially in our parts, to be the greatest King in the world; all this was written in their letters, and read by the Lord of his words to his Majestie. He commanded to aske me in what parts Venice was seated, and what King governed it; and I told him that it was in the Kingdome of Italie, and that it was a Republike or free State, not governed by any King. When the King heard this, he greatly wondered; so that he began to laugh so exceedingly, that hee was overcome of the cough, which made him that hee could hardly speake to his Great men.*

The accounts provided by these merchants of Venice are particularly valuable because Pegú was soon to be so utterly destroyed that hardly a trace of it has survived. Not until four years later did the first English visitor on record arrive. Ralph Fitch sailed from India on 28 November 1586, entered the Irrawaddy delta and took the usual channel to Pegú via

The Lord White Elephant

Sacred beings and creatures that are white appear in cultures all over the world. In North America, for instance, the Lakota believed that the sacred pipe had been brought among them by the White Buffalo Woman. Where the Iroquois held white dogs sacred, in Japan it was white horses; and the most famous story in the Izumo cycle concerns a white rabbit that turns out to be a deity. In England, superstitions that white horses, dogs and rabbits (but *black* cats) are lucky may represent the remnant of a similar set of beliefs. (Many older people there still try to ensure good luck by remembering to say, on the first day of a month, "White rabbits, white rabbits, white rabbits" before speaking to anyone.)

However, although the eyes and parts of the skin are pale, the white elephant is not white. What made it venerable was a set of beliefs. In Hindu mythology the creature was already one of the symbols of *chakravarti*, or universal kingship. In Buddhism there was the scriptural story that, before giving birth to the child who became Gaudama Buddha, Queen Maya had a dream in which a spirit came down into her womb in the form of a white elephant holding a lotus flower in his trunk; and there was the further belief that in a previous existence Gaudama Buddha himself had been a white elephant. The creature was consequently considered worthy of the highest respect among mortals: a male was accorded the status, trappings and rituals due to a king, a female was treated in the same way as a queen, and a calf would be suckled by women. Arriving in Pegú in 1587, Ralph Fitch saw how the four white elephants belonging to Nandabayin were cared for :

They doe very great service unto these white Elephants; every one of them standeth in an house gilded with gold, and they doe feed in vessels of silver and gilt. One of them when hee doth goe to the River to bee washed, as every day they doe, goeth under a Canopie of cloth of gold or of silke carried over him by sixe or eight men, and eight or ten men goe before him playing on Drummes, Shawmes, or other Instruments: and when hee is washed and commeth out of the River, there is a Gentleman which doth wash his feet in a silver Basin: which is his office given him by the King. There is no such account made of any blacke Elephant, bee he never so great.

(Purchas, X)

In 1805 Bodawhpaya became the possessor of a white elephant - only a cow, but the king was overjoyed:

Besides that he now expected to conquer all his enemies, he confidently supposed that he would enjoy at least 120 years more of life. As a symbol of this number the members of the royal family were making ready 120 glass lamps and other things to the same number.... when the elephant disclaimed all pretensions to divinity by a sudden death, caused by the immense quantity of fruit and sweetmeats which it had eaten from the hands of its adorers.

(Sangermano, 1893)

This was a disaster. Bodawhpaya feared imminent dethronement and death, but relief was at hand:

for, a few months later, some white elephants were discovered in the forests of Pegu. Instantly, the most urgent orders were issued to give them chase; and after several unsuccessful efforts one was at length captured. It was to arrive at Rangoon on the 1st of October 1806, the very day on which I sailed from that port for Europe.....

The last Burmese royal white elephant died and was buried by British troops a few days after the fall of Mandalay in 1885.

Syriam. The city was still a flourishing port, but the river was silting up so much that by the end of the century large ships would be unloading at Syriam and sending cargoes upstream in river-vessels; and Syriam was to become correspondingly more important. From the point where he arrives in Pegú, Fitch's account so closely resembles Fedrici's that we must conclude that it was largely borrowed.

For Pegú the end was fast approaching. Conflicts both internal and external were raging all the time. Gasparo witnessed the mass execution that followed the suppression of a rebellion led by an uncle who ruled Ava. Nandabayin had all suspected sympathisers in Pegú burnt alive along with their wives and children and then went up to Ava where, mounted on elephants, he and his uncle fought in single combat. The uncle was defeated and fled; but while all this was going on, Siamese forces were advancing from Ayuthaya, and they ravaged the Pegú countryside and carried off thousands of rural folk as prisoners. Because Nandabayin did not trust the Mon population of Pegú he had large numbers of them executed, many others managing to escape to Siam. So many people were slaughtered in battle, or executed, or abducted or forced to seek asylum, that Pegú was soon depopulated both within and outside the city walls. To make matters worse, up in the hills between Pegú and the Irrawaddy the bamboo flowered.

In any one area the bamboo will flower only once or twice per century and when this happens the bamboo thickets all wither and die back, leaving the forest floor thickly carpeted with little yellow flowers, each containing small but highly nutritious seeds. The field rats congregate and gorge themselves, grow fat and multiply rapidly; their young are large and vigorous and are also quick to multiply; and so it goes on until, after perhaps two years, the bamboo seeds are all gone and the jungle is seething with millions of hungry rats. In starving hordes they swarm down from the hills, strip the fields, overrun the villages eating everything they can reach, and even attack urban granaries. In 1596 a plague of enormous rats descended upon Pegú from the west and, as large areas of Lower Burma became virtual deserts, there came the first of a series of famines. During this time the kings of Toungoo and Arakan joined forces against Pegú, the former sending an army down the Sittang valley and the latter providing a fleet which took possession of Syriam. They then besieged the already stricken city, which fell in 1599. A visiting Jesuit priest familiar with Pegú's former glories lamented its predicament:

Yet now there are scarcely found in all that Kingdome any men, but a few which with the King have betaken themselves to the Castle, which with Women and Children are said not to exceed seven thousand. For in late times they have been brought to such miserie and want, that they did eate Mans flesh and kept publike shambles thereof, Parents abstained not from their Children, and Children devoured their Parents. The stronger by force preyed on the weaker, and if any were but skinne and bone, yet did they open their intrailes to fill their owne and sucked out their braines.

The women went about the streets with knives to like butcherly purposes.
(Purchas, Vol.X)

Towards the end of the year Nandabayin finally surrendered. He was put to death, his city was looted and reduced to rubble and many of the survivors were carried off to Arakan. But most had not survived. Another Jesuit named Boves was in Arakan when the new year ushered in a new century. He accompanied an Arakanese force that was on its way to the scene of battle, and has left us a description of the killing fields of Pegú. Down in Syriam, it was not silt that made navigation a problem:

It is a lamentable spectacle to see the bankes of the Rivers set with infinite fruit-bearing trees, now overwhelmed with ruines of gilded Temples, and noble edifices; the wayes and fields full of skulls and bones of wretched Pegúans, killed or famished and cast into the River, in such numbers that the multitude of carkasses prohibiteth the way and passage of any ship; to omit the burnings and massacres committed by this the cruellest of Tyrants that ever breathed.

Somehow Pegú was brought back to life, Ava continuing for a while to be only a provincial capital. In 1613 King Anauk-hpet-lun reasserted the monarchy and recaptured Syriam from a ruthless Portuguese mercenary called Felipe de Brito y Nicote (a film-script of whose life-story would probably be rejected by Hollywood as too far-fetched, his life being too full of melodrama and violence, his end too protracted and excruciating). The king then set about regaining lost territories and must have intended to restore Pegú to its former glory, for this was where he received envoys and where he eventually installed his household, which hitherto he had maintained in Ava.

❧❧❧❧❧❧

After the Portuguese freebooters came the Dutch and English East India Companies, whose traders operated with the encouragement of their home governments. One employee of 'John Company' was happily prospecting for trade in the Chiengmai area when it was recaptured by King Anaukhpet-lun's forces, who took the poor fellow and his unsold goods back with them to Pegú. Now a prisoner of the king, Thomas Samuel was treated well and allowed to trade but was forbidden to leave the country. When he died soon afterwards, the Company received the news from returning merchants and sent two employees to reclaim its goods. The pair, Henry Forrest and John Staveley, were also treated as prisoners and endured a lengthy and frustrating stay, but very little remains of the letters they sent back to the Company office in Masulipatam, on the Coromandel coast. The extant documents nevertheless constitute only the second eye-witness account by Englishmen, after Ralph Fitch's thirty years earlier. They recount how the king sent four galleys to welcome them in the first week of 1617. A few days later they were sent for by the king's brother

The Lord White Elephant (from Yule)

whom they found seated in a large bamboo house

in great state bedeckt with jewels in his eares with Gold Rings, with rich stones on his fingers, being a white man and of very good understanding..

(Purchas, V)

The two gave presents both to him and to the nobleman assigned to escort them to Pegú because

in this place heere is nothing to be done or spoken, or any business performed without Bribes, Gifts, or Presents.

Those three nouns hint at a great deal of annoyance and frustration. On arrival in the city they were ordered to build a house for themselves at their own expense, and when it was finished they were instructed not to leave it or even talk to anyone until they had seen the king and given him their present. As the year drew to a close they did manage to see the king but were unable to get him to attend to the matter in hand. They complained to the Company:

The country is far from your worships expectation, for what men soeuer come into his Country, he holds them but as his slaues, neyther can man goe out of his Country without his leaue, for hee hath watch both by Land and Water, and he of himself is a Tyrant, and cannot eat before he hath drawne bloud from some of his people with death or otherwise.

(Quoted by Hall, 1928)

Three months later, Forrest and Staveley were 'like lost sheep, and still in feare of being brought to the slaughter', but one wonders whether they were entirely blameless: two years in all had passed when the king ordered them out of the country - presumably because of their behaviour, for in describing Forrest later on his Company boss used such epithets as *riotous, vicious, unfaithful, debauched, audacious* and *dishonest.*

King Anauk-hpet-lun was eventually killed by his own son, who was immediately ousted and executed by an uncle called Thalun, and it was this king who in 1634 made a decision that can be seen as fateful and far-reaching for Burma: he decided to move the capital up to Ava. It stood on a more navigable river; it was in the middle of Burman rather than Mon territory; and it commanded that river junction where the Myitnge carried the Kyaukse rice cargoes down to the Irrawaddy. On the other hand the move was, in effect if not in purpose, a withdrawal from outside influences that served only to prolong ignorance of the world and to foster the traditional xenophobia of the Burmese Court. In the age of sail, Ava was quite simply too far upstream.

᠄᠄᠄᠄ᢀᢀᢀᢀ

In 1630, the year after Thalun was crowned in Pegú, beyond the mountainous ridges to the west a European visitor had arrived at the court of Thiri-thu-dhamma, king of Arakan. The kingdom had long led an unsettled existence. Thanks to its skilled shipbuilders and warlike seamen, Arakan had for centuries been able to carry out depredations at sea and in the Ganges delta, but had in turn been subject to invasions not only from Bengal but also by Shan and Burmese raiders. From 1532 onwards the Portuguese too began to carry out coastal raids, so it is hardly surprising that there is a gap in the records of almost two centuries between the departure of the Italian Nicolo di Conti in 1435 and the arrival of the Portuguese monk Sebastião Manrique. He was a member of the Augustinian Order who had become a friar in Goa and had been sent first to Bengal; when he arrived in Arakan he was probably approaching forty years of age.

Over the previous fifty years or so the Portuguese freebooters had become residents rather than marauders, and by now they were being employed by Thiri-thu-dhamma, who used their firepower and seamanship to safeguard his kingdom against the growing might of the Mogul empire. In September 1629 Manrique sailed in a Portuguese vessel from Hughli to Dianga, near Chittagong; and during his stay there he heard that the anti-Portuguese governor of Chittagong, a cousin of Thiri-thu-dhamma, had written to the king alleging that the Portuguese militia had secretly arranged to allow Mogul forces to capture Chittagong. Knowing that this false allegation, if believed, would spell disaster for Arakan's Portuguese community, Manrique and a certain Captain Tibao set out by land for the Court of Thiri-thu-dhamma in order to counter the charge. Three days' march southwards took them to Ramu, where the local governor supplied them with an escort to assist them through the rugged terrain, the haunt of wild elephants, tigers and rhinoceroses. The pair set out on 7 July 1630 with their Magh (north Arakanese) escort.

We started with this company and two Elephants with howdahs. As it was raining we decided to go in a covered boat over the two leagues upstream to the foot of the mountains, the Elephants being sent round by land. On reaching our destination at the foot of the hills we had to wait over an hour until the Elephants came up. We then disembarked and commenced to load the principal articles of our baggage on one of the Elephants, the other being kept for me and the Captain to ride upon; we were to go inside the howdah, which was fully furnished with mattresses, rugs, and cushions and well closed in with wax-cloth above and curtains on the sides, so that the rain, which was still heavy, did not molest us.

We were all busied in loading up when suddenly a fierce tiger, as large as a young bull, attacked us, out of the jungle. He seized a Magh soldier who was nearest to him, picked him up as if he was a dog, and carried him away with such speed that by the time his companions came to his assistance the tiger had nearly disappeared into the forest with his victim. Nevertheless some men followed it up with their spears, shouting and yelling, while my companions' escort also gave chase, letting off some rounds from their muskets. The noise of the shots so frightened the fierce beast that he dropped his prey in order to flee more rapidly, and hence they recovered the lucky soldier, almost disemboweled and so lacerated down the back that the sinews were exposed. His companions proposed to take him to the boat, but the Christians, who had found him, objected on the grounds that in transporting him he would expire, and it would be better to attend to his wounds first. To this the Maghs assented readily, as most Oriental nations believe that every Portuguese is a Tabibo, id est physician. But the Christians' intention was to effect a cure of his soul.

(Manrique, 1649)

[The word lucky is not a misprint: Manrique persuaded the victim to recite the Creed, and before he died baptised him, naming him Buenaventura 'for his good fortune in having been, through the divine pity, received into the body of the faithful'.]

Learning that the king was not in his capital but at the holy shrine Hpaya-gyi, which housed a massive statue of Gaudama Buddha, Manrique and his companion sought him there. This Mahamuni image, said to be a true likeness, was and still is the most revered representation of the Buddha in the region; and it was here that King Thiri-thu-dhamma was at his devotions. The bigoted friar seems to have avoided going to the shrine, which he would no doubt have called a work of Satan, and so leaves us no description of it; but the image will reappear in a later chapter. Manrique and Tibao did obtain a royal audience, however, during which the friar managed to persuade the king to reconsider the evidence concerning the alleged treachery, and the danger was thus averted. Manrique stayed in Arakan for several years and, just before leaving for India, attended the long-delayed crowning of Thiri-thu-dhamma in 1635. By this time the king had been postponing the ceremony for about ten years because of a prediction that once crowned he would soon perish. He was murdered in 1638, the year from which the Arakanese mark the beginning of their kingdom's decline. Manrique lived on for thirty years, but was also murdered. Having gone eastwards to the Philippines and China before returning to Rome and seeing his *Itinerario* published in 1649, he occupied important posts there for twenty years before being sent on some secret mission to London, where he was killed by his own Portuguese manservant in 1669. But we have jumped ahead, and must now return to the Burma of King Thalun.

໑ພວນຈ

The Dutch had already established a trading post when in 1647 the English East India Company sent three representatives to open one. Thomas Breton and his two colleagues reached Syriam aboard the *Endeavour* to find not only that King Thalun's son had raised a rebellion against his father but also that, since the king's law still forbade a foreigner to leave without his permission, the three would have to go up the river to deal with the king personally. The voyage so far had had its share of misfortune: in one way and another the captain, the chief mate,the surgeon and three of the ship's best seamen had all died on board, and many of the crew were very ill. Nevertheless when the royal summons eventually came they set out on the two-month journey up the Irrawaddy. Their troubles were not yet over, for on the way one senior crew member fell overboard and drowned, and '20 dayes journy short of Ava' a Peguan boatman carelessly set one of the ships on fire and much of its cargo of textiles went up in smoke. Reporting in a letter dated 11 February 1648, the Company's factors said:

Of what necessaries wee had of our owne wee are utterly stripped, even to our dayly weareing clothes, not haveing left us anything to lie upon in this wilderness save the bare ground; nor have wee any other remedy till wee repaire to the other boate, which conteyneth the remainder of our goods. The ruines of what wee have left, though of very little vallue, yet wee conceive them worth the carriage to Ava; but such is the cruelty of these people that, seeing us in necessity of a boat, will not be hired to furnish us for less then 500 viss; which, though it sincke deep into the worth of our burnt goods, yet is better given then that they should be altogeather lost.

(Hall, 1928)

After that letter there is no further reference to the journey in the fragmentary records, though it is clear that Breton and his companions did arrive and that the venture was a financial success after all. As far as we know, Breton was the first to reach Ava since Nicolo di Conti; but neither has left us a description of that city. Two years later the Company's

Masulipatam office acquired and equipped a new vessel for the Syriam run and hopefully named it the *Ruby*. Though the outbreak of the Anglo-Dutch war in 1652 would soon slow down English trade in eastern waters, in that same year a certain Martin Bradgate was sent over to Syriam. King Thalun had died four years earlier, and now his son Pindalé sat on the throne in Ava. Bradgate took some goods up to the capital, but found on arrival that the Company godown and all its stock had been destroyed by fire. After building a new one he spent much of his time in Ava, having no doubt realised that in a culture where all intermediaries expected 'Bribes, Gifts, or Presents' the cheapest and quickest way of getting anything done was to deal directly with the king. But if Bradgate ever penned a description of Ava, it has not survived.

∽∽∽∽∾∾∾∾

Just as foreign visitors could be detained at the king's pleasure, so any ship beached in bad weather or docking without prior arrangement became Burmese (that is, the king's) property by law. Because of the way Burmese officials treated foreign mariners, English ships began giving Burmese ports a wide berth.

A few years after Bradgate's trip to Ava, 'John Company' pulled out of the Syriam trading-post and another forty years pass before we find a detailed account of another journey to Ava, this time by a mission sent to King Minre-kyaw-din. The Court of Ava had for a long time been unsuccessfully pressing the Company to reopen trade when in 1692 a small English sloop had to put in to Martaban, having run out of fresh water and wood. The ship had duly been impounded, its cargo seized and the crew detained. Understanding that the men were being held as hostages pending the establishment of a trade agreement, in 1695 the Company sent a mission of private traders led by Edward Fleetwood and James Leslie to Ava with a great many presents, a letter containing trade proposals, and a request for the return of the ship, her crew and her cargo. Fleetwood kept a diary in which he recorded all the procedures that had to be observed; and here we find the mission on New Year's Eve taking to the Court of Ava the letter and the king's present, placed in small bamboo baskets and carried by 160 'coolies'. His attention to detail hints at the tediousness of the traditional ritual:

> *The Letter was carryed by Mr. King on horseback before the Present; and myself, attended by the Linguist, followed the Present: when we came to the Garden Gate, where the King was, we alighted; where we were met by one of the Ovidores, who was there ready to conduct me in, and to direct me in the manner of approaching the King; here I took the Letter from Mr.King and stayed almost a quarter of an hour, before the Gates were opened, When we fell down upon our knees and made three Bows, which done we entered the Garden, the Present following, and, having gone about half-way from the Gate to the Place where the King was seated, we made three Bows again as we had done before; and were ordered to sit*

down; after we were sat down, the King ordered the Ovidore to receive the Letter, and about half a quarter of an hour after, asked me the three usual questions viz. How long had I been in my passage from Madrass to his port of Syrian? How many days from Syrian to Ava? And, at my departure from Madrass, If I had left my Governour in good health? I told his Majesty, that I had been about 30 days in my passage from Madrass to Syrian; about 42 days from Syrian to Ava; and that at my departure from Madrass (thanks to GOD) I had left my Governour in good health, supplicating the Divine power for the continuation of his Majesty's health and happiness; After this, I sat about half a quarter of an hour longer, and then was dismissed.

(Hall, 1928)

There followed weeks of present-giving and negotiation before the petition was - unprecedentedly - granted on condition that the Company reopen its Syriam branch. Fleetwood did not manage to leave Ava until 9 February, yet his diary does not contain any description of Ava. The usual red tape and extortionate demands prevented him from leaving Syriam until 17 March; and by this time the monsoon was setting in, so his ship did not reach Fort St.George, the Company's headquarters, for another ten months. To cap it all, two years passed without any sign of the impounded ship, cargo or crew; another man was sent to Syriam, but he seems to have kept no record of the mission.

∽∽∽∽∾∾∾∾

The British were by now encountering serious armed resistance in India, and the main commodity that the Company wanted from Burma was not rubies (the quality of exportable stones being poor*) but saltpetre, a major ingredient of gunpowder; however, the Court of Ava had made the export of saltpetre a capital offence. There was also a demand for lac, a component of sealing-wax. These two substances symbolise very neatly the establishment of the Raj and its subsequent maintenance - first conquest, then administration. As for imports, the recent conflict must have been followed by poor harvests, for our next description of Ava comes from Alexander Hamilton, a mariner bound for Pegú with a cargo of Indian rice. Despite being attacked by French vessels at sea, having his cargo stolen and his ship scuttled, he reached Pegú in a Dutch vessel sold to him by his French captors.

Hamilton arrived in Syriam in 1710, soon after John Company reopened its branch there; and though he did not go up to the capital himself, he provides a reliable decription of Ava. 'This relation,' he explains, 'I had from one Mr.Roger Alison, who had been twice Ambassador from the

---

*Tavernier (1684) explains: *This is one of the poorest countries in the world, producing nothing but rubies, and those not in so great a number as is generally believed.... (and)... you rarely meet with a fine one weighing three or four carats, by reason of the great difficulty of conveying them away till the king has seen them, who always retains all the fine ones he meets with.*

Governor of Fort St.George, or his Agents at Syrian, to the Court of Ava'-
Fort St.George being the Company's base in Madras:

*The King's Palace at Ava is very large, built of Stone, and has four
Gates for its Conveniencies. Ambassadors enter at the East Gate, which
is called the Golden Gate, because all Ambassadors make their Way to
him by Presents.*

*The South Gate is called the Gate of Justice, where all People that
bring Petitions, Accusations, or Complaints, enter. The West is the Gate of
Grace, where all that have received Favours, or have been acquitted of
Crimes, pass out in State, and all condemned Persons carried out in Fet-
ters; and the North Gate fronting the River, is the Gate of State where his
Majesty passes through, when he thinks fit to bless his People with his
Presence, and all his Provisions and Water are carried in at that Gate.....
and tho' the Palace is very large, yet the Buildings are but mean, and the
City tho' great and populous, is only built of Bambow Canes, thatcht with
Straw or Reeds, and the Floors of Teak Plank, or split Bambows, because
if Treason or other capital Crimes be detected, the Criminals may have no
Place of Shelter, for if they do not appear at the first Summons, Fire will
fetch them out of their combustible Habitations.*

(Hamilton 1727, Vol.II)

Hamilton also describes such things as methods of jurisdiction, tattoo-
ing and dress, but perhaps the most interesting part concerns Burmese
women:

*The Women are much whiter than the Men, and have generally pretty
plump Faces, but of small Stature, yet very well shap'd, their Hands and
Feet small, and their Arms and Legs well proportioned. Their Headdress
is their own black Hair tied up behind, and when they go abroad, they
wear a Shaul folded up, or a Piece of white Cotton Cloth lying loose on
the Top of their Heads. Their bodily Garb is a Frock of Cotton Cloth or
Silk, made meet for their Bodies, and the Arms of their Frock stretcht
close on the Arm, the lower Part of the Frock reaching Half-thigh down.
Under the Frock they have a Scarf or Lungee doubled fourfold, made fast
about their Middle, which reaches almost to the Ancle, so contrived, that
at every Step they make, as they walk, it opens before, and shews the right
Leg and Part of the Thigh.*

*This fashion of Petticoats, they say, is very ancient, and was first con-
trived by a certain Queen of that Country, who was grieved to see the Men
so much addicted to Sodomy, that they neglected the pretty Ladies. She
thought that by the sight of a pretty Leg and plump Thigh, the Men might
be allured from that abominable Custom, and place their Affections on
proper Objects, and according to the ingenious Queen's conjecture, that
Dress of the Lungee had its desired End, and now the Name of Sodomy is
hardly known in that Country.*

The Women are very courteous and kind to Strangers, and are very

*fond of marrying with Europeans, and most Part of the Strangers who
trade thither, marry a Wife for the Term they stay.*

A little later, after describing marriage procedure and domestic arrangements, he adds wryly:

*If she proves false to her Husband's Bed, and on fair Proof convicted,
her Husband may carry her to the Rounday (Court council chamber), and
have her Hair cut, and sold for a Slave, and he may have the Money; but
if the Husband goes astray, she'll be apt to give him a gentle Dose, to send
him into the other World a Sacrifice to her Resentment.*

༄༅།

For the first quarter of the eighteenth century John Company showed
little interest in trading with Burma but, since Syriam was useful as a
ship-building base, continued to maintain a Resident there. Soon, however, even the shipbuilding became uneconomic - largely because of what
the Resident of the day, Jonathan Smart, called the 'exorbitant presents'
that still had to be made. By 1742 England, already at war with Spain and
likely to have France as an enemy too, was sorely in need of saltpetre.
Two years previously, however, the Mon of Lower Burma had rebelled
against Ava and their own king now ruled in Pegú, so it was from this
Pegú government that Smart would have to get permission to export
saltpetre; but by this time the upheaval in Lower Burma was such that the
Company sent to Smart a small detachment of sepoys to defend the trading post.

Ever since the heyday of Pagán, when King Anawrahta had destroyed
their capital Thaton, the Mon had struggled to maintain their identity. For
a long time, the Burman Court had been not only distant but slack and
ineffectual. Bands of Manipuri raiders had been coming and going almost
at will, on occasion reaching the very walls of Ava, and there was a Shan
rebellion not far north of the city. Taxation in Pegú was crippling, too, and
resentment of Burman rule had been running high. Foolishly imagining
that the local population would support him, the Ava-appointed governor
had proclaimed himself King of Pegú; but the people had killed both him
and an uncle who came down from Ava to appoint a successor. The masses
had gone through Syriam and elsewhere slaughtering all the Burmans they
could find. Smart seems to have sympathised with the Mon cause, and the
new king (a former monk) assured him that foreigners would not be mo-
lested. In 1743 the Burman forces descended on Syriam, plundering the
foreign godowns and robbing the churches - French, Portuguese and Armenian - but left John Company's premises intact. When the Mon successfully counter-attacked they must have thought Smart had been double-
dealing: although they left the staff unharmed, this time they burned the
trading-post down, and for a decade the Company had no further dealings
with Burma.

By 1752 the new Mon leader Binnya-dala was ready to subdue Ava once and for all. He had troops from a (now native) Portuguese population; some Dutch mercenaries; arms and ammunition bought from European arms-dealers; and a large flotilla. These forces converged on Ava and, after a three-month siege by land and water, the outer city fell and was fired. The high inner-city wall was breached a few days later, the king and his queens were sent down to Pegú, and the Court of Ava was burned to the ground. To establish Mon rule in the area, the commander remained with only a small garrison, the greater part of the army returning to Pegú. It was a fatal mistake.

Gate at Amarapura

The Asian walled city

The 'new city' of Pegú was built to a design that had been followed for centuries and which continued in use right up to the founding of Mandalay. Being square, walled, moated and comprising a grid of broad avenues in the centre of which stood elaborate palace buildings, Pegú seems to have differed from Mandalay mainly in its greater scale.

Duroiselle, superintendent of Burma's Archaeological Survey in the 1920s, considered that prototype cities had been found 'from Patna to Peking and - perhaps - as far as Nineveh'. Quoting at length Marco Polo's description of Kublai Khan's capital, now Beijing, founded in 1264 A.D., Duroiselle compares that city with Mandalay and concludes:

If we take into consideration that what Marco Polo describes on the top of the gates and on the walls were merely towers, answering to the pavilions or pyatthats *(a construction with multiple receding roofs) on the wall of Mandalay city, it will be seen how very much alike are the two descriptions. The points of resemblance in the general plan of both the cities are too numerous to be merely fortuitous. It will be remarked that, in both cases, the palace proper, which consists of a single storey, is built of wood on a masonry basement forming a rectangle; this is immediately surrounded by enclosure walls. The streets within the city are straight, cutting one another at right angles and leading from gate to gate; in both cities it is within the crenellated walls and the palace's enclosing outer wall that the streets are laid, and in the squares thus formed that the dwellings of the high officials are situated; both have a clock-tower or bell-tower to strike the time. The walls around the city form a square, each side of which has three gate-ways, the middle one of which being, in both cases, used by the king; the walls are battlemented, and watch-towers or bastions with multiple roofs are seen on the walls at the corners and over the gates, as well as between them; and a large moat has been dug all round the city.*

(Duroiselle, 1925)

Should further convincing detail be needed, here are two short extracts from Marco Polo's description as given by Duroiselle. The outer walls of Kublai Khan's capital have, says Marco,

a thickness of full ten paces at bottom , and a height of more than ten paces; but they are not so thick at the top, for they diminish in thickness as they rise, so that at the top they are about three paces thick. And they are provided throughout with loop-holed battlements, which are all white-washed.

Of the resplendent palace within, he says:

The roof is very lofty, and the walls are all covered with gold and silver. They are also adorned with representations of dragons, sculptured and gilt, beasts and birds, knights and idols and sundry other objects. And on the ceiling too you see nothing but gold and silver painting.

CHAPTER 2
Wild Justice
Ava, Shwebo and Sagaing, 1752 - 1783

> *Revenge is a kind of wild justice,*
> *which the more man's nature run to,*
> *the more ought law to weed it out.*
>
> Francis Bacon, *Essays: Of Revenge.*

In 1714, in a village of perhaps three hundred houses fifty miles north-west of Ava, a baby had been born to a family of good local standing. According to tradition, he grew up to be the leader of a band of huntsmen, an occupation that called for energy, cunning and courage. By his mid-thirties he had become locally powerful and, anticipating the fall of Ava, fortified his village and cleared its approaches. The village was originally called Mokso-Nga-Po Ywa ('the village of Nga Po the hunter') but came to be called Mokso-bo-(myo), 'Hunter-captain-(town)'. When Ava fell in April 1752, the Mon garrison left behind sent out detachments here and there to demand allegiance. The force sent to Moksobo was cut to pieces, and larger units sent to subdue the community were repulsed with great casualties. In next to no time this 'hunter' was gaining adherents and power, then proclaiming himself king with the name of Alaung-hpaya (Buddha-to-be) and building himself a palace at Moksobo.

By December 1753 Alaunghpaya was encamped outside Ava. One dark night the Mon garrison had the sense to pull out quietly and head back down to the delta. Alaunghpaya took over, repelled a Mon counter-attack the following year, went on to take first Pyé (Prome) then Dagon, which he renamed Yangon ('End-of-strife') - later anglicised by the British as Rangoon - and then lay siege to Syriam; yet in the midst of all this he found time to go all the way back upstream to Moksobo to deal with trouble-some bands of Manipuris and Shans.

Meanwhile a delicate situation was developing for the East India Company's representatives in Burma. Ever since its Syriam premises had been burned down a decade earlier, the Company had feared that the French were gaining too much local influence. While Alaunghpaya was establishing himself in Ava, the Company had taken possession of Negrais Island, which the English had long wanted as a naval base, and without permission had established a fortified settlement there. From this point onwards, it becomes clear that the Company's interests in the region were primarily political and only secondarily commercial. When two years had passed and Alaunghpaya's ascendancy was clear, the Company sent an embassy to conclude a treaty of trade and friendship with the king. Captain Baker and Lieutenant North set out up the Irrawaddy on 17 July 1755 with the usual 'present': this one included four cannons, eighty shot and four chests of gunpowder as well as textiles and other goods. By mid-August Baker was recording 'how tedious it was to go up this River'; by 8 September the embassy had still only reached the ex-capital Ava; and by this time some of the Company's ships lying at anchor down in Syriam had become involved in the hostilities there and were seen to be support-ing the 'wrong' side - the Mon. How would the Burman king react in these circumstances?

When Baker and his men finally reached the new court at Moksobo, Alaunghpaya was surprisingly accommodating and good-humoured. He listened attentively as the Company's letter was read out, but did bridle at its offer of assistance in dealing with 'rebellions, domestic feuds and for-eign enemies', laughing aloud at the very thought that he might need help and proceeding to boast about his own prowess. At the time, however, his favourite queen was seriously ill; when death came he was grief-stricken and the embassy was sent away with the treaty unsigned. Baker's descrip-tion of the area is that of a man with one eye on trading possibilities, his sketch of the new capital (which he spells *Momchabue*) being very brief:

> *Momchabue is the Place where the present Prince resides; it is a walled town, built with Brick and Mud, about 12 feet thick, and 20 high; and as I compute, about 1000 paces each side, being a regular square; and con-tains about 4000 Families. It is seated in an even Country, about 12 miles from the Water-side, but a very sandy Soil, though it abounds in many places, with a sort of Black Earth, which, when boiled, and otherwise prepared, produces great quantities of Salt, and out of the neighbouring parts is got, with but a reasonable degree of trouble, good Salt-petre...*
>
> (Dalrymple, 1793)

Baker also gives us a sorry picture of Ava. It was smaller than Moksobo and

> *'Tis said it has been a rich and populous Place. Indeed the remaining ruins afford reason to believe the latter, and common Report is sufficient to confirm us, in the belief of the former: Though I think (notwithstanding there are some two or three Edifices admired by the Country People) that there is not a single structure, or but one, that can possibly deserve the name of great, much less magnificent.(....) From hence the Merchants go by Land to and from SIAM. At this time it is not productive of a single Commodity, and though it has formerly been the Mart for Trade, that is at this time so dead, there is now scarce any there.*

Baker got back to Negrais at the end of October 1755. By the follow-ing July the untiring Alaunghpaya had taken Syriam and started building up Yangon to supplant it as Burma's main port; and in May 1757 he at last captured Pegú. The besieged Mon citizens, though reduced to eating rep-tiles, had put up a valiant fight; but when the end came there was such

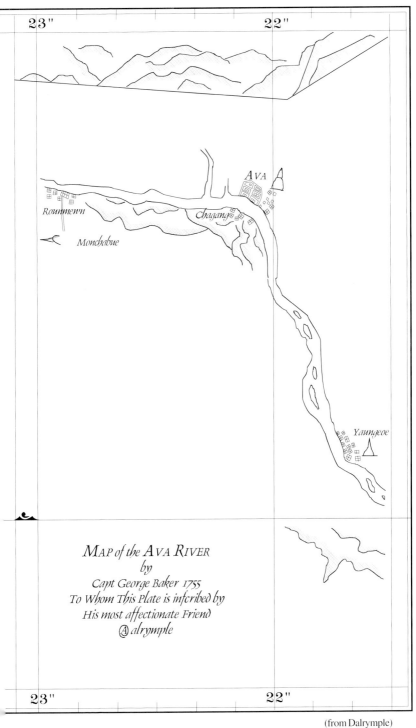

MAP of the AVA RIVER
by
Capt George Baker 1755
To Whom This Plate is infcribed by
His most affectionate Friend
A. alrymple

(from Dalrymple)

massive slaughter that Mon resistance virtually ceased to exist for years to come.

∽∽∽∽∽∽∽

Almost immediately Alaunghpaya wrote to the Company to say that he wanted its representative to meet him on his triumphal progress by river to Pyé, and in June Ensign Robert Lester was sent with two copies of a 'Treaty of Friendship and Alliance between the King of Ava, and the Honourable United East India Company'. This time the 'present' included a four-pound gun and carriage, a new carriage for a nine-pounder, two barrels of gunpowder, a pair of blunderbusses and a light musket, as well as some textiles.

There were the usual frustrations, the 'many hard things amongst these People that would try the most patient man ever existed' and, this being monsoon time, the 'excessive hard rains with much Thunder and Lightning' but at last his boat came out into a wide river, where he 'found the King, in his Barge, with great numbers of other Boats attending him'. The next morning his local assistant came and

he told me, that on going into the King's Apartment in his Barge, I must leave my Sword and Shoe behind, and on approaching near the King, to the Place appointed for me, I must kneel...

Lester objected but eventually acquiesced and found that, as before, Alaunghpaya's behaviour was a mixture of good humour and vainglory. The king enjoyed a laugh at Lester's expense:

As I had not room to stretch my legs out, and I was somewhat uneasy, I saw a small Stool behind me, which I took, and sat on, this caused laughter among the Great Men about me, the King asked the reason, and was informed, on which he rose up and came close to me, and laughed very heartily, and asked me what was the reason that Englishmen could not kneel? I told him we were not accustomed to it; on which he pointed to the Yard of the Boat, which was close by, and told me I might set there...

This departure from the rigid Court etiquette suggests that the king could be flexible, even sympathetic, on occasion. He was also full of questions, but could not resist boasting that even a nine-pound cannonball fired straight at him would do him no harm. Nor could he resist teasing white foreigners who did not 'black', i.e. have themselves tattooed. He asked Lester:

Why don't you black your Bodies and Thighs as we do (at the same time rising up and shewing me his Thigh)? Let me feel your Hand, feeling my Fingers and Wrist, and said we were like Women, because we did not black..

But he did sign the treaty which, among other things, ceded to the Company the island of Negrais (Haing-gyi), which commanded the mouth of the Bassein river.

A mere trade monopoly a century earlier, the Company was now fast becoming a powerful political force that would impinge more and more upon Burma's affairs. In that same year (1757) it gained control of Bengal; and when in the following year Alaunghpaya conquered Manipur, the two powers were already in dangerously close contact. There was no confrontation on this occasion, but in the next hundred years Anglo-Burmese friction would spark off two wars. In May 1759 events in India forced the Company to pull most of its personnel out of Negrais, but in October it sent in a small staff to maintain its footing there.

These employees were unaware that in the meantime Armenian merchants jealous of the English had been poisoning the king's mind by accusing the Company of various malpractices. The king ordered a massacre. At breakfast on 6 October one of the Company's honoured guests, the governor of Bassein, gave a signal. A large number of Burmese hidden outside came pouring in, and there were more than a hundred fatalities, mainly among the Company's Indian staff; but some, escaping by boat, lived to tell the tale.

After putting down a half-hearted uprising in Pegú, Alaunghpaya went on to conquer the southernmost parts of Burma and Siam. Over-eager for conquest, he made the mistake of heading north for the Siamese capital Ayuthaya too late in the dry season. He cut a bloody path through to the capital and laid siege to it but found it stoutly defended, and by this time he was unwell. As the rains came on, he reluctantly withdrew, leaving a rearguard to cover his retreat. On the long march back he died on his litter, but his death was kept secret until the columns reached Yangon. His body was taken upriver and laid to rest in Moksobo, which in time came to be called Shwe-bo (Glorious Commander). After an action-packed reign of only eight years, the hunter was home from the kill.

⋘⋙

When the Company's next embassy set out in 1760, Captain Walter Alves' mission was of course to protest formally to the new king about the Negrais massacre, but also to seek to ensure further trade. This time the king was to be found not in Shwebo but in Sagaing: on succeeding to the throne, the eldest son Naung-daw-gyi had executed a couple of officers he did not like, whereupon the army under an efficient and popular general had rebelled and occupied Ava, so Naungdawgyi was now ensconced on the opposite bank of the Irrawaddy besieging these rebels. When Alves arrived, the siege had already been going on for months and Sagaing had just been declared the capital:

> On the 22d of September, I arrived at Siggeyn, a place directly opposite to Ava, on the other Side of the River, and where the Buraghmah King had been some time, in order to forward the Reduction of Ava, which he

had besieged then for two Months with 100,000 Men, as I was told and whose Batteries were within fifty Yards of the Walls, and though there was no Cannon in the City, nor a Ditch about it, yet the Besieged kept them off with Musketry; and when they endeavoured to scale the Walls, the Besieged plyed them so with boiling Dammer, mixed with Oil, that they always fled with Precipitation; some Poor Creatures, that were miserably scalded in these Attacks, I saw in Hutts on this side of the River.

Alves, being one of those who had managed to escape from Negrais, knew more than most about that affair and could hardly be contradicted. But the king greeted his protest with surprise rather than disavowal: those who had been killed had been 'born to die there', it was their *kan*, their fate - and as for those responsible, well, soldiers were not expected to distinguish between the guilty and the innocent.

"For instance" says he "As soon as ever they get into Ava, I have given them orders to spare nothing that has life, and to burn and kill and destroy everything in it, though I know that ... the (rebel) general and the soldiers are to blame..."

Nevertheless, the king was fairly well disposed towards Alves and an agreement was reached whereby trading could resume provided it was not administered from a base as far-flung as Negrais. The king quite rightly wanted, though he did not say so, to keep a close eye on the Company from now on. In due course the Company chose to operate from Yangon; and it was not until December that the half-starved general and his men broke out and were cut to pieces.

⟨⟨⟨⟨⟩⟩⟩⟩

More than two decades pass before we have our next foreigner's-eye-view of the Court of Ava, and this time the visitor was an Italian missionary. Naungdawgyi had died in 1763 and, Alaunghpaya having decreed that each of his sons should succeed him in order of seniority, the king's immediate younger brother Myédu took the throne. Within a few months he had decided that Ava should be rebuilt as his capital and , when a white elephant was presented to him, Myédu assumed the name Hsin-byu-shin, 'Lord of the White Elephant'. He proceeded to raid Manipur, bringing back captives to help repopulate Ava, and then succeeded where his father had failed: after an epic battle that ended in 1767 he took Ayuthaya, which would never again be Siam's capital. Meanwhile, however, the Chinese had been attacking Hsinbyushin's own capital, their incursions ending in 1769 when the invaders sued for peace and agreed to a settlement. When they finally tramped off up the valley of the Taping, thousands died of hunger and disease on the way through the high passes. Near the end of Hsinbyushin's reign, the Shwe Dagon Pagoda was severely damaged by a great earthquake and, once he had put down a mutiny of the Mon troops he had levied for the war against Siam, he went down to Dagon in great pomp to restore it. Raising the golden spire to more or less its present height, he gilded it with his own weight in gold and crowned it with a new *hti*. Hsinbyushin died in 1776, seven years before the Italian padre's arrival. It was seven years of almost farcical turmoil followed by a chilling act of vengeance.

Contrary to Alaunghpaya's decree, it was not a younger brother of Hsinbyushin but his own son who came next to the throne. A twenty-year-old called Singu, he did manage to subject Manipur once again, but shrank from full-scale war with Siam. He liked having a good time, was drunk as often as not, and spent too much time away from the palace. This laxity allowed a faction from Paung-ga, a village near Sagaing, to smuggle their own eighteen-year-old pretender Maung Maung right into the palace and literally put him on the throne. On hearing of this, Singu fled but was persuaded to return, only to be killed by a minister who nursed a grudge. Poor young Maung Maung was a miserable failure and knew it. He tried to persuade some more senior kinsman to take his place but it was the eldest of Alaunghpaya's surviving sons, Bo-daw-hpaya, who put an end to the farce by having Maung Maung drowned and putting himself on the throne. Singu had reigned for six years, Maung Maung for just a week.

Bodawhpaya took no chances. He immediately carried out the traditional massacre of kinsmen - Singu's queens, for instance, being burned alive along with their babies. Then, having generously rewarded a distinguished old general for his support, he discovered that his own half-brother was in cahoots with the old man in a plot to supplant him. These two, along with their sympathisers and all *their* families and attendants, were also put to death. Even so, a further attempt to take the palace was launched from the village of Paung-ga, but the small force that scaled the wall was easily overpowered. When the surviving raiders had been executed along with those of the palace guard deemed to have been at fault, Bodawhpaya turned his attention to the village itself; and it is our Italian Barnabite missionary, Padre Vincentius Sangermano, who provides an account of the vengeance of the king. He arrived in Yangon in 1783 and went straight up to Ava, which he cannot have reached before September. But if he arrived a few months too late to witness the massacre, he was close enough in time and place for his account to be reliable:

> *Still was the fury of the king unsatisfied, for he now gave full scope to that cruel and inhuman disposition, of which he had already discovered sufficient signs. Notwithstanding the innocence of the great majority of the inhabitants of Paonga, he caused them all to be dragged from their dwellings, not excepting even the old men or tender infants, nor respecting the character of the priests and Talapoins (monks), and then to be burnt alive upon an immense pile of wood which had been erected for the purpose. The village was afterwards razed to the ground, the trees and plants in its gardens cut up and consumed by fire, its very soil was turned up with the ploughshare, and a stone erected on the spot as a mark of perpetual malediction.* (Sangermano, 1893)

Bodawhpaya now slept in a different room each night. It seems that ever since the shock of finding his brother and the old general plotting his downfall he had resolved to trust no-one; and eight months after coming to the throne, he chose a new site for his capital. Padre Sangermano probably* saw the immediate effects of the upheaval caused by this transfer - a practice that must have seemed as pointless to him as it does to us, for his account deals with the sort of questions that we would ask today,e.g. : Why abandon a ready-made city that was strategically well-situated ? How was the new site chosen? What sort of population was he dealing with? How was their transfer effected? How did they react? What happened to the abandoned city?... and so on:

..he resolved to abandon his present capital and to build another, thus the more easily to obliterate the memory of his predecessors, and fix the eyes of the multitude upon himself alone. Pretexts were not wanting to give a colour to this proceeding. It was said that the city and palace had been defiled by the human blood shed within its precincts, and therefore it no longer became the monarch to inhabit it; and hence it was ordained that a new imperial residence should immediately be constructed. To this proposal none dared to object, and all the Mandarins and royal ministers strove who should best give effect to the orders of the king. As in this country all is regulated by the opinions of the Brahmins, so that not even the king shall presume to take any step without their advice, therefore was counsel taken of them, and thereupon a site selected for the new city, on an uneven spot three leagues from Ava, upon the right or eastern bank of the river.

As usual, the new capital was a square walled city, each side being a mile long, and within an inner wall was built the teak-wood palace. When it was finished, Bodawhpaya went in state to take up residence in May, 1783; but what about the citizens?

After seven days he returned to Ava, in order personally to urge the removal of all his subjects to the new capital, which he effected on the 14th of the next month. Thus were the miserable inhabitants compelled to quit their home with all its comforts, and exchange a delightful situation, salubrious in its air and its waters, for a spot infected with fevers and other complaints, from the stagnant waters that surround it. (....) Vain would it be to describe the sufferings and fatigues, the oppressions and exactions, which this transmigration caused, to those whose eyes have not witnessed the extreme rigour with which the royal orders are here

---

* *Sangermano's dates do not quite tally with those of the Royal Orders of Burma (Than Tun, Vol.IV). These are the king's decrees and reports on their implementation that were kept in the Shwe Daik, the library that held the palace archives. Since none of the originals have survived, there are now only copies (sometimes only copies of copies) to rely on, and they are not always accurate. Sangermano's dates may therefore be more reliable here.*

executed.

Bodawhpaya's new capital, which he named Amarapura, may have seemed remote to the British but was reasonably cosmopolitan. Although the Burmans kept the walled city largely for themselves, around it there lived various ethnic groups, each in its own quarter:

Of the new inhabitants some took up their abode within the walls; and these were for the most part Burmese and persons attached to the royal family or to the Mandarins: to others were allotted dwellings without the city, whence arose various suburbs,or, as they are called by the Portuguese, campos. *Besides the Burmese, the principal foreign nations who occupy special districts are the Siamese and Cassè, who were brought captives to this country in the wars of Zempiuscien (Hsinbyushin), and have greatly multiplied in number. Perhaps still more populous is the suburb of the Mohammedan Moors, who have settled in the Burmese capital, as in every other part of India. Their profession is mostly traffic, and they enjoy the free exercise of their religion, having many mosques. To these must be added the suburb of the Chinese, whose industry is peculiarly remarkable, and that wherein the Christians dwell. The entire number of the inhabitants of Amarapura amounts to about 200,000.*

Finally, what became of Ava? Padre Sangermano's mournful account can still shock the modern reader:

No sooner was Amarapura inhabited, than Ava, famed not only as the residence of so many kings, but also for its pleasant and convenient situation and the magnificence of its public buildings, was instantly abandoned. Indeed Badonsachen caused its total destruction, by giving general permission to overthrow at will the superb Baò, or convents of Talapoins (monks), some of which were gilt all over, within and without, with the finest gold, the magnificent wooden bridges, the public halls and porticos. All the cocoa-trees, which, planted along the interior of the walls, overtopped them with their green shadowy branches, and gave the city a cheerful and sweet prospect, were cut down and given to the elephants for food. In fine, part of the walls was torn down by order of the king, and the river, being sluiced in, reduced the whole to an uninhabitable pool.

Despite Bodawhpaya's thoroughness, however, a time would come when Ava would rise again.

The Great Bell at Mingun

A Burmese Lady, mid-19th century

The ruins of Ayuthaya

CHAPTER 3
Colossal Wreck
Amarapura and Mingun, 1783 - 1819

> *And on the pedestal these words appear:*
> *"My name is Ozymandias, king of kings:*
> *Look on my works, ye Mighty, and despair!"*
> *Nothing beside remains. Round the decay*
> *Of that colossal wreck, boundless and bare*
> *The lone and level sands stretch far away.*
>
> Percy Bysshe Shelley, *Ozymandias.*

Bodawhpaya was wary. For several decades Arakan had known only instability and lawlessness, and life there had become so intolerable that a deputation of Arakanese lords had come to Amarapura to ask him to take control of their country. He was afraid not of the Arakanese army but of the advantage it held in being protected by the fabled Mahamuni image, said to be a likeness of Gaudama Buddha himself and to possess unearthly powers. Before sending an army he therefore sent his own experts, disguised as monks, to neutralise these powers. Only then, towards the end of 1784, did he despatch four divisions, three of which marched through the western passes while the fourth took the heavy guns by sea past Negrais Island. The four forces linked up, attacked and took the capital Mrauk-U (Myo-haung) without much difficulty, and Bodawhpaya's troops returned in triumph bringing not only the royal family and 20,000 prisoners but also the priceless image itself, a massive figure cast in bronze and almost four metres high. It was an almost incredible achievement to manhandle that dead weight over the ridges of the Arakan Yoma, down through the jungles and up to Amarapura, where Bodawhpaya received the image with great reverence.

Among the rest of the booty was a thirty-foot cannon and thirty bronze images. These figures had already seen a great deal of service under various masters. Cast in Cambodia and set up - probably as guardian statues - in Angkor Wat, they were already old when in 1431 the Siamese army sacked the whole glorious temple-city and took them back to Ayuthaya as part of the spoils; when the Siamese capital was overwhelmed by Bayinnaung's forces in 1564, the figures were carted off to Pegú; when Pegú was in turn razed by the Arakanese in 1599 the bronzes were taken to Mrauk-U and now they had arrived in Amarapura. Bodawhpaya had a pagoda built to house the revered image, and within the precincts of that Mahamuni (or Arakan) Pagoda six of the thirty Cambodian figures survive to this day.

Bodawhpaya's success in annexing Arakan made him over-ambitious. With thoughts of extending his empire to include China, India and even England (the traditional Burmese map looked nothing like the real world), he set out to conquer Siam as a first step. In this he might have succeeded if he had not panicked at a crucial moment and fled the field; retiring to Yangon, he announced on the way that he had defeated the Siamese. However, his conquest of Arakan had created tensions on its border with British Bengal, where bands of Arakanese were fleeing across the frontier into the Chittagong area and raiding Arakan from that base. The first Anglo-Burmese clash occurred in 1794 when a few thousand of Bodawhpaya's troops entered British territory in pursuit of one of these bands. The British complied with a demand for the extradition of the fugitives and in the following year sent an embassy to what was still known as the Court of Ava.

Hitherto, British embassies had been largely concerned with commerce. Burmese kings had treated the *kalabyu* (white foreigner) traders with a sort of benign arrogance that occasionally bordered on contempt, their ministers and officials exacting as much as they could in the form of taxes and presents. Furthermore, kings did not consider themselves bound to abide by their own agreements, let alone a predecessor's. The nature of this latest mission was not commercial but political, however, and it was headed by an imperial officer, Captain Michael Symes. His main purposes were to discuss the border situation, to establish diplomatic relations and to try to get British ships exempted from the traditional treatment - the seizure of vessels, crews and cargoes mentioned earlier; but commerce was also on the agenda. Symes was treated in a way that appeared inconsistent: as a visitor he was greeted with charming hospitality, but as an envoy he encountered what he called 'insufferable arrogance'. The reason was that he was representing not King George III but merely the Governor-General of India, and Bodawhpaya quite reasonably did not expect Governors to presume to treat kings as their equals. The British understood this matter of protocol but deliberately continued to belittle the kings of Burma in this way.

Soon after their arrival Symes and his party were given an outing on elephant-back to go and visit the hsaya-daw (here, *Seredaw*), the capital's senior monk. They had already met him in a fine building with a multi-roofed spire about 150 feet high, but the hsayadaw's own monastery was even finer:

This building... is perhaps the most magnificent of its kind in the universe. It is constructed entirely of wood, and resembles, in the style of its structure and ornaments, that in which we had an interview with the Seredaw, but was much more spacious and lofty. The numerous rows of pillars, some of them sixty feet high, all of which were covered with burnished gilding, had a wonderfully splendid effect. It would be difficult to convey, either in language or by pencil, an adequate description of this extraordinary edifice. The profuse expenditure of gilding on parts exposed to the weather, as well as in the inside, cannot fail to impress a stranger with astonishment at the richness of the decoration, although he may not approve of the taste with which it is disposed. I could not have formed in my imagination a display more strikingly magnificent.

(Symes, 1800)

Cultured though he was in a western way, Symes was clearly ignorant of the nature of Buddhism. To him, gold was something to acquire self-ishly, not something to devote selflessly to the adornment of revered im-ages and edifices; and like so many European visitors, he assumed that Buddhism was a form of idol-worship. His attitude is plain when he de-scribes a visit to the still-unfinished Mahamuni (or Arakan) Pagoda, where he was first shown the captured Cambodian bronzes and then the 'idol':

Peculiar sanctity is ascribed to this image; and devotees resort from every part of the empire, to adore the Arracan Gaudma... (...) As we ap-proached, a crowd of people thronged after us with tumultuous enthusi-asm, striving for admittance to offer up a prayer to this brazen represen-tative of the divinity. We soon turned from these wretched fanatics, and the object of their stupid adoration ... (...) This temple, with its auxiliary buildings, which are yet in an unfinished state, will, when completed, be the most elegant in the empire....

[Unfortunately on 8 April 1884, one hundred years to the very day after the arrival of the great image in Amarapura, the building would be destroyed by one of the many fires that ravaged Burmese capitals. Ac-cording to the royal records (Than Tun, IX), of the gold that had dripped off the image in the conflagration, 2,190 pounds were recovered and made into 'a gold chain-mail that looked like a monk's robe' to reclothe the image. The shrine was rebuilt soon after the fire.]

Symes was repeatedly snubbed, and was kept waiting a long time (this was normal practice) for an audience with the king; but he maintained his composure and eventually he and his companions Buchanan and Wood were allowed into the royal presence, proceeding via the Hlutdaw (here, *Lootoo*), or Council Chamber:

..when we advanced to the outer gate, we were not obliged to put off our shoes, but were permitted to wear them until we had reached the inner enclosure that separates the court of the Lootoo from that of the royal palace, within which not any nobleman of the court is allowed to go with his feet covered.

Symes made no objection to removing his footwear, and records else-where how the party endeavoured - in spite of their tight-fitting clothes and unsupple joints - to sit with their feet tucked behind them so as not to give offence. On entering the palace the group saw on a high pedestal a large, richly carved and gilded throne, the seat of which was screened by folding doors; in galleries on either side stood four white 'umbrellas of state', symbols of royalty; and in front two low tables supporting several large gold vessels.

Immediately over the throne, a splendid piasath rose in seven stages above the roofs of the building, crowned by a tee or umbrella, from which a spiral rod was elevated over the whole. We had been seated little more than a quarter of an hour, when the folding doors that concealed the seat opened with a loud noise, and discovered his majesty ascending a flight of steps that led up to the throne from the inner apartment. He advanced but slowly, and seemed not to possess free use of his limbs, being obliged to support him-self with his hands on the balustrade. I was informed, however, that this appearance of weakness did not proceed from any bodily infirmity, but from the weight of the regal habiliments in which he was clad; and if what we were told was true, that he carried on his dress fifteen viss, upwards of fifty pounds avoirdupois of gold, his difficulty of ascent was not surprising.

This entrance, a traditional piece of royal theatre, was clearly calculated to impress all comers; so too was the king's attire:

His crown was a high conical cap, richly studded with precious stones. His fingers were covered with rings, and in his dress he bore the appearance of a man cased in golden armour, whilst a gilded, or probably a golden wing on each shoulder, did not add much lightness to his figure. His looks denoted him to be between fifty and sixty years old, of a strong make, in stature rather beneath the middle height, with hard features and of a dark complexion; yet the expression of his countenance was not unpleasing, and seemed, I thought, to indicate an intelligent and inquiring mind.

After the usual ceremony, during which the party gave Bodawhpaya presents of Benares gold brocade, the king withdrew and the folding doors closed. Symes had been expecting a proper audience, but the king had said not a word to him or his colleagues. Bodawhpaya still did not wish to deal with governors, even (or was it especially?) with the Governor-General of India. Once the royal family had climbed on to their elephants and were departing, it was time to collect the signed treaty in one of the Council chambers; even then the official delivering it refused to say that it was a letter from the king to the Governor-General of India. Symes declined to accept it until the official complied. On their way out the visitors saw in the outer courtyard the huge cannon that had been captured in Arakan and

afterwards conveyed by water to adorn the capital of the conqueror, where it is now preserved as a trophy, and is highly honoured, being gilded, and covered by a roof of a dignified order. It is formed of brass and rudely manufactured; the length is thirty feet, the diameter at the muzzle two and a half, and the calibre measured ten inches. It is mounted on a low truck carriage supported by six wheels. Near it lay a long rammer and sponge staff, and we perceived several shot made of hewn stone fitted to the calibre.

By the time he set off downstream, Symes had spent more than three months in Amarapura. He had obtained permission for a Resident to operate in Yangon for the promotion of British commercial interests, but the king proceeded largely to ignore the other terms of the treaty.

⚜

The man appointed as Resident in Yangon the following year was a capable but arrogant officer more concerned with his own sense of importance than with the delicacies of intercultural diplomacy. On finding himself regarded as merely a superintendent of trade, Captain Hiram Cox protested both to the Burmese Governor and to his own Governor-General. Both made it clear that Cox was not an ambassador but a Resident, and the Yangon officials naturally said that only the Court of Ava could deal with such matters. Cox went upriver in defiant mood. On approaching Amarapura he found Ava largely deserted but Sagaing populous and bustling with trade. He viewed the remains of Sagaing's fort with the eyes of a military engineer, concluding that it was 'despicable both as to strength and situation' and even ascribed the existence of the numerous pagodas to nothing more than a royal whim:

On the summits of these hills near the city, are a great number of pagodas and religious buildings of various forms and style of architecture, some finished with domes, some pyramidal, some cones, with a profusion of gilding expended on them; they had been recently white-washed, and all of them seemed in good repair: those on the hills have traverse flights of steps, bounded by low parapet walls leading to them, which must have cost much labour and expense. Near the river are several new ones erecting, the devotion of his majesty having occasioned a rage for building temples and monasteries.

(Cox, 1821)

When he describes his first sight of the capital, there is a condescending tone, too, in the word 'smatterer':

In the course of the forenoon we reached the city of Amarapoo-rah, which, including the suburbs, extends four miles along the south-eastern bank of the river, and teems with religious buildings of various shapes. The palace, as seen from the river, appears a confused assemblage of buildings, glittering with a blaze of gilding. One part of it has a square building finished with battlements, and a flat roof with Tuscan Pilasters at the angles, something in the theatrical style, and evidently the essay of

*some smatterer in European architecture...(...) The main breadth of the
river opposite the city of Amarapoorah is about two miles; the intermediate space, however, at this season is mostly filled with high sandy islands....*

It was to one of these islands, and not into the capital, that Cox was
taken; and there he had to live. After two months he had to be rehoused
because the Himalayan springtime had begun to melt the snows, causing
the Irrawaddy to start its annual rise. The king himself was by now oper-
ating from a makeshift palace on an island nearer to the site of his pet
project: the construction of the largest pagoda in the world, which was to
be 500 feet high on a base 450 feet square. After seven years' work, however, only the gigantic brick base had taken shape. Cox is scathing about
Mingun, 'an assemblage of bamboo huts, with a few wooden houses':

*About the centre of what is called the city, is a wooden palace of his
majesty's externally of mean appearance; and along the bank near it were
ranged about ten large accommodation-boats for the royal family. They
have houses erected on them with gilt mouldings and ornaments, also two
large ones with high pagodas on them for his majesty's and the queen's
particular use..(...) A little beyond his majesty's palace is the site of the
intended pagoda; at present they are advanced but little above the foundation; and, as the dimensions are very great, it will require some years to
finish it. His majesty holds his court in a large one-poled tent on a sandbank in the river opposite...*

As an engineer himself, Cox had his doubts about the pagoda's guardian *chinthe*, which he calls 'two colossal figures of lions, or rather sphinxes,
in positions rather couchant than rampant' and whose height he estimates
as ninety-five feet:

*the eye-ball, which we had an opportunity of measuring, was thirteen
feet in circumference. (...) ..the sockets for the eye-balls are left vacant,
and to place the eye-balls in them will require some exertions of mechani-
cal ingenuity, which I should like to see...*

Cox describes an inner chamber and compartments designed to hold
such treasures as the king wished to place there, and reports finding piles
of lead beams and plates. Both the use of lead and the credulity of Cox's
guides occasion a great deal of sarcasm:

*The invention of lining the chambers with lead for the preservation of
the treasures, is an honour claimed by his present majesty, who has great
skill in these matters. That the design has a divine sanction we had ocular
demonstration, three piles of leaden plates gilt with gold leaf being shewn
us, which had been brought and arranged where we saw them at night by
angels. Our conductors assured us that the building was surrounded at
night by watchful guards, so that no human agents could have transported*

such weighty materials unobserved: it is, therefore, justly considered and believed as a miracle of divine favour. All this I was particularly desired to note down in my pocket-book which I did on the spot, and added to it an observation of my own, that a good deal of melted wax, such as is used by Burmhans for candles, had been dropt on the slabs; I, therefore, suppose the night must have been dark, and that the angels worked by candlelight. From the level of this terrace, a conical spire of solid masonry is intended to be erected, the weight of which I am afraid will prove too great for the leaden beams; but it would be a dangerous piece of impertinence for a stranger to offer any advice on these sacred matters, otherwise I could easily secure the safety of the superstructure, by shewing them how to turn arches over the hollow chambers.

The Burmese did know how to 'turn arches'; but with regard to loads and stresses Cox knew what he was talking about: the eyeballs never were hoisted into place, and the chamber would surely have collapsed. Being no diplomat, however, when he at length obtained a proper audience with Bodawhpaya on 11 October 1797 (he had arrived in Amarapura on 24 January), he caused acute embarrassment and offence by complaining to the king about the way he had been treated. In the circumstances the king took the most sensible action he could: 'as I was in the middle of a speech to him', says Cox, 'he rose from his throne and retired'. Cox returned to Yangon, was recalled to Calcutta and soon found himself in charge of a settlement programme for tens of thousands of refugees who had fled from Arakan into the south Chittagong area to escape forced conscription into Bodawhpaya's army for a war against Siam. He had settled about 10,000 of them when he died at the age of thirty-nine in a place which is still called Cox's Bazar.

⌘⌘⌘⌘⌘⌘

It was into this area that the Burmese army came in hot pursuit of escapees. Meeting firm resistance from British-commanded sepoys they withdrew, explaining that they had no quarrel with the British. The British wanted no trouble on the Burmese border - they had more than enough to deal with in India already - but convention demanded that frontiers should be respected. They therefore sent troop reinforcements to Chittagong and warned the Arakan authorities not to allow such military incursions across the River Naaf into India, but also sent an envoy whose main object was to forge an alliance; the aim was to establish a permanent embassy to the Court of Ava and a Consulate in Yangon, by now an important ship-building base, both to promote British commercial interests and to counter the growing French ambitions in the region. For this mission the Governor-General turned once again to Symes, now a Lieutenant-Colonel.

Symes well knew that, whatever the Governor-General's orders, his first task was to try to atone for the offence that Cox had caused. Given an embarrassingly large escort which he knew the Burmese would regard as threatening rather than just impressive, he arrived in Yangon and maintained as low a profile as possible. He also maintained his equanimity in the face of deliberate slights suffered as his flotilla approached the 'capital', the island on which the king now stayed. Unknowingly the party anchored overnight at an island where corpses were burned and criminals executed; in the morning the Court authorities instructed them to move because the island was 'unclean' and took them to another island where, completely ignored by the court, they stayed in boats and tents for another forty days. On 28 November 1802, six months after landing in Yangon, Symes and his aides were admitted into the king's presence. Having sent the customary presents ahead by land, the party was picked up by four riverine war-boats and taken to the royal dwelling, an unornamented white-roofed building which Symes likened to a vast barn. They were led through a very dirty courtyard into a pillared hall where the king and his court were already assembled. A chilly reception awaited them once the usual preliminaries were completed:

> Silence then prevailed for some time, which the king first interrupted by what I understood was a question to one of the ministers who sat near him, respecting the direction of the river Naaf, that divides the British and the Birmese territories, and whether it was not a considerable river. He then observed in an audible voice that the records of the Birmese Empire made no mention of war having ever subsisted between the English and Birmese nations, and that much mischief may arise from selecting an improper person to represent a state.

(Hall, ed. 1955)

It is not clear whether the person the king was referring to here was only Cox or any envoy who represented the Governor-General rather than the king of England, but what followed suggests the latter interpretation:

> He thought fit to pay me by name a compliment, and said that having again seen my face he should forget every cause of umbrage; (...) I made a bow and hoped that no misunderstanding might ever interrupt the harmony that had so long united two great and continuous empires, and that it was Marquis Wellesley's sincere wish to live on terms of amity with his Majesty. To this no reply was returned, and another silence ensued...

Symes was surprised and perhaps even saddened by the change that had come over the Court of Ava since he had last seen it seven years earlier: its 'appearance of disorder and meanness', its soldiers 'armed with old firelocks and shabbily dressed' and the gloomy hall whose pillars were 'naked trees' - all spoke of 'faded splendour' and 'diminished power'.

❧❧❧❦❦❦

One day during his long waiting-period, Symes had received a letter sent from Yangon by an intriguing character called Rogers. We shall not be meeting him again until twenty years have passed, but it is worth getting to know him now. Symes tells us of Rogers' background:

I received this day a dispatch from Rangoon by an Englishman named Rogers, a person of such singularity of character as to demand more particular mention. Mr.Rogers was bred a sailor and about 20 years ago was a mate on board the Worcester *Indiaman, from which he deserted in Bengal. Being destitute and friendless he found his way to this land of refuge for men of desperate fortunes, and here he has ever since resided. Pressed by poverty, and to elude his creditors, he some years ago became the vassal of the prince of Prome, the King's second son, and under the protection of this prince, has continued to carry on a petty trade, by which he has earned a scanty subsistence for himself and a numerous family. His knowledge of the Birmese language is considerable, and he is accounted among the natives an expert lawyer. He is abased by the English at Rangoon for being what they call 'Slave of a Native prince'. He is, however, a man of a vigorous mind, though from bad habits probably of loose principles, and not to be trusted but with great caution. In the prosecution of our interests in this country, he may eventually be very serviceable.*

By this time Rogers held an important administrative post. Cox had met him and thought him very capable; Symes agreed but did not trust him; the next envoy, Canning, took a violent dislike to him; and the early Baptist missionaries could not speak highly enough of him. But we must for the moment leave this intriguing figure and follow Symes.

⌇⌇⌇⌇⌇⌇

After all his patient efforts Symes took back to the Viceroy a reply which merely amounted to an expression of reconciliation and an invitation to continue using Burmese ports. Symes was convinced that if Britain was to protect her possessions and interests in the East, she would need to exercise influence at the Court of Ava; but the suggestion of establishing a permanent embassy to the Court had fallen on deaf ears because Burmese kings could not deal with mere viceroys. Bodawhpaya wished only to deal with His Britannic Majesty, so no progress was made in three further missions (in 1803, 1809 and 1811) undertaken by Captain Canning, who had accompanied Symes in 1802. Furthermore, there was still an uneasy situation on the India-Burma border, and in Bodawhpaya's last years the fragile peace began to crumble.

In 1811 a certain Chin Byan, the son of a refugee Arakanese noble, crossed the Naaf river with a large force, reoccupied his father's Arakanese lands and at one stage held most of the province. The Burmese court naturally assumed (though the Calcutta government denied it) that the British had connived. Canning was still in Yangon on his third mission at the time but refused to go up to Amarapura, fearing that he might be held hostage there until Chin Byan was either killed or handed over. In 1813 a Burmese envoy arrived in Calcutta demanding the extradition of Arakanese fugitives. Though this request was turned down, the British did cooperate by helping to bring about the defeat of Chin Byan; but other refugees continued to mount incursions into Arakan. In Amarapura a Royal Order dated 18 February 1817 required 'the English Company' to hand over two named refugees with their followers and to 'stop collecting taxes in Chittagong, Panwa and Dacca' because these areas were now 'part of the Burmese territory' (Than Tun, VII). It was a dangerous claim, given that in the same year the Burmese overran Assam; that they had already annexed Manipur, where they had left a puppet prince on the throne; and that they marched into Assam again in 1819.

Though the Company saw this extended Burmese presence along the Indian frontier as a threat to its own possessions, the stage was not quite set for war when, on 5 June 1819, Bodawhpaya died after ruling for thirty-seven years. It had been a lengthy and by no means inglorious reign, but he left behind a monument symbolic of overweening ambition: the vast base of an abandoned pagoda, guarded by two colossal *chinthe* with no eyes. On the other hand, the massive 90-ton bell that he ordered to be cast in bronze was a success and is still the largest working bell in the world.

If Bodawhpaya had obeyed Alaunghpaya's bidding he would have arranged for his younger brother to succeed to the throne, but instead he had made his own eldest son Crown Prince. When the brother objected, he was executed; when the Crown Prince died it was his own son, Bodawhpaya's grandson Ba-gyi-daw, who took his place; and, as we have come to expect, the new king wanted a new capital city.

Khmer Bronze

CHAPTER 4
Talk of Culture
Ava, 1819-1833

> *When I hear anyone talk of culture, I reach for my*
> *revolver.*
>
> Hanns Johst, Schlageter.
> (but often attributed to Hermann Goering)

> *When I hear the word 'gun' I reach for my culture.*
> I. J. Good, The Scientist Speculates.

It took Bagyidaw two years to decide that the Court of Ava should be relocated, and in that interval an Englishman named Henry Gouger arrived in Amarapura. He had been until now a private trader in Bengal, and therefore actually in competition with 'John Company', and was critical of some of its practices. Having been advised to seek a change of climate after an illness he had set out for Amarapura with a cargo of Manchester cottons and other British goods, thus mixing business and convalescence. Gouger seems to have got on with the Burmese far more easily than people like Cox and Symes. He was of course a private individual rather than the representative of a pushy foreign power, but he seems also to have been more sympathetic, more tolerant of cultural differences. Having made the acquaintance of the Governor in Yangon, he had a trouble-free journey upriver and arrived in Amarapura in September 1822. According to the Royal Orders (Than Tun, VIII) although the construction of the new capital had begun in June 1821, the official move did not take place until March 1824; when Gouger arrived people were already being obliged to move five miles downriver to Ava. His sympathies were with the common folk:

> *The removal of the palace means, in Burmah, the removal of the entire population of the Capital. The nobles did not care about it, as they were repaid for the little inconvenience it caused them, by filling their pockets from the corrupt distribution of the building sites of the new city, and the frequent litigation it gave rise to. To the people it was the source of ruinous loss and discomfort, to which none but an unfeeling despotism would have dared to subject them. It was melancholy to see them breaking up their old habitations, and seeking new ones at great cost and labour.*
> (Gouger, 1862)

Where Cox thought that the suburban teak, bamboo and thatch houses had 'but a mean appearance', Gouger found them convenient and sensible and had no objection to living in one:

> This plan of building is peculiarly well suited to a country liable, like Amerapoorah, to frequent shocks of Earthquake. One of these occurred while I was there, but, though it was rather a severe one, no damage was done; the houses merely rocked backwards and forwards without injury, and it seemed to cause very little alarm to the inhabitants. (....) The main streets were wide and cheerful, dotted here and there with noble tamarind trees, affording an agreeable shade, though the natives hold it to be unhealthy to live under the shelter of these trees. The town was surrounded by a high brick wall with battlements, and a wide ditch; this was nearly half a mile from the river, which, - above an island which has formed in the stream opposite the town, appears to be a mile broad. A large proportion of the population lived between the wall and the river, and it was in this suburb, on the river side, that I hired a house.

Nor did Gouger suffer any indignities or delays in getting to see the king. 'For some astrological reason' says Gouger 'His Majesty had vacated his gorgeous palace and was inhabiting a temporary one near to it, constructed of bamboo and thatch' until the new one at Ava was finished. It was here that Gouger had a relaxed and informal audience with Bagyidaw, and where he was astonished to meet someone whom we have met already:

> His Majesty addressed a few words to some one in the ranks behind me, which, to my no small astonishment, elicited an address to me in clear, good English accent - "Are you, sir, an Englishman?" Robinson Crusoe's surprise at the celebrated footprint in the uninhabited island could hardly have surpassed mine, for I thought myself 500 miles away from any of my own race. (...) He was a large, strongly-built man, slightly bent by age, attired after the fashion of the natives, already described - a long, ample silk cloth round the waist, a loose muslin jacket, tied with strings in front, covered his body, but did not conceal the white skin beneath, barelegged of course, and his long grey hair twisted into a knot at the crown, where it was confined by a strip of white muslin. His long grey beard was so thinned, according to the native fashion, that that portion only which appertained to the middle part of the chin was preserved, and this being of a texture stiff as horsehair wagged backwards and forwards in a most ludicrous manner whenever he attempted to speak. He spoke Burmese fluently, and (...) was addressed as "Yadza" (the nearest approach the Burmese language admits to "Rodgers") ....

By this time, the resourceful Rogers had been a British outlaw for forty years and must at least have been in his sixties. Ironically, the British would be making trouble for him soon, not deliberately but inadvertently, and not in a British court but in the Court of Ava. But for the moment we shall return to Gouger.

In next to no time Gouger had settled into his house, applied to see the king, attended Court the next day and been given an audience within the hour. He could not understand why British officials were being so unyielding over what came to be called "The Shoe Question". (*See box on pp. 134 & 135*) It was known that Burmans never entered royal or sacred ground without first removing their footwear as a sign of reverence, but British envoys regarded such a practice as beneath their dignity. Gouger's own views were refreshingly sensible:

..I cannot help stopping a moment, to exclaim against the folly of my countrymen generally, in raising a senseless clamour against a custom so truly agreeable in a tropical climate. I found the comfort of it so great, that from that day forth I never wore our detestable foot-gear of stockings and boots so long as I remained in the country. The cool light sandal of the native, slipped on and off with facility, was quite a luxury.. (...) Our Envoys have always complained of vexatious delays before they could secure a reception at Court. Nothing of the kind was experienced by the foreigner who had no state dignity to uphold.

His readiness to conform to custom helped him to prosper not only in public but also at Court, but if Bagyidaw was often affable he was also of uneven temper; and Gouger did not have long to wait for proof of this. The new palace at Ava , designed to eclipse the old one in size and splendour and considered by Gouger to be 'remarkably beautiful', was nearing completion and the architect 'stood deservedly high in his master's favour'. Above the throne towered the multi-roofed spire, and on its tip the gilded umbrella-like *hti* with its hoops of bells had just been put in place, and the delighted king often went to see how things were progressing.

On one of these excursions the town was visited by a terrific thunderstorm, the sacred tee was struck by the lightning, the massive iron stanchions supporting it bent nearly to a right angle, and the ill-fated umbrella of course reversed. It was indeed a melancholy spectacle to behold the fragments of this beautiful pinnacle, suspended at an immense height, a mark for all the fury of the storm. But the tempest was nothing in comparison with that which raged in the breast of the Tyrant when he beheld his glory blown to shreds, and an omen of evil brought upon his Throne. As he could not vent his fury on the elements, he turned it on the able but ill-fated Architect. I did not see him at the moment, but was told his rage was like frantic insanity. The poor man was hunted up and dragged to the place of execution, the Tyrant ejaculating every few minutes, "Is he dead?" "Is he dead?" as if grudging a prolonged existence even of a few minutes. But on the execution-ground a scene was enacted that illustrates my remarks about the universality of bribery. It is common, when the executioners have a victim of rank, or one able to pay, to suspend the blow till sunset, to give time to his friends to negotiate for his pardon. This chance was offered to the dejected Architect, who, almost as mad as his master, refused the boon, and insisted on their performing their office instantly; they complied, and the expected reprieve arrived too late.

Gouger went back to Calcutta to bring in another consignment of goods, and returned to Ava towards the end of 1823. He found Rogers still in good health but began to feel 'the first indications of an unfriendly feeling towards the British Government' as Anglo-Burmese relations deteriorated. Soon he found himself shunned and was advised to stay at home; and then in May 1824 he was arrested along with several other foreigners, including the American Baptist missionary Dr. Adoniram Judson and Rogers - 'a poor old man bending with age'. Rogers decided to poison himself rather than endure the hideous tortures that he knew to be usual, but he was unable to acquire the means in time. Along with Gouger, the Americans Judson and Price and a few others, he was thrown into the notorious *Let-ma-yun* ('hand-not-flinch') prison, so named because within its confines there were no holds barred.

∞∞∞∞∞

The reason for this internment was that the Court's enemies were closing in. Soon after the British had sent reinforcements to Chittagong, Bagyidaw had sent his great general Maha Bandula to Arakan with orders to conquer Bengal and bring the Governor-General in fetters to Ava. Burmese troops had promptly crossed the frontier and drawn first blood, whereupon John Company had declared war on 5 March 1824. Just before the imprisonment of the foreigners, Bandula had attacked at Ramu and almost wiped out the British opposition there; but the British were now attacking on two further fronts - in Assam to the north and on the seaboard in the south, where the aim was to take the ports and then strike up the Irrawaddy towards the heart, Ava. Bandula duly marched south.

General Campbell's army landed in Yangon, supported by a flotilla under the command of Captain Marryat, better known as a writer of sea stories and children's books. Here they found that Bagyidaw had deported the mainly Mon population, who would probably have welcomed the British, and that provisions were therefore difficult to come by. Worse still, the problem of disease had been grossly underestimated. The Burmese troops were depleted not only by disease but also by exhaustion, having just arrived from Arakan; but Bandula was by any standards a charismatic leader, resourceful and courageous, and his troops fought fiercely for him. Nevertheless there could be only one outcome, and when on 1 April 1825 he was killed by a shell at Danubyu, his army broke. Assam had already been taken and by the end of the month Arakan was also in British hands. There followed a period of stop-start hostilities during which the peace terms offered by Campbell met with procrastination. The cultural expectations on either side differed widely. Once, the Court of Ava sent two of their foreign prisoners as envoys and were astonished when, having had no success, the pair returned to their captivity. On another occasion the

Court sat stunned when one of its boats laden with the equivalent of £250,000 sterling was returned intact because what had been stipulated for reparations was a million pounds, not a quarter of a million. Though the Court considered this demand excessive, the war had actually cost about *thirteen* million in all, and of Campbell's 40,000 men (most of them sepoys) 15,000 were dead. For the European soldiers the main enemy had been disease. The figures speak for themselves:

EUROPEAN TROOPS

	In Yangon	In Arakan	Total
Battle deaths	166	nil	166
Hospital deaths	3,160	595	3,755
Survivors	412	409	821
TOTAL	**3,738**	**1,004**	**4,742**

The peace terms included the immediate release of all British prisoners, and in February 1826 Gouger found that he was being released while Rogers was not, the Court regarding him as a Burmese citizen. In conversation Rogers had often expressed a desire to see England again, and Gouger offered to plead with the British authorities for his exoneration, and even pressed him to agree so that he might at least live out his last days in British territory. Meanwhile, with Campbell's army closing in still further, the Court of Ava decided to release its prisoners and send a surrender note with the American missionary Mr.Price. (It would perhaps have been too demeaning to use a British prisoner for the purpose.) Campbell's military secretary recorded what happened next:

> *The army continuing to advance, was met at Yandaboo, only forty-five miles from Ava, by Mr. Price, and two ministers of state, accompanied by the prisoners* and the stipulated sum of twenty-five lacs of rupees; empowered to state without reserve, that they had given in ...*

Rogers was not one of the 'several others'. He had decided to stay with his family in Ava and, according to Gouger, the old gentleman 'ended his days in Burmah not long after'.

Apart from the £1 million indemnity, the Treaty of Yandabo required Burma to give up her claims to Manipur and Assam and to cede Arakan and Tenasserim in perpetuity to the Honourable East India Company, thus losing most of her coastline. Only then would the British withdraw to Yangon and embark their troops, leaving the rest of Lower Burma still in Bagyidaw's hands. It was also stipulated that there should be a British Resident at Ava. These conditions had not yet been fully met when a mission led by John Crawfurd arrived in Ava in September 1826. A great

---

* *Mr. Judson (an American missionary) and his wife, Mr. Gouger, a British merchant, and several others who had been taken during the war.*

(Snodgrass, 1827)

crowd gathered on the river-bank to see the strange steamship and the British *kalabyu*, and later on Crawfurd found that the king himself was 'extremely desirous of seeing the steam-vessel under weigh'. Though the journey from Rangoon had taken a month, Crawfurd reckoned that it would have taken only twenty days but for the frequent stops and the heavy vessel it had to tow part of the way.

Crawfurd was intent on securing a commercial treaty, but his hosts appeared to be in no hurry. Two weeks after arriving he was, as the king's guest, obliged to attend an annual regatta. His party was taken to a large covered boat anchored in mid-stream.

The King and Queen had already arrived, and were in a large barge at the east bank of the river. This vessel, the form of which represented two huge fishes, was extremely splendid: every part of it was richly gilt, and a spire of at least thirty feet high, resembling in miniature that of the palace, rose in the middle. The King and Queen sat under a green canopy at the bow of the vessel, which, according to Burman notions, is the place of honour...(...) Near the King's barge were a number of gold boats, and the side of the river, in this quarter, was lined with those of the nobility, decked with gay banners, each having its little band of music, and some dancers exhibiting occasionally on their benches. Shortly after our arrival, nine gilt war-boats were ordered to manoeuvre before us. The Burmans nowhere appear to so much advantage as in their boats, the management of which is evidently a favourite occupation. The boats themselves are extremely neat, and the rowers expert, cheerful, and animated. In rowing, they almost always sing, and their airs are not destitute of melody.

(Crawfurd, 1834)

This three-day event was picturesque but Crawfurd found the delay irksome. The next day was devoted to a fireworks display, which in protest he declined to attend, and another week passed before the Mission was presented to the king. When the Court officials tried as usual to make the party 'kow-tow' more than Crawfurd deemed appropriate, he insisted that 'no obeisance whatever should be made by us except in the King's presence, and that our shoes should not be taken off until we were on the point of entering the Palace'. Once in the precincts, he noticed that the multiple roofs of the huge timber building were covered not with wooden tiles but with 'plates of tin' - presumably corrugated iron - and that the Hall of Audience was 'without walls, and open all around, except where the throne is placed'. The palace had been occupied only two and a half years, and its resplendent interior was impressive:

The roof is supported by a great number of handsome pillars, and is richly and tastefully carved. The whole fabric is erected upon a terrace of solid stone and lime, ten or twelve feet high, which constitutes the floor: this is so smooth, even, and highly polished, that I mistook it at first for white marble. With the exception of about fourteen or fifteen inches at the

Bandoola's look-out tree at Donoobew--Mounting four guns (from Snodgrass)

bottom of each pillar, painted of a bright red, the whole interior of the Palace is one blaze of gilding. The throne, which is at the back of the hall, is distinguished from the rest of the structure by its superior brilliancy and richness of decoration. The pedestal on which it stands is composed of a kind of mosaic of mirrors, coloured glass, gilding, and silver, after a style peculiar to the Burmans.

When Bagyidaw tottered in under the weight of his raiment, he was waving what looked like 'the white tail of the Thibet cow' - a whisk which, like the white umbrella, was a symbol of royalty. Every courtier performed the *shik-ko*, raising his joined hands to his forehead and bowing three times to the ground. The shoeless visitors had clearly decided in advance how they should salute the king.

No salutation whatever was dictated to us; but as soon as his Majesty

Meeting of the British and Burmese commissioners at Neoun-ben-zeik. Principal figure, the Kee-wongee (from Snodgrass)

presented himself, we took off our hats, which we had previously kept on purposely, raised our right hands to our foreheads, and made a respectful bow.

They paid the Queen the same compliment when she appeared with the royal couple's only child, a little princess about five years old, and there followed the usual ceremonial activity, including the giving of presents; but Crawfurd was not in a good mood. He was convinced that he knew the reason for the Court's delaying tactics:

The festivals, which continue for three days, are distinguished by the epithet of Ka-dau, *which word means "pardon asking". Our presentation was evidently put off from day to day, that we might appear among the crowd of suppliants asking forgiveness for past offences!*

He was later led to believe that a further piece of deception was being carried out—that Burmese history was being written in such a way as to foster the Court's grand illusions. He finishes his entry for November 2 as follows:

I learnt last night, from good authority, that the Court Historiographer had recorded in the National Chronicle his account of the war with the English. It was to the following purport:- In the years 1186 and 1187*, the Kula-pyu, or white strangers of the West , fastened a quarrel upon the Lord of the Golden Palace. They landed at Rangoon, took that place and Prome, and were permitted to advance as far as Yandabo; for the King, from motives of piety and regard to life, made no effort whatsoever to oppose them. The strangers had spent vast sums of money in their enterprise; and by the time they reached Yandabo, their resources were exhausted, and they were in great distress. They petitioned the King, who, in his clemency and generosity, sent them large sums of money to pay their expenses back, and ordered them out of the country.

This may have been a piece of humorous Court chit-chat; it may even have been an account put about orally in an attempt to reassure the people; but it certainly does not appear in the palace archives known as the Royal Orders. About the king himself Crawfurd had mixed feelings, finding him on the whole somewhat clownish:

His manners are lively and affable, but his affability often degenerates into familiarity, and this not unfrequently of a ludicrous description. A favourite courtier, for example, will sometimes have his ears pinched, or be slapped over the face. Foreigners have been still more frequently the objects of such familiarities, because with them freedoms may be taken with less risk of compromising his authority.. The king is partial to active sports, beyond what is usual with Asiatic sovereigns,- such as water excursions, riding on horseback and on elephants, elephant catching, &c. Among his out-door amusements there is one so boyish and so barbarous, as not easily to be believed, had it not been so well authenticated:- this is the practice of riding upon a man's shoulders. No saddle is made use of on these occasions, but for a bridle there is a strap of muslin put into the mouth of the honoured biped.

On a later public occasion, however, he admits to a grudging admiration:

After the elephant combats were over, the King prepared to take his departure. His elephant, one of the noblest animals I have ever seen, having the trunk, head, and part of the neck of a white flesh colour, and in other respects altogether perfect, was brought up close to the shed under

---

* i.e. of the Burmese era

which we were sitting, and he mounted it with great agility, placed himself upon the neck of the animal, took the hook in his hand, and seemed to be perfectly at home in this employment. We afterwards saw the Heir-apparent, a child of thirteen years of age, guiding his elephant in the same way. This practice is, I believe, peculiar to the Burmans; for in Western India, at least, no person of condition ever condescends to guide his own elephant. There is at least some manliness in the custom...

This heir-apparent was Bagyidaw's young brother, Prince Tharrawaddy. Though only a teenager, he had developed a fine sense of theatre. When he gave an audience to the Mission he was not only richly dressed with gems at his throat, on his fingers and on his scabbard; he also knew how to make an entrance, for when the folding doors opened

the Prince was seen in an adjoining chamber seated upon a gilt couch, cross-legged, and under a pair of mirrors. This was intended for effect, and was certainly not unsuccessful. In a few minutes he got up, with a sword in his hand, walked briskly forward, and seated himself on the throne in the front hall. (...) He...acted his part with great propriety.

⟡⟡⟡⟡⟡⟡⟡

Crawfurd appended to his account a description of Ava by his colleague Lt. de Montmorency. This is full of information useful to an invader, dealing with walls, parapets, embrasures, moats, causeways and so on, but we can get some idea of the size and nature of the city. The walls were about five miles in circumference and, while most of the houses inside were 'mere huts', 'the dwellings of the chiefs are constructed of planks, and tiled, and there are probably in all not half-a-dozen houses constructed of brick and mortar'. There were ten markets within its walls and one in the suburbs, and these were well supplied with Chinese and Lao products and 'British cottons, woollens, glass, and earthenware'. The Lieutenant then turns to the temples:

In Ava, of course, there are many temples, the tall white, or gilded spires of which, give to the distant view of the place a splendid and imposing appearance, far from being realized on a closer examination. Some of the principal of these may be enumerated: the largest of all is called Loga-thar-bu and consists of two portions, or rather of two distinct temples; one in the ancient, the other in the modern form. In the former, there is an image of Gautama in the common sitting posture, of enormous magnitude. Colonel Symes imagined this statue to be a block of marble; but this is a mistake, for it is composed of sandstone. A second very large temple is called Angwa Sékong; and a third, Ph'ra-l'ha, or "the beautiful". A fourth temple, of great celebrity, is named Maong-Ratna. This is the one in which the public officers of the Government take with great formality the oath of allegiance.

Crawfurd went to see as much as he could of the surrounding area, though his hosts did not want him to enter the walls of Amarapura; this was probably because the old city was largely inhabited by Chinese who, since they had built substantial houses, stayed put when the Burmans were transferred. He was told that the old capital now contained only two or three hundred houses. His party was, however, persuaded to go and see the Great Image and the Cambodian bronzes. Crawfurd thought these looked 'neglected', and certainly they seem to have dwindled in number:

They consisted of several gigantic statues in the human form, three griffins, and one three-headed elephant. The human figures, all more or less mutilated, were lying neglected on the floor: they were represented in a standing attitude, on pedestals, had crowns on their heads, and might measure in all about eight feet high. These, when the image of Gautama was in Aracan, are said to have represented warders or guardians of his temple. The Burmans call such images "Balu", a kind of demon or malignant being. One of them had a third eye in the forehead, and, I thought, might be intended for the Hindoo god Siwa.

Exploring a little further Crawfurd and a colleague rode out (on horse-back, not on elephants) to a point on a hillside in Sagaing; they were impressed not only by the view but also by the number and scale of its religious monuments.

..a beautiful and magnificent prospect of the lower country is presented: this consists of the towns of Ava and Sagaing, the river with its islands, the lake Remyat-gyi'-ang, with the stupendous temple of Kaong-m'hu-d'hau on its banks close below. Both ranges are covered with temples innumerable. Sometimes the sides of the decomposed rocks are excavated to the distance of twenty or thirty yards, and these shafts, cased with brick and mortar, form the principal portion of the temple, the outer wall and a portion of the roof only being visible. In one low temple of this description we found a recumbent image of Gautama, occupying the whole building, and of the enormous length of very nearly seventy-five feet, each foot measuring twelve feet. The soles were sculptured in the manner in which the foot of Guatama (sic) is always represented, with a great variety of emblematic and hieroglyphic figures.

Here too he saw 'several half-finished structures of enormous magnitude, the founders having died while they were in progress, and no one afterwards thinking it worth while to complete the work'. He assumed that in Buddhism there was great merit in building a pagoda but little or none in restoring an old one, and mentions the one at Mingun as the 'most remarkable example of this'; but like many foreign visitors he found the neglect of old pagodas difficult to accept.

He was also finding it difficult to accept the Burmese Court's way of doing business, with its evasions, its procrastinations and its obfuscations.

ᕗᕗᕗᕗᕕᕕᕕᕕ

With time on his hands, Crawfurd was able to include in his journal anecdotes about two families resident in Ava. The first concerns Shwe Maung and his children. About thirty years old, Shwe Maung was intelligent and healthy but had two physical peculiarities: he had too few teeth and, more obviously, far too much body-hair:

The few teeth he had were sound, but rather small; and he had never lost any from disease. He stated, that he did not shed his infantine teeth till he was twenty years of age, when they were succeeded in the usual manner by the present set. He also expressly asserted, that he never had any molares; and that he experienced no inconvenience from the want of them... (...) At his birth his ears alone were covered with hair, about two inches long and of a flaxen colour. At six years of age, hair began to grow on the body generally, and first on the forehead. He distinctly stated that he did not attain the age of puberty till he was twenty years old.

Except for his hands and feet and 'the red portion of the lips', he was now covered in fine hair four to eight inches long which was silvery grey all over the head. Just as some European kings had court 'fools', so Bagyidaw employed Shwe Maung now and then as a freak, to imitate the antics of a monkey; but the king had favoured him enough to make him a present of a pretty wife. Of Shwe Maung's four daughters the first two had died very young, the third (now about five years old) was the image of her mother and completely normal, and the fourth already had silky flaxen body-hair and only four teeth, two incisors in each jaw. She was now only about two and a half years old; when we next meet her she will be a mature woman.

The second anecdote is more gruesome. The American missionary Dr Price, a colleague of Judson's, had married one of his Burmese converts, and this lady was in advanced pregnancy when she contracted cholera and died suddenly. As if this were not tragedy enough, Dr Price was now in a predicament of potentially nightmarish proportions because of two Burmese customs still current at the time, the one concerning death from cholera, the other death in childbirth.

No person dying of cholera morbus, which is considered an infectious complaint, is allowed a funeral with the customary solemnities, but must be interred on the day of death. The body of a woman who dies in labour before the birth of the child, is subjected to a horrid rite...(...) The belief is, that the souls of women dying under such circumstances would become evil spirits, haunting the towns or villages to which the deceased belonged, if a certain ceremony were not practised to exorcise them. The horrid ceremony in question is as follows:- The husband, with dishevelled hair, and bearing a Dá, or sword, in each hand, goes before the coffin, in the procession, from his house to the funeral ground, using the gestures of a maniac, and cutting the air with the weapons in every direction. When the procession has arrived at the place, the case is enquired into by the public officers, and a regular deed of divorce between the husband and the deceased is drawn up. The body is then opened by one of the burners of the dead, the foetus extracted, and held up to the spectators. The husband, after this, walks thrice round the coffin, goes home, washes his head, and returns, when the corpse is burned with the usual ceremonies.

Since the poor woman had died both of cholera and in childbirth, and since the king himself had - as a gracious gesture to Price - ordered that the funeral should be a public occasion, there was nothing for it but to deceive the king on both counts. Fortunately one of Price's friends, a high-ranking public officer, came forward to declare that the deceased had soon after the infant had been born, simply died of her labours; and on his assurances the public funeral 'took place with all proper solemnity'.

No such gracious gesture was shown to Crawfurd, however. After weeks of repetitious and unsuccessful haggling he left Ava in February 1827 and advised Calcutta not to appoint a Resident to Ava. Here, he said, in what was 'little better than honourable imprisonment', a Resident would be not only 'distant by a navigation of 1,200 miles (near 500 of it within the Burman territory)' but also 'an object of perpetual jealousy to a Government indescribably ignorant and suspicious' (Crawfurd 1834, Appendix IV).

༄༅་་་་་

Tenasserim was now British territory and, while Crawfurd was steaming back down the Irrawadddy on board the *Diana*, Henry Burney was settling into an administrative post there. It was his celebrated aunt who had written *Evelina*, the novel that had been a great influence on Jane Austen. Burney had already served the Company well in Bangkok, where he too had recently led a mission, and now in his spare time he was studying Burmese history, learning the language and earning praise from his superiors. Up in Ava, Bagyidaw was continuing to avoid implementing Article 7 of the Treaty of Yandabo, whereby each party had agreed to depute a minister to reside in the other's capital. To treat Calcutta as a capital and the Governor of Bengal as equal to a king would imply that Burma was in effect an Indian state, and this was anathema to him. Nevertheless, he eventually complied, and it was Burney who was appointed as Resident to the Court of Ava.

On his way upriver he was struck by the poverty of the population and soon learned the cause: local officials were collecting the money needed to pay the indemnity demanded by the Company - and, after the officials and the queen had taken their own share, only half the takings were entering the fund. Burney arrived in April 1830. Though his position was clearly a delicate one he did not suffer from a language barrier, and got to know the people far better than Cox, Symes or Crawfurd had. After a cool welcome, Bagyidaw treated him in a very friendly manner and even conferred a Burmese honour upon him. On his part however, Burney considered the king to be 'a poor weak fool, incapable of comprehending any rational argument' (The Burney Papers, BXV), and goes on to say that the king 'feels and broods over the disasters of the late war, and of all his subjects that war has left the least impression of our superiority on his mind'. Of course, no Burmese king could ever publicly concede that he had an equal, even if he considered it to be true; but it seems that Bagyidaw's melancholia, which was soon to turn into insanity, was already affecting his judgement.

Perhaps because his private concerns conflicted with his official ones, Burney's attitudes appear ambivalent. With his linguistic and cultural knowledge he was able to open the doors of the Court and of ministers' private homes, and to form genuine friendships; yet over the Shoe Question he (so to speak) dug in his heels:

My objection to removing my shoes is formed on the fact that the Burmese require it not as the fulfilment of a mere custom, but as a means of exalting the King and gratifying their own pride and vanity by humiliating and degrading the British character. Besides, the Mussulmans of this place have persuaded the Burmese to carry the etiquette regarding the shoes of Europeans much farther than what it is, I believe, at any other Court in Asia. Even in the streets and highways a European, if he meets with the King or joins his party, is obliged to take off his shoes. Dr. Price (an American Baptist missionary) always walked and ran barefooted alongside the King's litter, and Mr. Lane on one occasion, when he was invited to see the ceremony of the King ploughing the land, which is annually performed here as well as in China and Siam, was obliged to remove his shoes and walk a mile or two over burning sand until he was quite lame. When Sir Archibald Campbell deputed Lieuts Rawlinson and Montmorency to this place in 1828, he prohibited them to take off their shoes, and they did not, therefore, see the King.

(Burney, Journal. Quoted by Hall, 1974:201)

The Mr. Lane mentioned here was a private English merchant living in Ava at the time. Distrusted in some quarters as a British spy - perhaps because he was unusually knowledgeable for a merchant - he had nevertheless prospered and had been befriended by Bagyidaw's uncle, the Mekkara Prince. This man was a most unusual Burman in that he was well-read in western science and philosophy. Lane had taught him such things as logarithms, and together they were preparing a Burmese-English dictionary. Burney went to visit this prince and found him 'a very intelligent and inquisitive character'. For more than an hour he plied Burney with questions:

He questioned as to the latitude and longitude of London, Calcutta, Ava and Bangkok, the cause of the polarity of the needle, the reappearance of the last comet, the properties of the Barometer and Thermometer both of which instruments were hanging in his room, and the nature of Algebra which science, he said, he much wished to learn. Indeed he sur-

Arrival of British flotilla 1824

*Breaching
a Stockade*

prised me with the extent of his knowledge and he seemed to comprehend and admit the correctness of our system of the Universe. We saw in a handsome bookcase with glazed folding doors his library books consisting of Rees's Cyclopaedia, Johnson's Dictionary, the Holy Bible with Dr. Judson's translations, all of which, he said, he had read very carefully. On the whole he is certainly the most extraordinary man we have seen in this country. He sent lately to Mr. Lane translations from Rees's Cyclopedia of two very scientific articles, one regarding the calculations of eclipses and the other regarding the formation of hailstones.

(Quoted by Hall, 1974: 207)

Burney's surprise should not be surprising, for most members of the Court of Ava were still unaware of the outside world. This meant, of course, that they were also ignorant of the norms of international diplomacy. On one occasion when Burney had tried to explain that it was not customary to extradite political refugees (as opposed to criminals), an exasperated minister had exclaimed:

'Your and our customs are so completely opposite on so many points. You write on white, we on black paper. You stand up, we sit down, you uncover your head, we our feet, in token of respect.'

(Quoted by Hall, 1974: 190)

The minister may have fastened on comparatively trivial cultural differences, but there can be little doubt that the friction between Britain and Burma, though caused by the expansionist aims of each, was exacerbated by the inflexibility of cultural expectations on both sides. The British deserve much of the blame for this state of affairs; but if the Court as a whole had been as willing to learn as the Mekkara Prince evidently was, the first Anglo-Burmese war might not have been necessary. As it was however, another war was not far off.

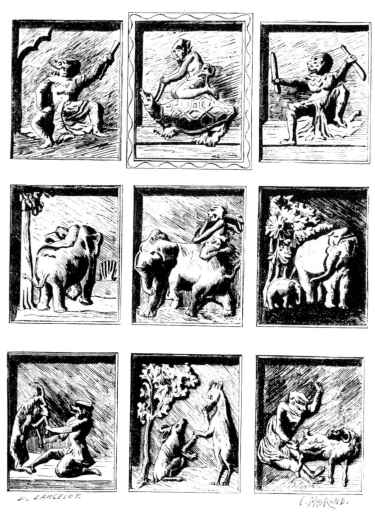

Copies of tiles at Amarapura

CHAPTER 5
Villainous Company
Ava and Amarapura, 1833-1857

> *Company, villainous company,*
> *hath been the spoil of me.*
>
> William Shakespeare , *King Henry IV Part 1, III, iii*

Bagyidaw's mental condition began to give cause for alarm, and often prevented him from taking part in Court business. Much as he liked Burney as an individual, he made it clear that he resented the British presence in Ava and formally proposed the removal of the Residency to Yangon. By 1834 he was losing his sanity, his behaviour being sometimes violent, sometimes reclusive, and Burney wrote to Calcutta supporting the king's proposal because the conditions of the post made it difficult for British officers to live there for more than two or three years at a time. What was 'so irksome and trying to the constitution' was not so much the physical conditions ('the thermometer often exceeds 100 degrees, and does not fall below 92 degrees before 12 o'clock at night', 'the want of wholesome vegetables', the lack of exercise, the impassable roads, and so on) as the psychological ones:

> *But what ought chiefly to be mentioned, when any important event or discussion arises here, the consideration that there exists no certain means of communicating with your own Government, which possesses less knowledge of the real character and customs of this than of any other Indian Court, greatly enhances in such a climate and situation, near a crazy King and an ignorant and trembling set of Ministers, the mental anxiety which preys upon the health of a public servant holding a highly responsible office.*
>
> (Bengal Secret and Political Consultations, Vol.380. Quoted by Desai, 1939)

The anxiety seems to have preyed upon Burney's syntax too, judging by that sentence. His request was turned down, but he had to go to Yangon for health reasons in any case. On returning to Ava in July 1835 he found that, according to the rumour circulating at the time, he had returned in order to arrange for a British force to invade China from Northern Burma. In reality, the Company was not on the warpath but seeking a trade route to the biggest potential market in the world.

Bagyidaw became so insane that he sometimes had to be restrained.

His brother Tharrawaddy, the bejewelled Prince whose entrance had so impressed Crawfurd, now embarked with his followers on a flotilla of hundreds of boats and went upstream to his great-grandfather's old capital, Moksobo. In itself, this act signalled his intention to make a bid for the throne, and in April 1837 he pronounced himself king, occupied the Ava palace and had Bagyidaw removed to an ordinary house outside the city walls. True to Burmese tradition, the new king announced that he was not bound by any treaty that he had not been a party to. After the usual tortures and executions, King Tharrawaddy declared that he wanted to see Ava in ruins, threatened to burn down the houses of any who chose not to follow him, and shipped his Court and most of Ava's citizens to Kyauk-myaung, almost sixty miles upriver. His intention was to build a new capital at Moksobo and to link it to the Irrawaddy at Kyauk-myaung by digging a canal.

Burney decided to move the Residency to Yangon as a temporary measure. He and King Tharrawaddy had parted on friendly personal terms, but the king's mind was firmly set against having a Resident in his capital; and he was also determined to regain - though not by force of arms - the territory ceded by the Treaty of Yandabo. By now Burney was beginning to think that military menace was the only language the Court of Ava would understand, and even the American missionary Dr. Judson favoured war as a means of introducing the 'civilising' influence of Christianity; but at this time neither Tharrawaddy nor the Governor-General wanted a war. When Burney gave up his post in 1838 and took a well-earned leave in London, the Residency sputtered on for only two more years under Colonel Benson and Captain MacLeod. Meanwhile, Tharrawaddy had given up his grandiose Moksobo project and taken up residence in Amarapura. There, in February 1839, construction work began on his new capital city.

It was not long before Tharrawaddy too started having fits of violent insanity. He was several times placed under restraint by his sons before he died (or perhaps was secretly done to death) in 1846, to be succeeded by his eldest son Pagán. Having withdrawn the Residency in 1840, the Company made no effort to re-establish diplomatic relations for twelve years, despite the indignant complaints made from time to time by British traders in Yangon. Then, in 1851, the Burmese charged the captains of two British boats with offences that included murder, gave them no trial and fined them heavily, whereupon they turned to the Government of India for reimbursement of £1920. The Company trimmed this figure to £920 and decided that, if the captains' protests of innocence were true, the Court of Ava should make good the loss. Since there was no longer a British representative at the Court, a certain Commodore Lambert was sent to Yangon with clearly specified duties. He was to check first whether the two captains' claims were justified and, if so, to seek compensation from the Governor of Yangon; and only if this failed was he to produce a letter that he had been given. It was addressed to the king by the Governor-General, Lord Dalhousie. Dalhousie was later to regret that Lambert had been chosen for the job, though he could hardly have known at the time how high-handed and belligerent the man would be.

As soon as his frigate H. M. *Fox* was at anchor in Yangon, Lambert ignored his carefully-sequenced orders. Without first checking the accuracy of the two captains' allegations, he wrote to the Governor of Yangon; and without waiting for an answer he sent via the Governor a letter to King Pagán's Prime Minister which enclosed Dalhousie's letter. His covering note to the Governor of Yangon explained:

> *I have the honour to transmit to you a letter for His Majesty the King of Ava, together with one for the Prime Minister of the King. I shall expect that every dispatch will be used for forwarding the same, and I hold you responsible for an answer being delivered in these waters within five weeks from this day.*

(Parliamentary Blue Book, 1852)

Lambert was in no position to hold any Burmese official responsible for anything, but in spite of his effrontery the king's reply was conciliatory: a new Governor would be appointed in Yangon and the requested compensation would be paid. Dalhousie thought this a very satisfactory response, war being a last resort; but Lambert seemed determined to provoke hostilities. He was not only arrogant but also ignorant - or more likely dismissive - of Burmese customs. When the old Governor was replaced, Lambert did not have the courtesy to present himself to the new one; instead he sent his officers, who rode their horses into his courtyard - a serious breach of etiquette. He also gave the new incumbent too little time to prepare the ceremony deemed appropriate to such a formal meeting, with the result that the British deputation was asked to wait until the new Governor was ready.

Impatient, the officers reported their annoyance to Lambert, who interpreted the delay as a deliberate insult and immediately over-reacted. By the end of the day he had warned Britons resident in Yangon to be ready to leave within hours; he had embarked several hundred of them aboard British vessels that were by now steaming away downriver; he had given orders that the king's own ship, lying at anchor nearby, should be seized as an indemnity against the £920 claim that had not yet been settled; and he had notified the Governor of Yangon and the Court of Ava that the coasts of Burma were now 'under a state of blockade'. Even when the British ships had moved well downstream, the Burmese made efforts to avoid an armed clash, but when Lambert continued to tow the king's ship seawards they felt obliged to open fire. Lambert describes what happened next on the morning of 10 January 1852:

> *Her Majesty's steam-sloop,* Hermes, *with the King of Ava's boat in tow, passed us at half-past nine, when the stockade opened a sharp cannonade on Her Majesty's ship* Fox *which was instantly returned with shot and shell, and the Burmese battery was in a short time silenced. On the smoke clearing away, not a person was to be seen on the shore or in the*

boats. Our fire, I have no doubt, must have done great execution, for I have reason to believe that at least 3,000 men were opposed against us. One or two of the enemy's shot struck the Fox, *but did very trifling damage.*

Even after this carnage the Governor of Yangon sent a message promising to satisfy all British demands, but Lambert ignored it. Governor-General Dalhousie, though still professing not to want war, changed his attitude within a month: he first informed Lambert that 'a considerable force' would be sent to Burma, and then presented King Pagán with a set of demands so stern that the monarch could not reasonably be expected to meet them. In effect, it was a declaration of war. The second Anglo-Burmese war began in earnest on 6 April 1852 when Admiral Charles Austen - whose sister Jane had been influenced by Henry Burney's aunt - assembled offshore the fleet of steam-driven warships escorting Major-General Godwin's Bengal and Madras Infantry Brigades. The vessels, ranged along the Yangon River, bombarded the shores and there was a brief engagement, which General Godwin did his best to glorify:

Rangoon. April 23, 1852.
.. The storming into the Great Pagoda was a beautiful sight. The 800 men had to descend from a height where a battery was (and where we lost a good many, the shots plunging in on us constantly); then to traverse a pretty valley to the ascent to the Pagoda. They marched through the battery, wound their way silent and steady, till they reached the foot of the rising ground on which the Pagoda stands.

Then came the rush up it, under cannon and musketry. In a few minutes the shout told all. The men then spread out, and drove all before them. My reward was, and ever will be, in that loud huzza which all the regiments in the rear heard and understood...
(Quoted by Woodman, 1962: 142)

Back in London, much of the record concerning Commodore Lambert's insubordination was carefully suppressed so as to make British aggression appear more justifiable. John Company's trading monopoly had lasted until 1813, when it was broken by the British Government, and six years after this Second Burmese War its powers would be taken over by the Crown. In the meantime, the Company was giving way to companies. British industries, many of them based in Lancashire and Yorkshire, regarded Upper Burma as their through-road to the Promised Land - China, the largest unexploited market in the world - and many politicians openly or tacitly supported British aggression where it led to profits. Even so, there were some angry denunciations in Parliament and the House of Lords. Richard Cobden, at that time Member of Parliament for the West Riding of Yorkshire and a man of strong moral principles, published a cogent and scathing attack in a pamphlet entitled *How Wars are got up in India*, but it won few converts.

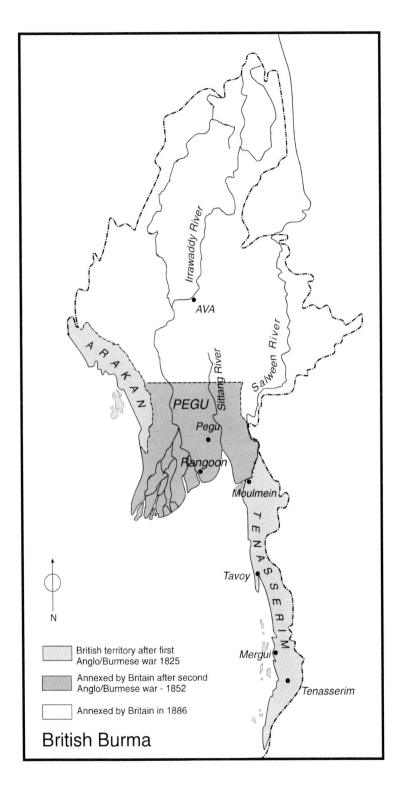

Irrawaddy River

A R A K A N

AVA

PEGU

Sittang River

Salween River

Pegu

Rangoon

Moulmein

T E N A S S E R I M

Tavoy

Mergui

Tenasserim

N

British territory after first
Anglo/Burmese war 1825

Annexed by Britain after second
Anglo/Burmese war - 1852

Annexed by Britain in 1886

British Burma

The whole of Lower Burma was soon overrun and declared as annexed to the British Empire. The invaders had learned from the experience of the previous Anglo-Burmese war: the provision of food and medical support was so much better this time that they suffered only 377 casualties in all, and the war cost less than one million pounds. In Amarapura meanwhile King Pagán was proving to be ineffectual and unpopular, and was also said to be of unsound mind. Even now, he was unwilling to come to terms with the advancing British. His half-brother Mindon, who had been allowed to use the title 'King' but was not *the* king, now decided to make a bid for the throne in the usual way : by travelling to Moksobo and gathering adherents there. His followers marched on Amarapura and in February 1853 dethroned Pagán, who was - unusually - spared and allowed the illusion of continuing power by being granted a small Court of his own. Invited to send envoys to Pyé (Prome), Mindon promptly did so, only to find that by now the British were fifty miles further upstream, at Myé-de. They had decided, although this did not accord with the terms of their own Proclamation of Annexation, to grab a further strip of teak-rich territory. The Court of Ava was now isolated not by choice but by enemies: to the north and east lay its old foes China and Siam, and to the south and west were its newer adversaries, the British. Half its empire was gone; there was no access to the sea; and although the waters flowing down from the roof of the world would continue to feed life, death could now strike swiftly against the current. Mindon did the only thing he could sensibly do: as a Burmese king he refused to sign a treaty, but as a sensible man he made no trouble and tacitly accepted the *fait accompli*.

❧❧❧❧❧❧

Mindon tried to persuade Dalhousie, the Governor-General, to restore Lower Burma to him. He made it clear nevertheless that he wished to remain on friendly terms with the British, and sent a Burmese mission to Calcutta. The mission was received graciously but Dalhousie was adamant, insisting that the new border should be fixed by treaty. "You may tell the envoys," he said to the interpreter Major Phayre, "that so long as the sun shines, which they see, those territories will never be restored to the Kingdom of Ava." Some months later he sent a mission to the Court of Ava to discuss the sort of treaty he wanted. Led by Phayre, who was well-versed not only in the language but also in the literature and customs of Burma, it was in effect a group of experts on geological, geographical, military and other matters, and its secretary was Henry Yule, a Captain in the Bengal Engineers. Though he was less sympathetic than Phayre to Burmese culture - he objected, for example, to Phayre's instruction that all officers should comply with the requirement to take off their shoes before entering a pagoda - Yule was a talented man. The narrative that he produced is valuable for the detail not only of its written descriptions but also of its pictorial ones, some of them drawn by himself.

The new king had not set about building a new city. According to the Royal Orders (Than Tun, IX) there had been some kind of Court petition in favour of keeping Amarapura as the capital, so it was there that on 13 September 1855 Mindon granted an audience to Phayre's mission. The king entered with the usual dramatic ceremonials:

At last the King's approach was announced by music, sounding, as it appeared, from some inner court of the Palace. A body of musketeers entered from the verandas in rear of the throne, and passing forward took their places between the pillars on each side of the centre aisle, kneeling down with their muskets (double-barrelled pieces) between their knees, and their hands clasped before them in an attitude of prayer. As the last man entered the golden lattice doors behind, the throne rolled back into the wall, and the king was seen mounting a stair leading from a chamber behind to the summit of the throne. He ascended slowly, and as if oppressed by weight, using his golden-sheathed sword as a staff to assist his steps.　　　　　　　　　　　　　　　　　　　　　　　　　(Yule, 1858)

Yule's closely-observed description shows how little the courtly ritual and dress had changed since Symes' day; and once again a Court official explained that Mindon's apparel was very heavy, asserting that 'the jewelled coat worn by his Majesty actually weighed nearly one hundred pounds'. On this occasion Mindon was joined by his queen, and several little princes were already in attendance. Two inquisitive little princesses also wanted to see what was going on. In the following passage, *Henza* (spelt variously *Hamsa, Hintha, Hantha,* etc.) refers to a mythical golden bird originally associated with the foundation of Pegu, also known as Hantha-waddy, but by this time used as a general symbol of sovereignty; and Yule's attention to the detail of the Queen's dress is remarkable:

The Queen seated herself on the King's right and a little in rear, assisting to hand in the gold spittoon and other appendages of a Burmese dignitary, which were presented by female attendants from behind. Between their Majesties in front of the throne stood a large golden figure of the sacred Henza *on a pedestal. After the Queen had finally taken her seat she fanned herself diligently for a few moments, and then fanned her husband, whilst one of the girls from behind brought her a lighted cheroot, which was immediately placed between her royal lips. (...) The Queen was not seen to...advantage. This was partly owing to the character of her head-dress, which would have been a very trying one to any lady. It was a perfectly close cap, covering ears and hair entirely, and rising above into a conical crest strangely resembling in form a rhinoceros horn,* with the point curved forward into a volute. Close lappets fell along the cheeks. The rest of her Majesty's dress had rather an Elizabethan character. The sleeves and skirt appeared to be formed in successive overlapping scolloped lappets, and the throat was surrounded by a high collar, also scolloped or vandyked, and descending to the waist. At the waist she wore a stomacher*

---

* Or perhaps rather the large nipper of a crab's claw.

or breast-plate of large gems.

Both cap and robe were covered and stiffened with diamonds, or what appeared to be such. The Queen is her husband's half-sister, as has always been the custom in the royal families of the Burman race, including that of Aracan when independent, and probably that of Pegu. One of the young girls who appeared at the lattice door in rear of the throne, dressed somewhat after the fashion of the Queen was, as we understood, the King's daughter. Another pretty little girl, with white flowers in her hair, who peeped in occasionally to get a glimpse of the Kalás, was said to be a child of the heir-apparent residing in the palace.

When the King had fairly entered, we all took off our hats, which hitherto we had kept on, and at the same time the whole of the native assembly bowed their faces to the ground and clasped their hands in front of them. The two rows of little princes, who lay in file before us, doubled over one another like fallen books on a shelf...

A Court official called a *than-daw-gan* then read aloud in an incantatory tone Dalhousie's letter and the list of his presents, the only one of which on show inside the audience hall was a model railway, which 'excited a good deal of interest among the Burmese'. (Dalhousie had only two years previously issued a famous Minute which determined the nature of the railway system that he was introducing into India.) Tradition laid down that a Burmese king did not address directly anyone who had sought an audience. It was the task of the *atwin-wun* to act as an intermediary. A traditional sequence of polite questions was put to those who came to sit at the 'golden feet' of the king:

*"Is the English ruler well?"**
Envoy. *"The English ruler is well." The Than-dau-gan repeated in a loud voice: "By reason of your Majesty's great glory and excellence, the English ruler is well, and therefore, with obeisance, I represent the same to your Majesty."*
Atwen-Woon. *"How long is it since you left the English country?"*
Envoy. *"It is now fifty-five days since we left Bengal, and have arrived and lived happily at the royal city."*
Thandau-gan. *"By reason of your Majesty's great glory and excellence, it is fifty-five days since the Envoy left the English country,"* (Bengal, *here interposed Major Phayre),* "and he has now happily arrived at the golden feet, therefore with obeisance,"* &c.&c.
Atwen-Woon. *"Are the rain and air propitious, so that the people live in happiness and ease?"*
Envoy. *"The seasons are favourable, and the people live in happiness." The Than-dau-gan repeated this in the same fashion as before.*

---

* Ingleet-Men *may apply to the Queen of England, or to the Governor-General. It is an ambiguous expression, purposely, I believe, adopted by the Burmese as a salve to their pride, compelled to hold intercourse with a dignitary who is not an anointed king.*

When Phayre and his officers had received in turn presents from the king, the royal couple rose and passed through the gilded lattice, music played again, the doors rolled out from the wall and the group were given permission to retire.

✦✦✦✧✧✧✧✧

Phayre's party, like those of Symes and Crawfurd, were permitted to do some exploring. In Sagaing, Yule noted that the massive brick rampart described by Cox was now 'decaying', and there was none of the bustling trade that Cox had seen. Since most of the pagodas were in ruins because of the great earthquake of 1839, Yule and his companions found little of interest until they had climbed 'a staircase of 275 steps' to a pagoda called "The King's Victory". Here it was not the pagoda but the view that enchanted them; Yule seems to have been stunned by a moment of beauty that led the hard-headed engineer to use such words as *magic, beautiful,* and *enchantment* - and then to have been embarrassed by the sensitivity of his own response:

The scene was one to be registered in the memory with some half-dozen others which cannot be forgotten. Nothing on the Rhine could be compared to it. At the point where the temple stood, the Irawadi forms a great elbow, almost indeed a right angle, coming down to us from the north, but here diverted to the west. Northward the wide river stretched, embracing innumerable islands, till seemingly hemmed in and lost among the mountains. Behind us, curving rapidly round the point on which we stood, it passed away to the westward, and was lost in the blaze of a dazzling sunset. Northwestward ran the little barren, broken ridges of Sagain, every point and spur of which was marked by some monastic building or pagoda. Nearly opposite to us lay Amarapoora, with just enough haze upon its temples and towers to lend them all the magic of an Italian city.

A great bell-shaped spire, rising faintly white in the middle of the town, might well pass for a great Duomo. You could not discern that the domes and spires were those of dead heathen masses of brickwork, and that the body of the city was of bamboo and thatch. It might have been Venice, it looked so beautiful. Behind it rose range after range of mountains robed in blue enchantment...(...)

A great deal of the beauty of the scene was, doubtless, due to the singularly fine atmosphere of the evening. But our impression was that the Lake of Como could not be finer, and those who had seen Como said that it was not.

Our description incited the Envoy and others to visit the temple next day. Seeing the whole in the hard light of the late morning sun, they set us down, I doubt not, as guilty of ridiculous exaggeration.

On another occasion Yule and three colleagues set out early by boat to go and see the old capital, Ava. Stopping for breakfast on the way, they found themselves part of an everyday scene that made a pleasant change from the affairs of Court; as with the little girl with white flowers in her hair, it was again a child that stole the scene:

On our way down to Ava we halted to breakfast at the Shwé-kyet-kya, or "descent of the golden fowl", a cluster of pagodas on a high promontory over the river, the face of which is revetted with a high wall. Here the river is hemmed into one distinct full channel between two decided banks, and there are no islands. A little further down on the same bank is the Shwé-kyet-yet, or "scratching of the golden fowl", (these names both refer to an uninteresting legend,) a large square pagoda on a hill top... (...)

We spread our breakfast on a square table-like platform in a zayát*, at the foot of the Shwé-kyet-kya. As we were seated round this, many old women entered, bringing with them baskets of plantains, &c., apparently their food for the day. They spread a mat in front of our table with much care, but we did not comprehend what they intended, till a youngish Poongyi entered and seated himself on the mat. We then began to entertain the distressing suspicion that we had in our ignorance taken the reverend man's pulpit for our pic-nic-table! Carefully holding the peculiar talipat fan, which the priests carry on occasions of duty, so as to screen the congregation from his view, he commenced reciting what seemed to be a liturgic prayer. In this the women took part by regular responses, joining their hands and bowing their heads towards him. It was interesting to see a fat little three-year-old child trying to join his chubby hands and bow like his old grandmother.

Further downstream the officers noted that Amarapura's main port area was still at the mouth of the Myitnge and that some of the ships lying there 'must have been close on 150 tons burden'; turning into this river they found the king's ceremonial barges, one of them twin-hulled and 'in decay'; and on reaching the deserted capital they found it ravaged by the forces of nature - not only by the creeping jungle and the encroaching river, but also by the throes of the earth itself:

The ramparts still stand, though in decay, and the greater part of the interior area is a mere mass of tangled gardens and jungle. A few of the principal streets are still kept, or keep themselves, clear of overgrowth, and the others are traceable as muddy lanes at right angles to each other, but they are silent and untrodden. One large white modern pagoda, built, or thoroughly repaired, since the earthquake, rises from the thick foliage, near the west end of the river face, and is the chief mark of the site of the city to voyagers on the river. It is surrounded by a very extensive cloister, having marble Gautamas in niches ranged along it. The river seems to be encroaching, and as the full sweep of its current from the north strikes here, it is surprising that it has not encroached more rapidly. The site of the Residency, long occupied by the respected Colonel Henry Burney,...

---

* *A public open-sided building used as a resting-place.*

has been long swept into the river. Passing a wide ditch and second wall, we entered the inner city in which the Palace stood. Little remains but the mere bases of numerous buildings, and platforms of brickwork. One high square tower, or belvedere, stands as the earthquake left it, greatly out of the perpendicular, and with the massive veranda pillars round its base staggering hither and thither, or prostrate in great unbroken masses of brickwork, giving a forcible idea of the violence of the visitation.

When Phayre's mission returned to Calcutta it carried with it a great deal of useful information, so Dalhousie did not consider it a total failure; but it had been unsuccessful in that it had not brought back a signed treaty. He was also disappointed that it had not gained access to the famous ruby mines at Mogok.

Back in Amarapura the petition to continue using the city as the capital was not successful for long. It is possible that Mindon had heard of the new wide streets and imposing buildings to be seen in Yangon, which the *kalabyu* now called Rangoon; perhaps he longed to recreate the grandeur of old Ava; or perhaps, like many a king before him, he was seeking to glorify his own name. Whatever the case, he several times told the Court of the dreams he had been having, in which Mandalay hill, a little to the north of Amarapura, figured prominently. The matter was considered by the Court. The hill was known as an auspicious place; also the king had been known to express his annoyance at hearing the hoots of the British steamboats as they plied the Irrawaddy. Court ministers now consulted the resident Brahmin astrologers and the monks, and it was determined that a site below Mandalay Hill - but not too near the river - would be the most propitious place for a new capital. On 13 January 1857 a Royal Order was issued to build the new city and on 13 February, the jungle having been cleared, the site was marked out and pegged.

Mandalay,1886. View from Mandalay Hill

Kuthodaw and A-htu-ma-shi Kyaung, 1886

CHAPTER 6
Better Sacrifices
Mandalay, 1857 - 1872

> *And almost all things are by the law purged with*
> *blood; and without shedding of blood is no*
> *remission.*
> *It was therefore necessary that the patterns of things*
> *in the heavens should be purified with these;*
> *but the heavenly things themselves with better*
> *sacrifices than these.*
>
> The Holy Bible, *Hebrews, IX, 22-23.*

It was a time of unrest in India. At one of the military training establishments near Calcutta, John Company was introducing, as a replace-
ment for the old smooth-bore musket, the Enfield rifle. Recruits would
soon be shown how each glazed cartridge was to be torn open with the
teeth or by hand before it could be used, and a false but clever rumour
would be spread abroad: the cartridges were coated with a mixture of pork
and beef fat. In May, the horror and fury of both Moslem and Hindu soldiers would explode into The Great Revolt - which the British would call
The Indian Mutiny. During the prelude of mounting unrest, with British
eyes not on Upper Burma but on India, Mindon's citizens laboured to
build the new capital, Mandalay.

In founding his city, Mindon was following tradition not only in design (*See box on p. 22*) but also in procedure. A Royal Order had been
issued on 1 December that the Court should 'study the magic by Bame
Sayadaw and three other senior monks at the time of making Ava capital
city for the second time in 1763 and the records of how this art was employed when Amarapura was built in 1782'(Than Tun, IX); a later order,
for the attention of 'All good guardian gods', promised 'offerings of food
and light with musical entertainments as well to the temporary shrines of
all Local Guardian Spirits'; and another a few days later, addressed to The
Thirty-Seven Nats (*See box on p. 72*) and other spirits, announced that the
city and palace of Mandalay would be most magnificent because Mindon
was at the top of the list of 'all reigning monarchs of the world'. This
flattery was largely a matter of convention, since the Court of Ava was by
now only too aware of the existence of at least one monarch more powerful than its own king; but the appeal to the Nats and spirits was in earnest,
and indeed it is likely that a more gruesome magical practice was carried
out when it came to constructing the great outer wall.

Mandalay was built from the centre outwards - stockaded palace first,

Nats

Buddhism points its followers away from the transience of this life towards the acquisition of *neibban* (or nirvana), an attainable state of peace in which selfishness - and therefore suffering - are absent. Most Burmese are practising Buddhists, but many also feel a need for some less sublime, more earthy system of beliefs to help them deal with the here and now. The very idea of a soul is foreign to Buddhism; but according to an older underlying animism the 'butter-fly spirit' (or *leippya*) does survive after death, and the natural world is also inhabited by its own spirits. These older beliefs resisted attempts to stamp them out, and to the human and natural spirits were added a set of supernatural beings derived from Brahmanism. To this day, therefore, most Burmese recognise at least three distinct types of spirit, or *nat*:

1. the spirits of the dead;
2. spirits inherent in the Earth (trees, rivers, mountains, buildings, etc.); and
3. the unearthly spirits surviving from Brahmanic cosmology.

Those with Western beliefs might find it interesting to compare the above types with the following:

1. ghosts and poltergeists;
2. naiads, nymphs, elves, etc.; and
3. angels.

Anawratha, the great king of the Pagán period who first formalised Buddhism in Burma, failed at first to extirpate the older belief systems; in order to subordinate them, he decided to establish a pantheon headed by Thagya Nat, who was the Sakya or Indra of the Brahmans. His 'official' set of thirty-seven *nats* has survived with modification over the centuries, some tragic historical figures having been substituted for some of the original ones. An agreed pantheon of thirty-seven is accepted all over Buddhist Burma today, over and above the more localised *nats* such as village and household spirits.

walled city later - and the king was living in a temporary palace; so it would seem that the offerings of food, light and music were made with regard to the palace under construction rather than to the as-yet-unbuilt city. It was traditional to protect the city by other means:

> On the foundation of a new capital, there are always a certain number of people buried alive. The idea is that they become nat-thein, that their spirits haunt the place where they were put to death, and attack all persons approaching with malevolent intentions. The notion is entirely due to the royal astrologers, the Brahmin pônnas, and as being repugnant to the tenets of Buddhism, is strenuously denounced by the true brethren of the yellow robe. But it fits in very well with the popular superstition regarding the existence of spirits, and has hence always firmly maintained its ground. (...) When the foundations of the (i.e.Mandalay's) city wall

were laid, fifty-two persons of both sexes, and of various age and rank, were consigned to a living tomb. Three were buried under each of the twelve city gates, one at each of the four corners, one under each of the palace gates, and at the corners of the timber stockade, and four under the throne itself. The selection had to be made with care, for the victims were required to be representative people, born on special days of the week, and the boys buried were not to have any tattoo marks on them, the girls not to have their ears bored. When it was known that the troops were making the collection, no one was to be seen about the streets, except in great bands in the middle of the day. The Government gave a series of magnificent dramatic performances, but no one went to see them. Eventually, however, the tale was made up, and the building went on apace. Along with the four human beings buried at the corners of the city were placed four jars full of oil, carefully covered over and protected from any damage that might come from the weight of earth pressing down upon them. These were examined every seven years by the royal astrologers, and as long as they remained intact the town was considered safe.

(Shway Yoe, 1882)

With regard to the human sacrifices Shway Yoe, *alias* J.G.Scott, who is still acknowledged as the greatest western authority on Burmese culture of the period, was nevertheless contradicted by some other well-informed contemporaries - and by the king himself:

We have it upon the authority of the King, that this ancient custom was not followed at Mandalay. Jars of oil were buried instead at the corners of the city, and guardian spirits were installed in little image houses under the care of inspired mediums. The King would have no victims associated with the outset of his reign.

(O'Connor, 1907)

The king certainly was a devout Buddhist, but devotion to Buddhism had never prevented Burmese kings from engaging in slaughter. It is likely that the Brahmins' recommendations were indeed carried out, but that the king dissociated himself from the sacrifices. (*See box on p. 75*)

The new palace was still unfinished when in March 1858 a mission from the United States of America arrived. It was greatly regretted that the visitors would be able to see neither the finished product nor the Lord White Elephant, which had once belonged to Bodawhpaya and had died of old age just before the move to Mandalay. Receiving the visitors in his temporary palace, Mindon disconcertingly studied them through a pair of jewelled opera-glasses before thanking them for their presents and questioning them about America and their religious views. Meanwhile in London Her Majesty's Government sat shaken by the appalling violence in India, and passed 'An Act for the Better Government of India' transferring the powers of the Honourable East India Company to the Crown and making the peoples in the Company's territories subjects of Queen Victoria,

Empress of India; and British Burma was of course still considered to be nothing more than a province of India.

Plan of Mandalay c-1900

Scale 1 inch = 1 Mile

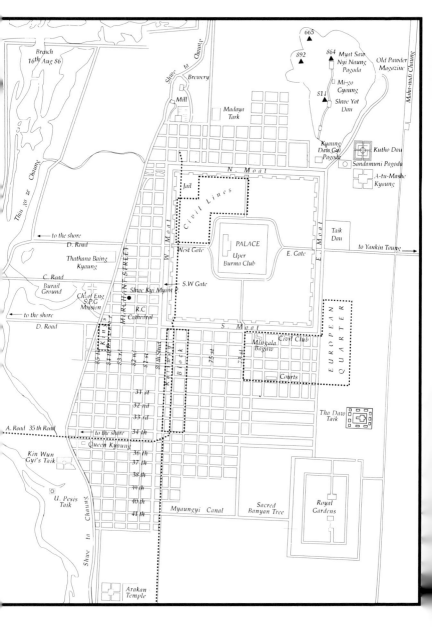

Foundation sacrifices

The Golden Bough tells of an old practice of

immuring a living person in the walls, or crushing him under the foundation stone of a new building, in order to give strength and durability to the structure, or more definitely in order that the angry ghost may haunt the place and guard it against the intrusion of enemies.

(Fraser, 1922)

Frazer noted that in what he calls 'modern Greece' the blood of a sacrificial lamb or cockerel was made to flow on the foundation stone and the animal was then buried beneath it. Centuries earlier, however, the victims had probably been human, for nearby in twentieth-century Romania Frazer noted a mitigated form of the custom in which a man's shadow was used instead of his life-blood. In fifth-century Britain a chieftain called Vortigern sought a boy victim when founding a new castle; but when in 1078 the stones of the Tower of London were being put in place, they were set in mortar that contained the blood of animals, not of humans.

In 1634, the year when Ava was founded, King Prasattong of Siam used four pregnant women as sacrificial victims in the rebuilding of Ayuthaya's city gates; and in Burma ,according to Mason (1860), a criminal was buried in each of the post-holes of Tavoy's gates when the city was rebuilt in the 1750s. By the time of the founding of Mandalay, no doubt

decent people hated the rite, but it does not follow that it was not carried out without the king's express sanction, in hole and corner fashion at night.

(Harvey, 1925)

It had long been an almost universal custom to distance one's leaders from awkward facts and decisions. In Burma, should this distancing have been left undone, any devout Buddhist king would have had to dissociate himself from the use of *myosadé*, human victims sacrificed to protect the realm. To quote Harvey again,

King Mindon ... was a truthful old gentleman but he had a way of considering himself entitled to deny a thing merely because he had shut his eyes to it. He used to say that he never had a man executed; it is true that he hated the death sentence, but he used to say, "Take him away. Let me never see his face again", and everyone knew what followed these words.

One is reminded of what happened to Archbishop Thomas á Becket when Henry II said in a moment of exasperation, "Who will free me from this turbulent priest?"

Horace Browne, destined to become the very last Resident at the Court of Ava, was in September 1859 merely Revenue Settlement Officer in Pegú. His 'ill-kept' diary, written up much later, tells how he was delighted to be asked to act as Secretary to the Commissioner of British Burma, Major Phayre, on an informal mission to try to persuade Mindon to sign a treaty. Browne was determined to make a good impression:

I enter on a course of study to fit myself for the totally different milieu *in which we shall find ourselves on the other side of the frontier. One must accustom oneself, for instance, to the use of the Court or polite language. The forms of speech in Burmese are threefold, according to the rank of the person addressed - inferior, equal, or superior to the speaker. Here the nature of things obliges us always to use the first form, whist we are addressed in the third. We must now acquire the habit of using the second and third forms ourselves. It would be a dreadful solecism to address His Majesty of Burma, or even his Ministers, in the same terms that we use when speaking to our subordinates or servants. I also furbish up my knowledge of the religious and political history of the people...*

(Browne, 1907)

Browne was thankful that the visit was an informal one. British officers in full uniform were ridiculously overdressed and must have endured great discomfort in the Burmese climate; Phayre's party were spared the worst with regard to dress, and Browne found that his linguistic homework had not been in vain:

...so we put on our lightest and loosest trousers, to facilitate the adoption of the crouching posture which etiquette requires of us in the presence of the King. The unfortunate precedents of the last two centuries oblige us to submit to this, to us trouser-wearing Occidentals, inconvenient method of showing our respect. With the progress of civilization in these regions let us hope that chairs may one day be provided for Queen Victoria's representative, but as yet they do not even exist in the palace of Mandalay. (....)

Once only the King addressed himself directly to me to test my knowledge of Burmese literature, and he gave me a certificate of high proficiency in the language by saying, "How well Browne speaks!" Very few allusions are made in public to the main object of our visit - the conclusion of a treaty.

While in Mandalay, Browne was visited by someone we have already met. The little girl described by Crawfurd, Shwe Maung's youngest daughter, must now have been about thirty-six years old:

We are visited more than once by that freak of Nature the celebrated Hairy Woman. Notwithstanding the extraordinary deformity which gives her a striking resemblance to a Skye terrier, there is nothing repulsive

THE TRAVELLER'S HISTORY OF BURMA

about her appearance. This is due to her graceful gestures and the sweet-ness of her voice. Being a retainer of the palace, she has acquired courtly manners, and the singular timbre of her voice makes it quite a pleasure to listen to her conversation. *

> * *In after-years, when I first heard Sarah Bernhardt, I was impressed with the idea that her silvery tones were not unfamiliar to me, and after a little reflection I said to myself, "Why, that is the voice of the Hairy Woman of Mandalay."*

Three years were to pass before Phayre persuaded Mindon to sign the treaty and accept a Resident in Mandalay, during which time the British more or less openly pursued the search for a trade route to China. Dr. Clement Williams, an Army surgeon fluent in Burmese who had won Mindon's favour by performing successful cataract operations in the palace not only helped substantially in the treaty negotiations but also went on to explore the upper reaches of the Irrawaddy, and found that steamers could go even farther upstream than Bhamó - i.e. even closer to China than had been thought. On receiving his recall to India in 1865 the re-markable Dr. Williams resigned rather than return to army life there, and instead became the Mandalay agent of the Irrawaddy Flotilla Company, which had just been formed in Rangoon on the initiative of the Govern-ment of India. The river provided the easiest access to China, and a single cost-efficient transport system was necessary for current and future Brit-ish trade.

Meanwhile, the palace had been completed, the city had been walled, and a riverside town was springing up; but one dark episode had saddened Mindon. Within the Court itself a rebellion had started in which two of his own sons had killed Mindon's brother, his intended successor. It was a traumatic event which, as we shall see, would have tragic consequences at the end of his reign. The rebels escaped on board the royal steamboat and headed downstream, but were arrested and interned in British Burma. Mindon was grateful for cooperation of this kind; but when the British Resident, Major Sladen, placed an agent in Bhamó whose task was to start surveying the final land link on the intended trade route to China, the Court was not amused. Mindon distrusted Sladen's motives but endeavoured not to sour Burmese-British relations. He seems to have been more concerned to de-insulate the Court of Ava and make Upper Burma a little less parochial in its outlook.

༄༅༅༅༅

Mindon was a popular ruler. Although a devout Buddhist he was by no means a bigot, one of his great virtues being his high regard for religious tolerance. The Reverend Dr. John Ebenezer Marks, the son of a Jewish family in the East End of London, had become an Anglican missionary and was now in Rangoon running St. John's College, a foundation of the Society for the Propagation of the Gospel. One of Mindon's sons went down to Rangoon and visited various establishments, including St. John's College. It was not long before Dr. Marks received a royal letter:

It set forth that His Majesty, with all his titles, had heard of the school of the English priest in British Burma, and the good that the school had done amongst the people, and desired (commanded) that I should go up to the new capital city of Mandalay, the centre of the world, and there, under His Majesty's patronage and support, establish a similar Christian school for the benefit of his people.

(Marks, 1917)

When Marks arrived in Mandalay on 8 October 1868 he had some of his students with him, and a few days later they went to see the king:

My boys and I went to the Palace in bullock carts, the most uncomfortable of conveyances. We had to climb in over the bullocks' tails, and the bamboo flooring sloped at a fearful angle. The wheels, consisting of one or two solid blocks, had probably been made round originally, but they had worked nearly square. The roads outside the city walls were terribly bad, so that by the time we arrived at the Palace gates we felt that our limbs wanted readjusting. (...) We went first to see the famous White Elephant...

Though the meeting was to be fairly informal, one of the princes placed before the king 'the emblems of royalty, the golden-handed sword, the gold betel-box, and the gold spittoon'; Marks remembered a touchingly amusing little anecdote:

His Majesty once, as a token of his goodwill, sent a gold spittoon as a present to Queen Victoria, who, in acknowledging the gift, thanked the King for the beautiful flower vase that he had so kindly sent her!

Once he had settled on his couch the king 'took up a pair of binocular glasses and had a good stare' and a herald intoned that, in obedience to Mindon's command, the visitors had come from Rangoon and now placed their heads under the Golden Foot, awaiting His Majesty's pleasure. Having greeted Marks pleasantly, the king assured him that his every wish would be granted. Marks promptly asked permission to work as a missionary in Upper Burma, to establish a church and an English cemetery and to build a school. True to his word, Mindon granted each of these wishes and went even further: schools for both boarders and day-scholars would be built Burmese-fashion, altered according to the Doctor's wishes and maintained at the king's expense. Dr.Marks interposed: he could easily get contributions from Rangoon, Calcutta and England.

The King looked proudly at me and said: "Nga min bè!" "I am a King, I want no assistance in my works of merit," for such he deemed the erection of church and schools. The only contribution that he allowed was that of Her Most Gracious Majesty Queen Victoria, who, when she heard of King Mindôn's liberality, of her own accord sent out a most beautiful font of variegated marbles, in token of her appreciation of the King's kindness.

Admittedly Mindon had an ulterior motive: he was still hoping that the troubles elsewhere in their empire would induce the British to yield Lower Burma to him, and that the opinions of this holy man might have the same weight with the British Government as those of a hsayadaw would have on the Court of Ava. As it happened, however, Dr. Marks had more influence on the Burmese than on the British monarch, notably in the prevention of some executions.

There were various methods of execution, the least excruciating of which was beheading. Because it was forbidden to spill royal blood, however, clubbing or drowning (or both in sequence) was a more appropriate method in such cases; and because it might prove difficult to bludgeon such a person into insensibility without causing some bleeding, it was necessary to spare the sensibilities of any onlooker by first putting the royal person into a red velvet bag and tying it up tightly. Of Mindon's sons, four (including a lad called Thibaw) were enrolled as pupils in Marks' new school; but another was, as one of the rebel leaders, due for execution. This was the Katha Prince. In a letter to his superiors Marks described how he interceded on behalf of the rebel prince and his followers:

To the Rev. the Secretary S.P.G.
Clergy House, Mandalay.
June 17th, 1870

On Wednesday, the 8th of June, I obtained information that a number of men who had been concerned in the recent contemplated rebellion of the Katha Prince were to be publicly beheaded that afternoon in the cemetery near our mission compound. My informant asked me to allow the princes, our pupils, to leave school earlier on that account, which I did. It occurred to me that possibly I might, as a Hpôngyi, *intercede on their behalf, and I resolved to do so....*

Marks took a colleague with him, hurried to the palace on foot and reached the portals before the princes under his charge arrived; and when they came, he used them as messengers. Dr. Marks needed to see the king on urgent business, they announced. Mindon immediately called him and his colleague inside and asked what was wrong.

I began by praising His Majesty's well-known clemency and humanity, and then prayed for the lives of the foolish men who were to be led to execution that day. The King said that judgment had not been given and that he knew of no execution. I assured His Majesty that my information was correct. The King asked if anyone else knew about it, and was told by an officer present that there was to be an execution that afternoon. The King at once sent him with his royal order to stop it. I thanked His Majesty earnestly for his merciful care for the lives of his subjects. The King replied very kindly, and after a few moments sent another officer, a Than daw zin, *or herald, with the following order: "Go, stop the men from being led out to execution; and if they have already left, my royal order to the* Myo wun *is that they are to be brought back and not to be killed."*

On leaving the palace Dr.Marks saw the crowds that had assembled to see the procession from palace to cemetery; on the next day he obtained a list of the pardoned prisoners, with the Katha Prince's name at the top; and he was also assured that 'everything, even to the scarlet velvet bag, was prepared ready for the execution...' The incident serves to show how the king might well be unaware, or at least claim to be unaware, of orders promulgated by his Ministers.

∽∽∽∽∾∾∾∾∾

By 1871 Mindon's religious and political activities were at their peak. He had sent Burmese scholars to India to learn telegraphy, and there was now a telegraphic link between his capital and Myé-de in British Burma. As a way of showing his independence, he was encouraging western nations other than the British to participate in his country's development. Most important of all, however, he was preparing to welcome from various parts of Asia (including the traditional enemy, Siam) Theravada Buddhist luminaries who were coming to attend the Fifth Buddhist Synod that he was convening; and to this end he had set scholars and stonemasons to work at the task of preparing and inscribing on marble slabs a definitive version of the entire *Tripitaka,* the Buddhist scriptures. This, 'the largest book in the world', eventually comprised 729 large tablets*, arrayed and housed at the foot of Mandalay Hill to form the Kuthodaw. He also prepared a new jewelled *hti* to replace the old one that crowned the great Shwe Dagon pagoda; although the British would not allow him to officiate, they consented to its ceremonial installation.

The opening of this synod was not far off when a 23-year-old American stepped from a Flotilla Company vessel on to the Mandalay shore. Frank Vincent had completed only two years of his studies at Yale when he fell ill. When his father sent the convalescent on a cruise, Frank was able to regain his health and see Southeast Asia at the same time. He wanted to see the king, had brought presents with him for that purpose, and through a rich Chinese intermediary had arranged an audience for the next morning. Disembarking, he set out up the sandbank on a Pegú pony brought by the rich man's servant and rode with him past Mindon's newly-built summer palace, 'lavishly ornamented with fancy wood carvings' and surrounded by a lofty bamboo fence. Crossing a plain which was flooded for the greater part of the year so that 'the natives are compelled to betake themselves to canoes and rafts *in lieu* of ponies and bullock-carts', he

---

* *As the number nine has almost universally been regarded as a mystical number and has fascinated mathematicians for centuries, I wonder whether the number of tablets is entirely coincidental: 729 equals 9 x 9 x 9.*

Approach to Shwe Dagon

British
Officers at
Shwe Dagon

observed the town that had grown up between the river and the walled city. Apart from the usual wood-and-bamboo raised houses there were neat two-storey Chinese shops, but one district had been razed by one of the town's frequent fires:

> The ground was covered with the charred and blackened remnants of huts and household goods, the dead trees were heaped about and still smoking, and, as if to heighten the mournful spectacle, here and there, at considerable intervals, might be seen little mat hovels which had just been erected by some of the sufferers, who had saved only enough to shelter themselves from the scorching mid-day sun.

> (Vincent, 1873)

Once he was in the king's presence, it became clear to Vincent that Mindon thought he had come on some kind of political or even intelligence-gathering mission. When the king urged him to encourage the American government to send people to settle in his kingdom, the young man politely said he would pass this request through the appropriate channels; but Mindon became persistent:

> Promising to make his wishes known to the proper authorities at home did not seem to be sufficient for his purposes, for he said he would keep me in Mandalay while I wrote, and until an answer came from America. At this I demurred of course, when His Majesty said if I would remain he would give me a house, living, and as many Burmese wives as I wished (a rather tempting offer, for the women of the upper classes are both pretty and modest), and, furthermore, he would 'make my fortune'. I was fast becoming very much interested, and slightly excited as well. His Majesty wished to make also a commercial treaty with America, and my services would be indispensable. Thus were alluring nets spread for my feet and enticing temptations presented to me.

When the excited and embarrassed young visitor resisted these temptations the king retired somewhat annoyed, but not before graciously giving him a sum of money to spend in Mandalay. At the last moment Vincent almost weakened:

> One of his queens or concubines (he has four of the former and about a hundred of the latter) who, though out of sight, had been fanning the King with a gorgeous fan of peacock feathers during the audience, now took a peep at us, of course exhibiting herself at the same time, and such a beautiful creature I have rarely looked upon before and perchance never shall see again. She was one of the veritable 'houris of Paradise', an oriental pearl of indescribable loveliness and symmetry. I will not attempt a description; but the King's liberal offers came at once to mind, and I felt what a great sacrifice it would be to return to my native land and refuse.....

Mindon was trying hard to win friends and influence people.[*] The following year (1872) he managed to send a mission direct to Queen Victoria, bypassing the jealous attentions of the Government of India - which, now that the company's territories were in the Crown's hands, was headed not by a Governor-General but by a Viceroy; but the Burmese nevertheless found themselves being presented to her not by the Foreign Minister but by the Secretary of State for India. Entertained in London, Manchester, Liverpool and elsewhere, the mission was everywhere courted by the Chambers of Commerce, which had been putting pressure on H.M. Government to open up trade with western China as soon as possible. This impatience had come about because, in order to protect his own trade, Mindon had been discreetly thwarting British attempts to complete the long-sought-after land link between the Irrawaddy and Yunnan; the delay had even led a Society of Arts lecturer to call for a survey of the Salween, the Mekong and Siam's Chao Phraya river as potential alternative routes. In London the chief Burmese minister, the Kinwun Mingyi, made speeches stressing the need for good relations between the two 'sovereign nations' and proposing the establishment of a Burmese Consulate there, but no such convention was signed. To the Empress of India, Mindon's independent kingdom in Upper Burma was still a mere province. In Paris and Rome, however, documents were signed which provided for reciprocal diplomatic, commercial and cultural relations.

Anglo-Burmese relations now began to deteriorate. The Secretary of State for India ordered a new survey of the proposed trade route to China and the task was assigned to Horace Browne, now a Colonel. The British Consul in Shanghai, Mr. Augustus Margary, was to travel westwards to meet Browne at Bhamó so as to act as his interpreter when they crossed into Yunnan. The two did meet, but when Margary and a few companions went ahead of their armed Burmese escort they were killed by a band of Chinese inside Burmese territory. Browne and the rest of the party escaped further attack only by firing the jungle, and according to Browne the Chinese aim had been to wipe out the party on Burmese soil so as to incriminate the Court of Ava. In that same year, 1875, the Resident in Mandalay received an order from India that was at the very least petulant and might be interpreted as provocative: he should no longer 'unshoe' or sit on the floor in the presence of the king. The British knew that the removal of footwear had long been a cultural requirement, and that in Burmese culture 'chair' was a foreign concept (*kala-htain* means 'foreigner-seat'). The 'justification' for the new order was that the members of a Burmese mission to India had worn their traditional head-dress, had kept their shoes on and had been given chairs to sit on; by some twist of logic, the order was saying that because the Burmese envoys had adopted the behaviour expected by the British, the British could now refuse to adopt the behaviour expected by the Burmese. The practical result was

---

[*] *Very soon after coming to the throne Mindon had sent, through an American Baptist missionary, a letter to Franklin Pierce (US President, 1853-57) suggesting that a US/Burma treaty should be established.*

that the Resident, Mr. Shaw, gained no further audiences with Mindon; meanwhile other representatives, especially those of the French, stepped up their diplomatic activity.

Mindon, who was understandably anxious to counter British influence by establishing links with the rest of the world, suffered an embarrassing loss of face in 1876. News arrived that an Ambassador on his way to Mandalay from Turkey had fallen ill, was now in Rangoon, and had requested the help of the Court of Ava. The required help was forthcoming, and it was not until an audience had taken place and the visiting party had returned to Rangoon that the 'ambassador' was unmasked:

> *This daring impostor proved to be an Abyssinian , or Arab, named Shereef Mohammed, a liberated slave, who arrived in Rangoon some time in the month of October. There he fell into the hands of some designing individuals, who, after representing to the King of Ava that a Turkish ambassador had arrived at Rangoon in a state of illness, induced him to send down to that place an official, named Moung Galay, with orders to cure and bring on His Excellency to Mandalay. This was actually done; and the Golden Foot, being flattered with the idea that the Commander of the Faithful had really sent an embassy, and that no doubt there were presents of immense value coming from some ship or fleet in the Irawaddi, entertained Shereef Mohammed right royally, presenting him with money for himself and precious stones for the Sultan, in anticipation of those which he believed to be on the way; and after transacting all the necessary business with His Majesty, the pseudo-ambassador and his attendants set off in all haste for Rangoon, where a quarrel about the division of the spoil led to a full exposure of the imposition. The cook of the "mission" had been promised a gift of 300 rupees on their return to Rangoon, and on applying for it found his claim repudiated. In a fit of rage he revealed the whole affair to the police.*

(Grant, 1879?)

Mindon's fortunes were on the wane, it seemed, for while this hoax was coming to light in Rangoon his chief queen fell sick and died. He had earlier tried to regain lost territory by peaceful means, and that too had come to nothing. He had even pestered Dr. Marks :

> *At last, one day, in a private room, he unfolded a plan by which I could, as he thought, be of great service to him. I was to go to England in his sea-going steamer, the Tsitkai-yin byan, taking with me two or three of the princes, and when I got to London I was to tell Queen Victoria how good he had been, and ask her to give back to his Government Bassein or Rangoon, that he might have a seaport of his own. Of course I pointed out the impossibility of my undertaking anything of the kind. He got very angry, and said hastily, "Then you are of no use to me." But he soon recovered his good temper and talked pleasantly as others came into the room. But I never saw him again.*

(Marks, 1917)

Marks, who had persisted in asking for the princes' school fees to be paid, had been told to leave; the school did not close, however, and the work of the S.P.G. continued. Within two years of his chief queen's death, Mindon himself was sinking fast. Ever since his brother and intended successor had been murdered by Mindon's own sons, the king had deferred any decision on who should succeed him. Although he had seventy sons, the newly-senior queen Hsin-byu-ma-shin was mother to none of them; but one of them, young Thibaw, was in love with Su-hpaya-lat, the second of her three daughters, and Hsinbyumashin meant to make full use of this promising situation.

On 12 September 1878 all the princes received an order to attend the fast-failing king and hear his wishes. The Nyaung-yan Prince and the Nyaung-ok Prince did not appear, however, because their mother had heard that there was mischief afoot: the senior queen had, with the help of the Chief Minister, devised a plan to put Thibaw on the throne. All this had been kept secret from Mindon but some of his womenfolk had eventually told him what was going on, whereupon the enfeebled king decided on a plan that would no doubt have torn his diminished kingdom apart: the country would be divided into three provinces, each to be ruled by one of the three most eligible princes. When the time for the pronouncement came, two of the princes were ushered in, and the absence of the third - Mindon's favourite, the Nyaungyan Prince - was explained away. Once the Chief Minister had persuaded the Hlutdaw to advise the king in favour of Thibaw, royal detainees who had been released were promptly re-arrested. Mindon knew nothing of all this, of course, but there was now a public appearance of legitimacy in the matter of the succession. Mindon died on 1 October without knowing what had happened to the Nyaungyan Prince and his brother. What had happened is the stuff of high melodrama.

Christian views of Burman culture

It is interesting that Gouger felt far more affinity with Rogers than with Judson. As a freelance trader Gouger had accommodated himself to the Burman lifestyle, and Rogers was to all intents and purposes a Burman by this time. Judson on the other hand, for all his good works and heroic efforts to spread the word of the Lord among them, remained unaccepted by the Burmans. Indeed he deprecated their culture and was in favour of British aggression as a way of opening the door to Christianity in the region. There was a tendency for missionaries, on coming face-to-face with a culture not only very different from Christianity but also able to repel it, to discount or even condemn uncritically ways of life that they were unable to subvert. In a book which she subtitled 'Missionary views of the Burmese in the nineteenth century', Trager (1966) further illustrates this aspect of culture-clash.

The cultural damage done by missionaries was not confined to their work overseas, for back home their views were passed on to children. Take for example one children's book that was in press in London when Mandalay fell to the British and was printed in tens of thousands. It begins by declaring its Gradgrindian intention 'to prevent a taste for FICTION, by cherishing a taste for FACTS'; it also aims, of course 'to interest its little readers in the labours of missionaries'. Here are some of the 'facts' it offers to them. The first extract purports to describe Burma's Buddhist monks; the second, Burmese people in general:

> *They pretend to be so modest, that they do not like to show their faces, and so hide them with a fan, even when they preach; for they* do preach *in their way, that is, they tell foolish stories about Buddha. ....*
> *... The Burmese are a blunt and rough people. They are not like the Chinese and the Hindoos, ready to pay compliments to strangers. When a Burmese has finished a visit, he says, "I am going," and his friend replies, "Go." This is very blunt behaviour. But all blunt people are not sincere. The Burmese are very deceitful, and tell lies on every occasion; indeed, they are not ashamed of their falsehoods. They are also very proud, because they fancy they were so good before they were born into this world. When they do kind actions, it is in the hope of getting more merit, and this bad motive spoils all.*

(Anon, 1886)

The modern reader will find the writer's ignorance and contemptuous attitude shocking enough, and will be further appalled that this material was written for young children; but such texts must have been fairly typical of the indoctrination that went on in many a church and Sunday-school in Britain, as their young charges were being prepared to take up the 'White Man's Burden'. The prejudices encouraged in this and other ways played their part in the fall of the Court of Ava.

King Thibaw

King Thibaw and his Queens

CHAPTER 7
The Sun Going Down
Mandalay, 1872 - 1885

> *Shall I tell you the signs of a New Age coming?*
> *It is the sound of drubbing and sobbing*
> *Of people crying, We are old, we are old*
> *And the sun is going down and becoming cold.*

Stevie Smith, *The New Age.*

The mission established by Dr. Marks was now in the hands of the Rev. John Colbeck, and the Residency was still held by Mr. Shaw. It is Colbeck who now takes up the story. These three extracts are from a letter dated 18 September 1878 but dealing with events that had occurred a few days earlier:

I was expecting and watching for the arrival of refugee princes escaping from an expected massacre; we did not know whether the king was alive or dead, and expected to hear a wild outburst of confusion every moment. I stayed up till the next morning at 3, and then turned in till 6 o'clock - nothing happened. Next day, according to secret information received, a "Lady of the Palace" came dressed as a bazaar woman, and shortly afterwards came about a dozen others; they were more than I had bargained for, but I had to take them in and secrete them as well as possible. A few minutes after them came in a common coolie, as I thought. I got up and said, 'Who are you?' He said, 'I am Prince Nyoung Yan; save me!' He was terribly agitated, had escaped from a house in which he was confined, and his uncle had been cut down - not killed - in opening a way for the prince to escape.

This made me a party of twelve: the prince and his wife, two daughters (princesses), one son (prince), foster-mother and her daughter and attendants... We knew search was being made for the fugitives, and so as soon as dusk came we dressed up our prince, Nyoung Yan, as a Tamil servant, and as it fortunately came on to rain, I smuggled him into the Residency Compound, right under the noses of the Burmese guard at the gate. He carried a lamp and held an umbrella over me, as it was raining, and I treated him in character, i.e., spoke to him as a servant, etc., until the coast was clear. We did it capitally, and even cheated the Indian servants of the Doctor, into whose house we first went. Prince Nyoung Yan, alias Ramasawmy, did his part well.

- - - - - - - -

Next evening I went to dinner with the British resident. This was a bona fide engagement. As it was dark, of course, I needed a light, so one of the Prince's servants became my servant, and a sweet but sad little Princess of ten years, dressed as a boy, followed me, carrying books for me. This is just in Burmese style. Priests get boys to carry books, etc., for them, so we got throgh the guard again; I thought they were going to stop us long before we got to the gate, but walked boldly on and the guard cleared out of my way. So Princess Tay Tain Lat got in safely to her father.

- - - - - - - - -

Next morning I sent Princess Tay Tain Gyee to the Post Office, which is inside the Residency Compound, dressed up as a boy. One of my own Christian boys from Kemmendine went with her and brought back a note from Mr. Shaw, the British Resident, saying she had got in safely. The Postmaster came to breakfast with me, and as he was going back to office I said he might as well take a boy with a box of books, etc. He said, 'All right,' and got in by another gate, also guarded. This 'boy', dressed as such, was the foster sister of the Prince, and a brave little woman she was. It was she who had come first of all to prepare the way for the whole family. If she had been apprehended, she would have been beaten to death very likely.

(Colbeck, 1892)

By such means, dozens of royal refugees were given shelter and spirited away. The Nyaungyan Prince and his brother were put on board a British steamer bound for Rangoon and were then taken to Calcutta for their own safety; but Shaw did not have long to wait for the massacre that he had been expecting. Not long after Thibaw had been enthroned and married his sweetheart Suhpayalat, dramatic bulletins started reaching Horace Browne in Rangoon. Twenty years earlier Browne had been complimented by Mindon on his Burmese; he had also been one of the survivors of the Chinese ambush when Margary was killed; now a rather blimpish Colonel, he noted the reports in his diary.

February 19, 1879. — Startling news has arrived from Mandalay. Shaw telegraphs that a general slaughter of almost all Thibaw's brothers and sisters, with their mothers, wives, and children - from eighty to one hundred in number - has taken place in the palace, only a mile from the Residency. The butchery was a cold-blooded affair, entirely unprovoked, not having been preceded by any plot or disturbance. The people are alarmed and terrified and the ministers disapprove. Shaw has threatened to haul down his flag if the massacre continues.

February 20. — Shaw telegraphs again, saying that he has expressed his horror at the massacre, and entreated ministers to intervene to save the survivors. If the slaughter continues he will not be justified in keeping the British flag flying. He has received in reply from the ministers a recommendation to mind his own business as Burma, being an independent country, has a right to act according to custom. He fears further massacres.

(Browne, 1907)

Browne was all for pulling out the Residency, kicking out Thibaw and putting the popular Nyaungyan Prince on the throne as a puppet of the Viceroy; but as this would involve the commitment of troops to Upper Burma at a time when the British army was already engaged in Afghanistan, and in South Africa had not only suffered defeat by the Zulus but was also expecting trouble with the Boers, the Viceroy merely advocated further diplomatic protests. Browne was also in favour of warning off the other European powers seeking favour at Court, especially the French, whose *Union Indo-Chinoise* included Laos and consequently shared a border with Thibaw's kingdom:

We ought to be able to say to all such intruders that they have no business in our back premises. Whilst Upper Burma was shut up in a corner house, and we held the key of the front and only door, we could look upon it as a negligible quantity; but now that a back-door is being opened out, leading into French territory, greater precautions are necessary.

Mr. Shaw died of rheumatic fever and Browne was posted to Mandalay to take his place; but this time he was not so keen to go. Four days after arriving he learned of more palace murders. The fifth day's diary entry records how unsatisfactory his tumbledown quarters were and how indefensible, both physically and morally, the Residency was: apart from a few living inside the Residency's fence of bamboo matting, there were only two British citizens now left in Mandalay: the missionary Mr. Colbeck and a Major Halsted (retired), said to be 'of weak intellect'. Two months later, while saying goodbye to some visiting officers at the riverside, Browne came across some 'preparations for a naval review':

There was an armed steamer surrounded by many war boats. Torpedoes were lying promiscuously about on the bank in the happy-go-lucky manner characteristic of Burman insouciance. I stumbled over one half buried in the sand, which was said to be charged with dynamite. The show was got up with the idea of impressing me and my friends with the idea that, despite our precautions against the smuggling in of munitions, Mandalay is well equipped with all the modern instruments of warfare.

Ever since the order forbidding them to 'unshoe', British representatives had of course been excluded from the Court, and a few days after the naval review a sour Colonel Browne departed.

August 29. — Today I bid adieu to the mud and mire, moral and material, of Mandalay city. As regards the unostentatiousness of my departure, which was desired by our Government, the officials here have certainly aided me to the best of their ability, for not a single one of them has taken the slightest notice of me since I informed them, a week ago, that I was about to leave.

᚛᚜᚛᚜᚛᚜

Early in the year news had reached Burma that a British force had been wiped out at Isandhlwana in a memorable Zulu victory, and it was said that Thibaw no longer considered British power to be of any great account. In Rangoon the British reacted with horror to the Mandalay massacre, while Thibaw boasted that having thrown the British out of Mandalay he would soon be in control of all Burma. In reality he had never yet ventured outside his own walls, and his restricted kingdom was becoming increasingly lawless.

For a lone Briton, Upper Burma was not a safe place to be, but one of Dr. Marks' schoolmasters in Rangoon had come up to Mandalay at a time when the Nyaung-ok Prince, having slipped out of Calcutta, had returned and was harrying Thibaw's kingdom. Trade was dwindling because of the closure of the Residency and the royal purse had become so light that a state lottery had been set up. There was also a smallpox epidemic at the time. The schoolmaster, who had introduced Association Football into Burma by teaching it to his pupils and others in Rangoon, was also acting as Special Correspondent for London's Daily News; and the first sentence of his first dispatch, datelined 15 March 1879, had been "Theebaw, the King of Burmah, is going mad with drink and fear" - which smacks a little of exaggeration for journalistic effect. When off duty this remarkably energetic teacher would often dress in Burmese style, and with his brown eyes and moustache would probably have passed as a *kalá* (Indian) at first sight; at all events, he was able to find his way around Mandalay and glean a great deal of information about Burmese culture. This man was J.G.Scott, whose account of human sacrificial rites was quoted in the previous chapter. The following is part of a letter he wrote in February 1880:

King Theebaw has at last left the Palace and visited Mandalay Hill. This may seem to you a very simple matter and hardly worth the trouble of recording. But when a King of Burmah leaves his palace and deigns to show himself to the world, there is a tremendous to-do. King Mindôn only came from behind his stockade two or three times, during the last ten years of his reign. King Theebaw till this present pilgrimage had never been out at all. If Golden Foot goes by water, all bridges have to be destroyed, for never can descendant of Alaungpayah pass beneath where mortal has trod above. All houses he may pass must have a wooden grating put up in front of them. A cat may look at a king anywhere but in Mandalay. About ten days ago, mounted on an elephant, and surrounded by a cloud of horsemen and men-at-arms and Ministers, he wended his way to Mandalay Hill there to worship at the pagoda.... Even as it is, Theebaw would scarce venture so far, were it not that the people now firmly believe in his fairy spear, his charmed slippers and his magic looking-glass, and above all in the fact that he has dished the British.

King Theebaw has suffered a great blow, his seven months' old son has died of smallpox.... He was rocked in a cradle encrusted with diamonds, rubies, sapphires and emeralds of incredible value. His outfit - he *was to be dressed* en Anglais - *cost five thousand rupees. All the people living round the palace stockade had to buy new cooking pots lest the smell of rancid oil from old dekcheese might offend the tender nostrils. And now the poor little thing is dead.*[*]

(Mitton, 1936)

Thibaw's lottery had become a craze in Mandalay, and each Minister in charge of selling tickets was ingratiating himself by using his own body-guards to force people to buy the tickets he had been allocated. One day in the autumn of 1880 Scott was chatting to some pretty market girls in the silk bazaar when he was suddenly seized and frogmarched outside by two men:

> *Both of them were naked to the waist, and on the nape of the neck they had a dragon tattooed.They were Palace soldiers. They did not give me time to question them. "If you don't come and take tickets at the Yay-Noung Prince's lottery office, we'll denounce you as a spy of the Nyoung-Oke's and you'll be crucified down by the bund." (...)*
>
> *My position was somewhat ticklish. The Yay-Noung's men had heard me talking Hindustanee to the bazaar girls. If I were brought up in Court there would be no escape for me; so I said, "All right; I was going there."*

On the way, Scott inveigled the two thugs into a drinking-house run by a Chinese friend of his:

> *I told my friend Swee Gwan to show us into an inner room, ordered some mild gin and brandy, and waggled my head at him. Chinamen are very quick of apprehension and Swee Gwan returned with some samshu (Chinese rice-spirit) and "Eagle" brandy; the latter as fiery as a blast-furnace.*
>
> *One of the two filled a tumbler with brandy and samshu, drank half of it, declared that he had never tasted anything so good before, and sub-sided on to the floor. The other confined himself to brandy, and grew talk-ative... (...)*
>
> *By the time my friend had finished his story, he had got well into his second bottle of brandy, and took no more interest in lottery speculations for that day. Shortly afterwards he fell asleep, Swee Gwan and I deposited him after dark in a convenient back-garden on the other side of the street, and put his friend in another some way off. The royal lotteries lost some money that day; but I did not hang about the Mandalay silk bazaar in Burmese dress any more after that experience.*

Under the pseudonym Shway Yoe, Scott wrote a classic book on Bur-mese culture in which, along with much else, he describes an informal audience with Thibaw, 'the Lord of the Rising Sun'. A year or so earlier

---

[*] *Pagán, the ex-king supplanted by Mindon,also died of smallpox a few weeks later.*

the king, on receiving a protest from Queen Victoria about the palace massacres, had sworn never to look on a white man again; but the need of royal revenue had led him to change his mind. Having obtained a suitable present and after paying the usual bribe to a minister, Scott and some companions arrived in a bullock-cart and went through the usual formalities. Unlike his predecessors, Thibaw came almost immediately; and unlike their predecessors, Scott and his friends were decidedly provocative:

King Thibaw comes alone , except that there is a page with cheroots. The gigantic gold spittoon and betel-nut box and other salivating and chewing paraphernalia, which were deposited before his late lamented father, are wanting. He knocks off the ash of his green cheroot on the carpet and presently lets it go out. Meanwhile the thandawsin, the royal herald, has commenced chanting our names, business, and the list of our presents. This is done in a high-pitched recitative, and takes a long time, for all the names, styles, and titles of his majesty are declaimed for a matter of quarter of an hour, each sentence ending with a long-drawn payá-a-ah.

At last it is over, and Thibaw asks if we are well. We announce that we are, and the interpreter, who throughout sees fit to translate bald monosyllables into obsequious, not to say grovelling periods, says that by his majesty's merciful permission we are in the enjoyment of perfect health. Thibaw then demands our business. The interpreter replies that we have come to view the glories of his majesty's mighty kingdom, and to lay our heads under his golden feet. This is a lengthy formality, for an epitome of the titles comes in with every answer. Thibaw looks very ill at ease, and has an occasional glance at us out of the tail of his eye. Having enquired about the well-being of the Queen, the Viceroy, the Chief Commissioner of British Burma, and his dear brothers in Calcutta, who, he hopes, are being well treated, as befits their rank, it seems as if there was going to be a sudden end to the audience, to avert which we wildly grasp at the idea of saying that we had taken tickets in the royal lotteries, but had not been successful in the drawing. His majesty twirls his cheroot over his shoulder, which is a sign that he wants a light, and says he is very sorry, but hopes we will try again. We announce that we are going to make another attempt, and add, in the desperate hope of getting his majesty into a controversy, that lotteries are considered a very bad thing for the people in Europe. The interpreter gazes for three-quarters of a second reproachfully at us and says, that by reason of his majesty's great might, glory, and clemency, we are encouraged to make a fresh venture, and that we are lost in wonder at the wisdom which has fallen upon such a method of increasing the revenue....

(Shway Yoe, 1882)

The visitors were considering breaking Court etiquette by addressing the king directly, when Thibaw made some closing remarks and left. Once outside, they were given teacups which were filled from a teapot: what they found themselves drinking was 'brandy and water of considerable potency'. Perhaps it was not only the palace guards who suffered from the demon alcohol, for according to Scott a great change, the result of drinking too much 'plebeian gin', had come over the king within three years of his accession.

The four jars of oil that had been buried at the corners of the city wall had already been examined twice at seven-year intervals. While they were intact the city would be safe. When the 1880 inspection was due the omens were sinister: the smallpox epidemic was at its height, one of the most cherished of the crown jewels (a huge ruby) had disappeared and a tiger had escaped from its cage in the royal gardens, killing an attendant and eating much of the corpse before the beast could be recaptured. When the court Brahmins found that all but one of the jars had leaked, they decided that something drastic had to be done.

A full conclave of the astrologers voted by a large majority for the change of the capital. This, however, neither the ministers nor Thibaw Min would hear of. Mandalay is very different from Amarapura and Ava. There are too many solid brick houses and mills and public manufactories... The pônnas therefore held another meeting, and it was decided that the only other alternative was the offering of propitiatory sacrifices. At the instance of the Pônna Wun, a truculent old villain, it was resolved that the number should be the highest possible: a hundred men, a hundred women, a hundred boys, a hundred girls, a hundred soldiers, and a hundred foreigners. This the king agreed to, and a royal mandate was signed, and arrests forthwith commenced. A frightful panic spread in Mandalay after the first day. Every steamer leaving the capital was crowded to suffocation, boats went down the river in dozens, and there seemed every possibility that Mandalay would be deserted.

Scott tells us that at this point the ministers became alarmed, cancelled the order and denied that it had ever been issued; and certainly the command is absent from the Royal Orders (Than Tun); but the original command, the arrest of more than a hundred people and the consequent panic - these were attested facts. Now that news travelled so fast, the Court feared that the outraged British would have an excuse to come steaming upriver and marching northwards in force, as they might well have done if they had not been so occupied in Afghanistan and South Africa. They would wage another war in Burma, but not just yet.

༺༺༺ ༻༻༻

For some years French imperial expansion had been worrying the British who, with no Resident at the Court of Ava, had been forced to rely on rumour and inference. They now suspected that the French, once they had subjected the province they called Tonquin and all was quiet in their Indo-Chinese Union, would attempt to supplant British influence in Upper Burma, take over the profitable commerce already established on the Irrawaddy and pursue the elusive trade route to China. In 1883 Thibaw sent a mission to Europe, where the envoys stayed a suspiciously long time in Paris. When the British Ambassador asked what was going on, the Prime Minister, M. Jules Ferry, was at first evasive but then admitted the intention to place a French Consul-General in Mandalay. As a friendly neighbour France had every right to do this, of course, but the idea of the French - of all people - cornering their market was anathema to the Chambers of Commerce in Rangoon and Britain, where it was obvious to many that sooner or later Upper Burma would have to become either British territory or a protectorate, and the sooner the better. However, to cite French ambitions as a potential cause of war would only have risked making an enemy of France herself.

Except for Mandalay, Thibaw's kingdom was by now in a near-anarchic state, with armed bands marauding even nearby in Sagaing, and Burmese Governors were advising the skippers of British mail steamers not to tie up to the bank at night but to anchor under steam in mid-river. The palace gaols were full of political prisoners and dacoits, and one infamous minister persuaded Thibaw that among their number were conspirators who, if freed, would dethrone him in favour of the Myingyan Prince. The city gates were therefore locked and a 'break-out' was engineered in which up to three hundred escapees were massacred. The next day, 23 September 1884, the corpses were thrown on to carts and dumped on the burial ground to the west of the city, where they lay for some days before being put into shallow graves. Inside the city, the palace was festive night after night with music and plays; outside, the pigs and pariah dogs were unearthing the flesh and feasting. Shocking though this was, however, and even though an estimated quarter of a million people had moved south into British territory, the violence had to be regarded as an internal matter that in itself was no cause for war.

The French Consul duly arrived in Mandalay in June 1885 and within three weeks had obtained the go-ahead to build a railway to link Mandalay to the *British* railhead in Toungoo and to set up a national bank, in return for a percentage of the profits on certain commodities. This was galling enough, but the situation became serious when in that same month there came into British hands in Rangoon a letter that had been written by the French Prime Minister six months previously. It was addressed to Thibaw's Foreign Minister, and showed that M. Ferry had been less than open about French intentions in Burma:

With respect to transport through the province of Tonquin to Burma, of arms of various kinds, ammunition and military stores generally, amicable arrangements will be come to with the Burmese Government for the passage of the same when peace and order prevail in Tonquin....

(Parliamentary Blue Book, C-4614, 1886)

A pretext for hostilities was inadvertently supplied by The Bombay Burmah Trading Corporation. Established in 1863, the BBTC had been founded on a concession awarded by Mindon to an enterprising Scot named William Wallace to extract and export teak, and throughout Mindon's reign the relations between Court and Corporation had been friendly and mutually beneficial; but when early in 1885 Thibaw found his coffers almost empty, he coolly asked the BBTC for a loan of twenty-two lakhs of rupees - £220,000, roughly equal to five years' advance payments. The loan was refused and Thibaw's ministers promptly made life difficult for the Corporation, which asked the Chief Commissioner to intercede on its behalf. Mandalay then accused the Corporation of illegally exporting 56,000 logs, and raised the demand to twenty-three lakhs plus some minor sums. Denying the charge, the BBTC suggested an independent enquiry but the Court of Ava would neither submit to arbitration nor drop the charge, so a subsequent request from Mandalay for a small sum on account had to be ignored on principle. It was this dispute, fastened upon by the British authorities, that was the occasion (hardly the *cause*) of the Third Burmese War.

Although the Government of India was not keen on another Burma war and Burma's Chief Commissioner Charles Bernard shared this reluctance, the Chambers of Commerce in both London and Rangoon were clamouring for action. In London there was now a new and more hawkish government whose Secretary of State for India, Lord Randolph Churchill, lost no time in sending an ultimatum to Mandalay: it warned the Burmese government to take no further action against the BBTC and required the Court to receive an envoy from the Government of India, to accept a permanent English agent in Mandalay, to provide facilities for the 'opening up of British trade with China via Bhamó' and to 'regulate its external relations in accordance with our advice'. To comply with such truculent demands would in effect be to surrender one's sovereignty, and the ultimatum was - in spirit if not in form - tantamount to a declaration of war.

The deadline for acceptance was 10 November. Some 10,000 troops were meanwhile to be transferred to Rangoon, a sure sign that Thibaw was not expected to accept the terms. As late as 3 November the British Ambassador in Paris received a note from a Burmese representative assuring him that Queen Victoria's envoy would be received in Mandalay with all due honours, that relations ought to be established between the Court of Ava and the Court of St. James and that negotiations could take place in London. To the last, the Court of Ava was insisting on negotiating as a sovereign government. It was not, and refused to become, an adjunct of India.

Churchill was implacable. On 6 November, four days before the deadline, British troopships dropped anchor off the Irrawaddy delta; five days later the troops were in Thayetmyo at the border where, awaiting the arrival of two machine-gun launches and two gunboats, some refitted steamers of the Flotilla Company lay at anchor with their 'flats' (barges) in tow, laden with artillery. General Prendergast arrived on 13 November and all was now ready. Proceeding upriver in line astern, the flotilla was more than five miles long. The next day, the gunboats *Irrawaddy* and *Kathleen* came upon one of the king's steamers, moored along with its attendant flats. When shore batteries opened fire the *Irrawaddy* responded by raking the Burmese vessels with machine-gun fire, causing many crew members to abandon ship. Among these were two Italian officers, Molinari and Camotto, and when the latter leapt overboard he left behind some military drawings, a diary and some letters. In a letter dated a week earlier he had written:

> *To me is entrusted the great and arduous task of closing the river Irrawaddy, the great and only communication of the country. Molinari is charged with the fortresses, etc.*
>
> (Military Proceedings, Burmah, 1885-6)

One of the moored flats had indeed been fitted with sharpened teak posts and when scuttled would probably have sunk any steamer that ran on to it, so the speed of Prendergast's advance may well have prevented delays and consequent loss of life; but the outcome can never have been in doubt. One Burmese detachment put up stout resistance at Minhla, thick fog was a hazard, and a channel had to be found past a scuttled steamer near Sagaing, but there was little further difficulty. South of Ava a state barge came downstream bearing envoys who sued unsuccessfully for an armistice. The Royal Orders for 24 - 28 November (Than Tun, IX) consist entirely of a flurry of telegrams to and from the Court. The first command begins 'Check the advance of the invading heretics Stop' and only three days later comes 'Cease fire and surrender Stop'.

The forts at Ava. Shwe-kyet-yet and Tha-byé-dan were disarmed by Colonel Sladen, formerly Resident at Mandalay and now Political Officer to General Prendergast. Colonel White, given the task of disarming the fort at Sagaing, found his Burmese counterpart quite nonchalant and the soldiers and local people cheerful.

> *I sent an order to my predecessor, the Burmese general, to come and hand over to me. He was discovered in his hut eating his dinner, and when told to come at once he said he would like to finish his dinner. However, it was hinted to him that his dinner of tomorrow night might be unnecessary if he got my dander up, so he leisurely lit a cheroot and lounged out, and immediately sat down and appeared entirely unconcerned. Long before I got to his fort I told him I would show him where I had intended to assault it, and took him to the place. He said, "Yes, you could have got in there."*
>
> (White, 1885)

On 28 November at 9a.m. the flotilla reached the Mandalay shore, where thousands had come to watch. A letter was sent to Thibaw's chief minister asking him to bring the king aboard by midday, as had been arranged by telegram the previous day. Word arrived that the minister himself would come at 3 p.m. but, since there was a local rumour that Thibaw was going to escape to the ancestral capital Shwebo, when midday came and went troops were disembarked and sent to surround the walled city. As he knew the town well Sladen rode, through streets lined with curious spectators, ahead of the detachment advancing towards the central southern gate. With a handful of aides he crossed the moat, finding more large crowds 'in quiet amazement wondering what was going on', and hurried to the east gate of the palace enclosure.

> *The gate was open and I might have entered. The idea struck me that we were too late, but the palace guards were on duty, and no actual evidences of discomfiture or desertion were apparent. Only a few minutes intervened before the Minister's elephant was seen in the distance coming in full haste. After greeting, his first words were - "On no account let the troops enter the palace. Will you come in with me alone?"*
>
> (Sladen, 1885b)

Leaving a note asking Prendergast to hold back the troops, Sladen went in and was relieved to find the king still in residence; attempting to maintain a royal bearing, he received Sladen in the presence of his wife Suhpayalat, her wily mother and the usual palace guards.

> *The king spoke nervously at first, and asked whether I remembered him; then he went at once* in medias res, *and in a very formal and impressive manner he said, "I surrender myself and my country to you. All I ask is, don't let me be taken away suddenly. Let me have a day or two to prepare. I will leave the palace and go into a summer-house in the palace enclosure." Subsequently he gave me to understand that he was anxious on the Queen's account to remain until her confinement, an event which was expected in three or four months. It would be in vain to describe my own feelings during this interesting and trying interview. My reply to the request for grace was ... that, all interests considered, the best course for the King was to prepare for an immediate departure from his capital and country.*

However, since the city was by now surrounded and the interview was becoming painfully protracted, Sladen agreed to leave him as a prisoner undisturbed in his palace overnight, provided that he understood that Sladen would return with Prendergast in the morning to take him away.

To this he assented, and when I hinted at the possibilities of attempted flight, he said seriously, "Where can I go to? I have no wish to go anywhere. I wish to remain now that you are here. I know you will see that I am not ill-treated. I will go anywhere with you. Will you come with me when I am taken away?"

Once outside the palace gate, Sladen informed Prendergast of the agreement. Although the Indian troops were allowed only as far as the outer enclosure Thibaw panicked, convinced that these *kalá* were going to put him to death. Sladen had also agreed that the palace maidservants should be allowed to come and go - an unwise concession, as Sladen's own account shows:

Note by General Prender-gast on my draft copy. By request of Colonel Sladen and the Ministers, women were allowed to go in and out of the west gate of the palace, which they said led only to the Queen's rooms. I remarked that "women are very clever, how shall we be sure that someone who should not go out will not pass as a woman?" One of the Ministers proposed that the sentry should ex-amine them all - a delicate task for a private soldier.

Their place seems to have been taken by a number of common women of the town, who, by some means or other, had gained admittance through the western gate of the palace,and had already commenced to seize and carry off everything they could lay their hands on in the royal apart-ments. The King argued in his own mind that if people of this class could enter the palace at will, men and troops might soon follow, and his life was not safe. The Queen and Queen - mother called me away to their own portions of the palace, in order that I might see for myself what was going on there.

Underneath Prendergast's note Sladen added a further note admitting that he had been wrong to request that women of the palace should be 'allowed exit and entrance through the western gate leading into the Queen's apartments'. The notes indicate that something had gone badly wrong (*See box on pp. 101 & 102*) and that there had been a strong difference of opin-ion between Sladen and Prendergast; also, the phrases 'common women' and 'some means or other' may be euphemistic, for another authority records that

by the morning, of three hundred maids of honour only seventeen re-mained in the palace, while it was filled with women from the town who were neither maids nor honourable.

(Scott, 1924)

Sladen woke to find a minister begging him to come and reassure the king and, seeing the women still pouring in, went to fetch a guard of *English* troops. On his return he found that Thibaw, with his queens Suhpayalat and Suhpayagalé and the dowager queen Hsinbyumashin, had retired to the little summer palace, taking with them their remaining valuables and maidservants. After posting his guard around the building, Sladen handed the royal prisoners over to General Prendergast.

The sun was now high and it was necessary to get the royal party to the steamer waiting three miles away. At three-thirty that afternoon Prendergast and his staff appeared at the top of the palace steps followed by the forlorn royal group and their servants carrying bundles. Between files of English troops they walked eastwards to the Red Gate, used only by the royal and the exalted; but here Thibaw refused to get into the *dooly* that awaited

THE BURMAH EXPEDITION: Deposition of King Theebaw—General Prendergast gives him ten minutes' grace. (London Ill. News)

him. It was only a sort of sedan chair, but it was Indian and it looked too much like a stretcher. Walking was out of the question for a king, so traditional bullock-carts were used. Some commentators accused the British of heartlessness in using this form of transport but, as 'Shway Yoe' pointed out,

except elephants, they were the most aristocratic conveyances in the place, and the pity that was lavished on the deposed king because he had to ride down to the steamer in a "bullock-cart" was mere absurdity. To have put him on an elephant, even if it had been the Lord White Elephant, would have been cruel irony, and to have made him ride a pony would have been simply to parade his fall before the populace. His mode of departure was the most honourable that could be given him.

(Scott, 1886)

The sun was low as the procession passed through the town, but the discerning onlooker might have noticed that above Thibaw's carriage there were only eight white umbrellas instead of the nine that had been his due as King of Ava. Some womenfolk wailed as he passed, but there was no violence. Nevertheless, when the royal prisoners boarded the steamer *Thooreah* (*The Sun*), the vessel put out into mid-stream for safety. Unable to head downriver now that it was getting dark, it rode at anchor; and not until the sun came up did *The Sun* go down. In Rangoon the royal party was met by British administrators:

As junior officer in the Secretariat, I was told off to board the Thooreah *on her arrival. I was thus the first officer in Rangoon to see the ex-King and his Queens. King Thebaw was in appearance a Burman of very ordinary type. He looked neither dissipated nor cruel; nor did he show any emotion or feeling of his melancholy position. (...) Queen Supayalat's features were more finely marked than is usual with Burmese ladies. She bore no appearance of special depravity, but she certainly looked a little shrew. (...) The royal exiles were transferred to the R.I.M.S.* Clive, *and, after remaining for a few days in Rangoon, were taken to Madras. They were finally transferred to Ratnagiri in the Bombay Presidency, where King Thebaw and Supayalat still live. The poor little second Queen, of whom nothing, good or bad, has ever been heard, died last year.*

(White, 1913)

Having left his palace on 29 November 1885 Thibaw never saw it again, and it was in Ratnagiri that he died on 15 December,1916. It was a cruel irony that The Lord of the Rising Sun, the last of the Burmese kings, should not only be banished to India, but should have to while away thirty years in the land of the *kalá* and end his days there. The widowed Suhpayalat was permitted to go to Rangoon, where she spent the rest of her life quietly in a small private house.

Prendergast and Sladen

In the difference of views between the General and the Political Officer there was probably more than now meets the eye. Prendergast's biographer claims that, when the time came to draw up the official *History of the War in Burma,*

> *the Quartermaster-General's Intelligence Department compiled an account of the war without referring to the General who commanded the expedition - nor did they inform him that they were about to prepare the book, and when the* History *was published in 1887 they failed to forward a copy to General Prendergast.*
>
> (Vibart, 1914)

Very soon after the annexation of Upper Burma, both Prendergast and Sladen were removed from the scene. The General was relieved of his command and posted to India where, according to Vibart, he did not learn of the existence of the *History* until three years after it was printed. His subsequent efforts to correct what he saw as a seriously inaccurate account were first ignored and then met with bland assurances; and yet when, *twenty-six years after it was printed*, Vibart obtained a copy of its military sections - the political part being withheld as confidential - not a word had been changed. It is true that soon after the taking of Mandalay, Prendergast had been accused of some military shortcomings: it was said that his campaign had taken too long, that his attempt to disarm the Burmese militia had been ineffective, and that he had subsequently exceeded his brief by going far upstream to take Bhamó. But although he seems to have had reasonable military explanations, he was replaced on 31 March 1886. As for Sladen, less than a month later he was persuaded to resign; Lord Dufferin considered him 'a foolish, vain man' but admired his courage, and recommended that he should be made a Knight.

One reason for the shabby treatment of Prendergast was that he had fallen foul of the Press. Field Press Regulations required reporters to submit their copy to military censorship, and for sending a despatch without complying with this regulation Prendergast had the Rangoon correspondent of *The Times* of London summarily sent back downriver. The correspondent, E.K.Moylan, never forgave him. His *Times* despatch turned out to be accurate, covering not only the looting of the palace by several hundred women but incidents elsewhere, and giving an impression that Prendergast was not in control of events.

> *All the incidents which Moylan mentioned had occurred. Guards had had to be placed on the Italian and French consulates; robbery and murder had taken place in the streets; the princesses had lost their jewellery; at the 'Incomparable Pagoda', in the north-east of the city,a magnificent diamond had been stolen from the forehead of the Gautama by Burmese soldiers who were placed there to guard it, and a second large diamond and other jewels stolen from a pagoda in the south-west suburbs.*
>
> (Stewart, 1972)

The Times was henceforth unsympathetic to Prendergast, and Lord Randolph Churchill (who for political reasons had hoped for an earlier victory) was no more kindly disposed. Stewart provides a detailed account, but much still turns on the events of that chaotic night of 28/29 November, 1885. Unlike Prendergast, who no doubt had more pressing matters on his mind, Sladen kept a daily record of events; but if one turns to the entry for that night in his manuscript diary (Mss. Eur. E. 290/65) one finds that the crucial part of his entry was deleted, first in his usual pencil and then in ink. On the page in question, reproduced below, the heavy deletion of twelve vital lines comes between the phrases 'In great trepidation' and 'great confusion'. How much of the disorder Prendergast (as opposed to Sladen) was responsible for is by no means clear; what is certain is that he was never able to clear his name with respect to the Mandalay expedition. A century later it was pointed out to me by a Burmese resident of Mandalay that of all the major British figures after whom Burma's streets, markets and so on were subsequently named, Prendergast's was conspicuous by its absence.

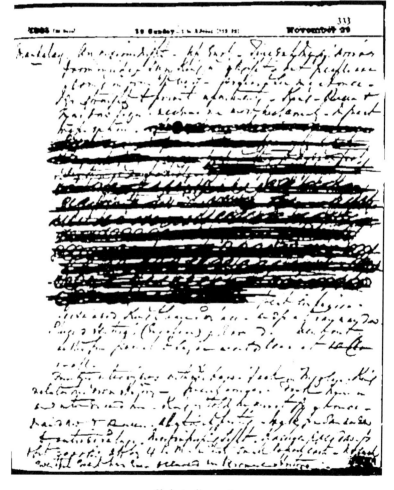

Sladen's diary entry

CHAPTER 8
Following the Sun
Upper Burma, 1885 - 1889

> *a power ... whose morning drum-beat, following the*
> *sun, and keeping company with the hours, circles*
> *the earth ..*
>
> Daniel Webster, *Speech in the US Senate, 7 May 1834*

The *Thooreah* was the first commercial ship to leave Rangoon for Mandalay after the deportation of Thibaw. On board was M. de Bouteiller, appointed to succeed the ailing M. Haas as French Consul in Mandalay. The newcomer had arrived in Rangoon only to learn that the king had been deposed, and the British authorities had tried to persuade him that there was no point in going upriver; but he argued that there were French citizens and a Consulate there, and as yet there was no successor to Thibaw with the power to dismiss him. No sooner had he arrived at his Consulate, however, than Her Britannic Majesty's Government issued a decree of annexation: Upper Burma was to come under British rule as part of its Indian Empire, except that (for the time being, at least) the Shan States would be treated as tributary principalities rather than British territory. French influence in Mandalay was at an end.

One of the first civilian visitors in Mandalay after the deposition was Grattan Geary, the editor of the *Bombay Gazette*; like any good journalist he went to see things for himself, taking the quickest route:

> *I left Bombay on the 7th December, 1885, and proceeded to Burma by the most expeditious route, via Calcutta.*
>
> *A very good idea of the transverse extent of the British Indian Empire may be formed by setting out in the mail-train at Bombay on a given evening and proceeding as fast as steam will permit to the further frontier of British Burma, and beyond to Mandalay and to Bhamo, which are now dependencies of the Empire. Sixty hours' rail to Calcutta, sixty hours' steaming to Rangoon, a night's rail to Prome, a week's steam to Mandalay. Three or four days' further steam will take you to Bhamo, a thousand miles up the Irrawaddy, where you may rest for a few days before crossing the intervening territory to the Chinese frontier. Count up the hours and the miles, and you will see that you have got over a good deal of this planet's circumference.*

> (Geary, 1886)

On arriving in Mandalay, Geary found a town full of soldiers, surrounded by a countryside full of dacoits. Dacoity was to be a problem for the next six years, for many of the Burmese conscripts who had defected with their arms at the time of the surrender had banded together and were roaming over large areas; and some had allied themselves to one of the pretenders to the throne, of whom there were at least five. Within the city, however, Geary found great beauty:

This Hall of Audience is the finest structure of all that go to make up the totality of the palace. A beautiful pinnacle of wonderful lightness and grace surmounts it. Corrugated iron has been turned to ornamental use in filling in the light timber framework which soars up to bear the resplendent golden umbrella that crowns the whole. The fluting of the corrugated iron harmonises very successfully with the bold and aspiring lines of the structure. Iron wire ropes of great tenuity run from the ground to the slender spire, and give it a certain amount of support; they, too, harmonise with the general flow of the lines upwards and seem to be a necessary and artistic detail of the general design.

The Palace consists of a series of pavilions and other buildings, differing in size and detail, but all composed of teak, elaborately carved, and painted red when not covered with gilding. The application of gold is on so liberal a scale that the eye gets tired of it, and the Indian red of the bases of the pillars is a welcome relief. The ingenuity of the designer and the skill of the workmen give variety and interest to every varying detail. There is no monotony, and no straining after the grandiose. Some of the buildings, if reproduced in gold and silver work, would make exquisite caskets for the boudoir of a queen.

Unfortunately it was precisely the palace premises and the monasteries, the only substantial buildings of any size in Mandalay, that offered the most suitable accommodation for the occupying forces. It must have been galling for layman and *hpongyi* alike to see the twin pillars of their culture used as quarters by the British administrators and even desecrated by the *kalá* and *kalabyu* soldiers. The building where Thibaw surrendered was vandalised:

The King's Summer House, in which Theebaw used to spend the evenings and the nights in the hot weather, is a bright little kiosk of silver and looking-glass, in a small ornamental piece of water surrounded by a large number of alcoves. In each of these latter was a highly decorated couch intended for the Phoongyes, who visited His Majesty and received largesses at his hands. In each alcove was a handsome glass chandelier. A roystering company of Madras Sappers rushed round, and smashed every lamp, for the enjoyment of seeing the showers of glass fall to the ground. This seems to have been the worst if not the only act of wanton destruction committed within the precincts of the palace.

If the Burmese did not see much vandalism, there was enough un-

The Palace at Amarapura
Burmans on U Bein Bridge

King Mindon
Image of Mahagiri Nat, Pagan, c. 1826

seemliness and incongruity to make them flinch. The brilliant pageantry of the palace gave way to the business of military and civil administration. Sir Harry Prendergast and his officers were in residence there when on 15 December 1885, about the same time that Geary arrived in Mandalay, the Chief Commissioner Mr. Bernard and his staff joined them. One of his staff was Herbert White, who felt the strangeness of the situation:

My abode was immediately under the wooden tower in the south-east corner of the palace, whence Queen Supaya-lat is said, the legend is apocryphal, to have viewed the march of the British force from the shore to the city. Behind me was the shed of the White Elephant, which died a few days after the occupation, feeling, no doubt, that his use was at an end. Opposite, fronted by a pillared terrace, in the midst of which played a fountain, was a charming pavilion faced with white stucco, of modern design and construction, used by the King as a morning room. Mr. Bernard adopted it for the same purpose. We were all most kindly made honorary members of the Head-quarter Mess, established in spacious rooms adjacent to the Royal Theatre. There, with the chief military officers, we dined every night, and often played a quiet rubber. (...) Most strange and almost incredible it seemed to range at will the halls and corridors, where hardly a fortnight before the Lord of many White Elephants had kept his State. (...) Rooms so lately tenanted by King, Queens, and their butterfly attendants, aglow with light and colour, were now occupied as sober offices and quarters. Khaki uniforms, boots, and the ringing of spurs replaced gay pasos and tameins and soft pattering of naked feet.

(White, 1913)

The king's audience-hall was used as a church, the queen's hall as a club-house. The Church also made use of monastery buildings outside the walls, including the *kyaung* where Thibaw had been a novice monk. Winston, a Wesleyan minister arriving in Mandalay a year later - by which time the widespread unrest had made it necessary to increase the Upper Burma garrison to more than 17,000 troops - was given a lodging in a building belonging to a large monastery, and was surprised at the amount of space available in such buildings outside the palace headquarters:

Within a very short distance of us, in buildings of a similar kind, ... the whole of the 2nd Battalion of the Hampshire Regiment, several hundreds strong, were lodged. It was said by the chief Buddhist authorities about the time of the annexation that there were close upon six thousand monks in Mandalay, but there are monastery buildings to accommodate many times that number. In addition to all the monks, the entire British force of English troops, Native Indian Sepoy troops, and military police in Mandalay, altogether several thousands strong, were lodged in monastery buildings, and still there was plenty of room to spare.

(Winston, 1892)

Peaceful buildings that even the king would have entered barefoot were now shuddering to the thump of army boots, and loud with military activities or off-duty revelry.

Close by the quarters of the Hampshire Regiment was a pagoda of fantastic shape. Being a brick building, and not liable to catch fire, it had been put in use as the armourer's shop, and there the regimental blacksmith was at work with his anvil and tools, his portable fireplace and bellows, and close beside him, as he worked, was the beautiful marble image of Buddha for which the pagoda was erected.

The regimental canteen, from whence proceeded of an evening the loud laughter of the soldiers in their cups, and the singing of many a long-drawn-out song in the true English vernacular, was originally a building consecrated to Buddhist meditation, asceticism and prayer.

It was the number and the beauty of such buildings that had caused someone to dub Mandalay 'The Vatican of Buddhism'. Winston, unlike some other western observers, was impressed most of all by a building called the A-htu-ma-shi Kyaung, the 'Like-of-which there is not' monastery, usually called the Incomparable Pagoda. At Mindon's command and with the involvement of a European architect, it had been built in 1857 in memory of Mindon's father, whose throne was placed within it. It was a most unusual construction which from a distance resembled a low white pyramid, a quite un-Burmese shape. Underneath its raised floor the Hampshire Regiment held its church parades, Winston tells us, because the large area (200 by 150 feet) was cool and airy. If many westerners found the un-Burmese exterior ugly, they felt quite differently about its interior. In 1885, one unnamed English observer had considered its great hall to be not merely the finest in Mandalay:

It would be no great stretch of truth to say that it is the finest in the world. The building is composed of a series of bold terraces, seven in number, rising one above another, the central one being the highest. The golden hall is carried on thirty-six pillars, some of which are seventy feet high, the ceiling reaching its greatest elevation in the high central terrace. And there a colossal figure of Gautama sits, meditating beside a golden throne intended for the King. The boldness of the general design, the noble proportions of the immense hall, and the great height of the golden roof soaring over the throne and the statue, fill the mind with surprise and pleasure. Pillars, walls, and roof are richly gilt, glass inlaying heightening the brilliancy.

(Quoted by O'Connor, 1907)

According to Bird (1897) the building was a hundred feet high, the structure being of massive teak 'to which bricks of large size were nailed, and the whole neatly covered with stucco work'. Winston admired this 'magnificent decorative plaster work'. Five years later the whole monastery was gutted by one of Mandalay's many fires, and only the masonry balustrade and the outside staircases - with some of the stucco work - remained.

⌘

In November 1886, some months before Winston's arrival, the administrator Henry White left his palace paperwork and card games to accompany Colonel Stedman and his men on an expedition into Shan country. For three days of continuous late rain the party scrambled up rocks and muddy slopes. Many fell sick with malaria, but at last the ground levelled out and the sun broke through the cloud. Having now reached the Shan plateau, they revelled in the fresher climate and rode on to three villages, the third of which was the most attractive:

> *On that delightful plateau, some three thousand feet above the sea, the winter climate is perfect. We rode through forest paths and fairy glades, wild roses clustering in the hedges. At Pyintha and Singaing, we first saw the bazaar, held every five days, a custom peculiar to the Shan States and Further East. Buyers and sellers came from all the countryside, often from distant places. It is much like market-day in a country town in England. (....) Pyin-u-Lwin, a charmingly situated village of some five-and-twenty houses, with a market-place and a gambling ring, won our hearts. Though we did not actually discover Pyin-u-lwin, we were among its earliest visitors. (...) Soon after our return, on Colonel Stedman's recommendation, a military post was established at Pyin-u-lwin, and called Maymyo, after Colonel May, of the Bengal army, a Mutiny veteran, the first Commandant.*

> (White, 1913)

Colonel May had been in command of a regiment there in the previous year, and had been the first to recommend the spot as a haven from the humidity of the Delta and the heat of the plains below.

⌘

Down in the heat of Mandalay in March 1887 a new Chief Commissioner of Burma arrived. Wishing to make amends for the damage done by the occupying forces, Charles Crosthwaite quickly made the acquaintance of the head of the monkhood, the *thathanabaing*, and was impressed by his courtesy and good humour.

> *One of my first acts at Mandalay was to issue orders for the repair of monasteries occupied by our men and for making compensation in some form to the monks, and at least twice afterwards I reiterated and enlarged these orders. No doubt this matter of the monasteries was a grievance. But, as so often happens, it was made more of by busybodies and correspondents interested in defaming the administration than by the sufferers. It was an unfortunate necessity of war.* (Crosthwaite, 1912)

The old *thathanabaing*, it is true, made no complaint about this matter. He was more concerned about the conversion of the walled city into the cantonment that came to be called Fort Dufferin, after the Viceroy of the time. The inhabitants of the city were being moved out, and it was this population that the monks had depended upon for their daily food, the old gentleman explained. When Crosthwaite pointed out that the king himself had moved the populace from capital to capital, the *thathanabaing* had a good answer ready:

He replied that the king removed the kyaungs *with the people, and put them up on the new sites at the public cost, and also compelled his Ministers to build new monasteries. He was amused by my suggestion that the Commissioner and the secretary who accompanied me should be ordered to erect some monasteries on the sites to which the people were being moved. He saw the humour of it.*

Relations with the Chinese constituted another task for Crosthwaite, both diplomatically with respect to as-yet-undemarcated borders and locally with regard to the opium trade. The boundary problem would involve interminable surveys and discussions, and would not be finally resolved until 1961; the more immediate concern in Mandalay was the Chinese community's complaint that it was now impossible to get hold of enough opium to continue the traditional trade. It was mainly the Chinese, of whom there were perhaps ten thousand in Upper Burma, and some of the hill peoples that smoked opium. Very few Burmans did so, because it ran counter to Buddhist precepts; this was why the previous Chief Commissioner had placed severe restrictions on its use:

"No shops whatever will be licensed for the sale of opium, inasmuch as all respectable classes of Burmans are against legalizing the consumption of opium in the new province. Any one found selling opium to persons other than Chinese, or transporting opium in quantities above three tolahs, or keeping a saloon for consuming opium, will be liable to a fine not exceeding Rs. 500 or to a three months' imprisonment, or to both. As traffic in opium was absolutely prohibited under the Burmese Government, there will be no hardship in thus proscribing opium dealings."

Those were the existing regulations, but Crosthwaite thought it necessary to keep the Chinese community sweet; in any case, he considered such a law unenforceable. There was a meeting in Mandalay at which, he says, he 'was able to reassure the Chinese'.

Elsewhere the unrest continued, conducted by a variety of local leaders ranging from royal pretenders to patriotic leaders to plain bandits who nowhere acted in coordination but were everywhere supported by the conspiracy of silence maintained by the countryfolk. Across such a hostile countryside it was essential to establish efficient communications. The northward extension of the railway from Toungoo to Mandalay was effected so quickly that an engine covered the 220 miles of new track on 1 May 1888 and a regular service came into operation the following March. Four years later Winston noted that the postal, telegraphic and telephone services in Upper Burma were all in good working order, and added:

> *In fact, so civilised has Upper Burma become, that a movement is on foot for a private company to lay down several miles of tramway in the streets of Mandalay, and start a service of trams; and another scheme has been submitted for lighting the principal streets with electricity.*
>
> (Winston, 1892)

Travel was becoming not only easier and more comfortable but also more fashionable. An English Baptist missionary who had organised his first railway excursion in 1841 had also foreseen that long-distance travel by boat and train would be a growth industry. By the time of his death in 1888, the year when Mandalay saw its first locomotive, screw-driven steamships had been crossing the Atlantic for almost fifty years, work had just begun on the Trans-Siberian railway, 'globe-trotting' was already popular among the well-to-do in Europe and North America, and he, Thomas Cook, had become the world's most famous tourist agent. The pneumatic tyre was also first used successfully in that year, and someone had already started a craze for making immensely long journeys by bicycle, for the same year saw the publication in London of a book called *Around the World on a Bicycle*, by Thomas Stevens (Sampson, Low, Marston). To the Court of Ava had come first of all the merchant venturers and traders and then the haughty envoys; now it was the age of the tourist. Visitors to Burma just *had* to see Mandalay: they arrived aboard the Irrawaddy Flotilla Company's luxurious steamers, on the much faster but much less comfortable trains, and even on bicycles. Alice Hart came up by steamer.

⌒⌒⌒⌒⌒⌒

Mrs. Hart was accompanying her husband on a tour of Burma in 1895. On returning to England she was so appalled at people's ignorance about Burma that she wrote and published an account of her experiences there. Like Yule so many years before, she was greatly impressed by her first sight of Sagaing, and her description of the view from the 'King's Victory' pagoda resembles his, except for the signs of industrial development:

> *On the level plain on the opposite bank once stood the splendid city of Ava, now a heap of ruins, the unsightly remains of which are hidden beneath a green garment of jungle. To the left, where the river bends suddenly to the south, are seen the spires of Amaurapoora, dominated by the swelling dome of the Pato-dau-gyi pagoda. The long line of white smoke winding snake-like among the ruins, testifies to the advent of science, civilisation, and steam ....*
>
> (Hart, 1897)

Again like Yule - and a host of others - she greatly admired the 'exquisite workmanship' to be seen in the monasteries and royal buildings. She adds in a footnote that

when the Burmese troop of artisans, from the Empire of India Exhibition, were conducted to Windsor to see the Queen, they expressed great surprise that Windsor Castle, the palace of the Empress of India, was not gilded!

Unlike many visitors Mrs. Hart spent a lot of time observing ordinary people at their daily tasks and describes them for us: in the market 'the girls in charge of the jewellery stalls are magnificent', she says,

and with the great holes in the lobes of their ears filled with rosettes of diamonds and rubies, they answer the questions of the globe-trotter with an air of supreme indifference, but if he means business, they are willing, nevertheless, to sell the jewelled ear-tubes out of their ears.

In the houses of downtown Mandalay the cottage trades were open to view:

There sits a woman weaving a brilliant damask, not by means of the noisy Jacquard loom, but by deftly passing a hundred shuttles in and out of the silken warp; close by are women winding dyed silk yarn on bamboo wheels, while naked children play around, and the men sit contentedly by, idly chatting and smoking big cheroots. In that shop they are cutting out and embroidering clogs; in another the yellow robes of phongyees hung out to dry proclaim the worker's trade to be that of a dyer; in one street all the men are engaged in hammering out and gilding pagoda htees, and in another making teak boxes, guaranteed to protect clothes and paper from the ubiquitous white ant.

Above all, the sensitive Mrs. Hart talked to people and listened to their views on life under their new masters - views which she clearly sympathised with. People admitted that fire prevention and control were better now, that travel was easier and that rice was fetching better prices; but they maintained that, culturally and even financially, they were poorer than in Thibaw's time:

Thousands of poor were fed by the largesse of the King: these people were employed by the English Government in road-making during the acute distress which prevailed after the collapse of the monarchy. For centuries the Burmans have been accustomed to hold their King in the deepest reverence as the head of the nation. Court etiquette was a fine art, pageants were a part of the popular pleasures, and the King's presence at the fêtes of boat-racing or elephant-taming made gala days. Notwithstanding the occasional massacres and murders within the royal stockade, the people of Mandalay had, they contend, a good time. Pwés were given every evening, boat-races and football competitions were held constantly, and gay-heartedness was characteristic of the people. The monarchy fell, and the English possessed Mandalay. A new city has sprung up on the old rectangular plan in the suburbs outside the moated walls; the roads extend for miles and are lit with street lamps. Pigs and dogs, the only scavengers in the olden days, have given place to a drainage system, and police patrol the streets and protect property from dacoits. For all these improvements the people are taxed; taxed, they say, for lighting streets to enable the English to go to their evening parties when the natives go to sleep; to make roads for the carriages of the English, while the old cart tracks were good enough for their own bullock gharries: they complain that they are not allowed to set up a temporary booth in the street, and have a pwé whenever they please, and they remember regretfully the bounteous liberality, the gorgeous ceremonials, and the gilded palaces of their kings.

The Burman and the British conceptions of progress or civilisation differed fundamentally, she noted, because they were derived from philosophies that were diametrically opposite. In this respect, the immigrant Chinese and imported Indians were closer to the British than to their Asian neighbours the Burmans:

The English trader's object is to make money to send it home, and to get away as soon as he has made his "pile": the aim of the Indian Government is to make Burma, its richest province, contribute largely to an empty exchequer. It is not without reason the Burmans say, "We are getting poorer": the Englishman, the Chinaman, and the Madrassee are gradually coming to possess the land, and unless the happy-go-lucky Burman learns to toil, to struggle, and to fight, he will inevitably be crowded out. His views, that the bounteous earth supplies food enough for all her sons, and that to get through life with as little labour and as much laughter as possible is the true philosophy, that to strive after wealth and possessions is pure folly engendering care, are out of date, and will not hold their ground side by side with those of the Britisher, whose object is to get, to gain, and to hold. Poor Burma !

༺༺༺༺༺༺༺

Just before Mrs. Hart's book was printed she was able to add a little news : the great bell at Mingun, which had fallen during the great earthquake of 1838 without sustaining damage, had just been raised and suspended from new supports. Her manuscript had not yet reached the printers when, at precisely 5.30 a.m. by St. Pancras Church clock on a grey wet morning in July 1896, three men jumped on to their bicycles and sped off through the City of London. Almost a year later they were still pedalling, but now heading north in hot sunshine along a recently-laid railway line.

From Kyaukse onwards the land grew nothing but pagodas. Of these there was a rich crop, though some were running to seed. Fancying we distinguished a rideable road, we left the rails and went to it. It was the famous King's Highway. We knew we were somewhere near Mandalay. Once this road must have been imposing, but now it had fallen into decay, and was only picturesque in ruins. There was a broken wall on either side, and it burst into ornamentation at the slightest provocation. Little cracked shrines and large cracked shrines stood lonely among enormous weeds. One image had lost its arm; time had damaged the eyesight of another; many were minus a nose. (...)

The road had originally been of thin square-shaped bricks, laid edge-ways; but kingly feet and courtiers and, in less reverent days, rough bullock-carts, had knocked the way out of all shape. We cycled along it for a mile and then went back to the railway.

Huts became numerous, crowds of houses turned their back windows on the railway in trans-Thames style, and we saw an Indian cab. There was a railway crossing. We wheeled from the line to the right; we wheeled to the left. We were on a macadamised road.

"It's Mandalay!" we shouted; and whiz, whiz, we went at scorching speed. In five minutes there was the sun-baked citadel in front of us; there were the towering arches to the great gates; the big moat gleamed like a mirror; there was a group of pretty Burmese girls coming down the road in their bright silks: rudely, but as a sign of gladness, we scattered them....

(Fraser, 1899)

After a week or so in Mandalay where, as honorary members of the Upper Burma Club, they 'could sit with legs cocked up on long-armed chairs and inspect the adjoining scenery over tumblers' (the adjoining scenery being the Queen's Audience Hall), Fraser and his two companions pedalled off towards China. More than another year would pass before they again saw the clock of St. Pancras Church, after a 774-day journey during which they had cycled 19,237 miles - the longest bicycle ride on record at that time.

᧞᧞᧞᧞᧞

Before meeting our next globe-trotter, a young lady on her way to Maymyo, we must go back almost a decade to 1889, when Rudyard Kipling arrived in Burma. He was accompanying some friends on a voyage from Calcutta to the United States, and their ship put in at Rangoon for a while. Kipling went across the bay to Moulmein where, on his way up to a pagoda, he had (in his own words) 'fallen deeply and irrevocably in love with a Burmese girl at the foot of the first flight of steps'. A year later when he was alone and unwell in London, vivid memories of that day came back to him and he put pen to paper. In June 1890, when he was just twenty-four, the most famous of his *Barrack Room Ballads* appeared in print: 'Mandalay'. The fact that on his short stopover Kipling never went upstream on 'the road to Mandalay' is irrelevant: his ballad is told by an imagined Cockney 'Tommy' who *had* gone upriver as one of Prendergast's soldiers but was now, like Kipling himself, having to endure 'the blasted Henglish drizzle'. No sooner had the poem appeared than it was set to music; although Kipling said he had written it to the rhythm of an old waltz tune, the ballad has lived on as a thumping party piece with a marching beat. We can now return to our lady visitor.

Kipling's ballad was still popular when in November 1897 a young Englishwoman with a delightful sense of humour boarded a ship in Liverpool. Her sister's husband was serving in Maymyo and they had invited her to join them for a holiday. In Rangoon, accompanied by an *ayah*, or maid, Beth Ellis boarded the Mandalay train and arrived in the heat of the afternoon after 'twenty-two hours boxed up in a railway carriage with a chattering ayah'.

When I arrived in Mandalay I was filled with an overwhelming gratitude towards Mr. Rudyard Kipling for his poem on the subject. Rangoon, fascinating and interesting though it be, is yet chiefly an Anglo-Indian town, but Mandalay, though the Palace and the Throne room have been converted into a club, though its pagodas and shrines have been desecrated by the feet of the alien, and though its bazaar has become a warehouse for the sale of Birmingham or Manchester imitations, yet, spite of all, this former stronghold of the Kings of Burmah still retains its ancient charm.

When first I experienced the fascination of this wonderful town, my feelings were too deep for expression, and I suffered as a soda water bottle must suffer, until the removal of the cork brings relief. Suddenly there flashed into my mind three lines of Mr. Kipling's poem, and as I wandered amid "them spicy garlic smells, the sunshine and the palmtrees and the tinkly temple bells", I relieved my feelings by repeating those wonderfully decriptive lines; I was once again happy, and I vowed an eternal gratitude to the author.

Before the end of my two days stay in Mandalay I began to look on him as my bitterest foe, and to regard the publication of that poem as a personal injury. The Hotel in which we stayed was also occupied by a party of American "Globe Trotters". In all probability they were delightful people, as are most of their countrymen. They were immensely popular among the native hawkers,who swarmed upon the door steps and verandahs and sold them Manchester silks and glass rubies at enormous prices. But we acquired a deeply rooted objection to them, springing from their desire to live up to their surroundings.

We should have forgiven them, had they confined themselves to eating Eastern fruits and curries, wearing flowing Burmese silken dressing gowns, and smattering their talk with Burmese and Hindustani words. But these things did not satisfy them. Evidently they believed that they could only satisfactorily demonstrate their complete association with their surroundings by singing indefatigably, morning, noon, and night, that most unBurmese song, "Mandalay".

They sang it hour after hour, during the whole of the two days we spent in the place. In their bedrooms and about the town they hummed and whistled it, during meals they quoted and recited it. At night, and when we took our afternoon siesta, they sang it boldly, accompanying one another on the cracked piano, and all joining in the chorus with a conscientious heartiness that did them credit.

We tossed sleepless on our couches, wearied to death of this endless refrain that echoed through the house: or, if in a pause between the verses we fell asleep for a few seconds, it was only to dream of a confused mixture of "Moulmein Pagodas", flying elephants, and fishes piling teak, till we were once again awakened by the uninteresting and eternally reiterated information that "the dawn comes up like thunder out of China 'cross the Bay".

(Ellis, 1899)

As if she had somehow divined that within her own lifetime the British would have left Burma, Miss Ellis could not help but find an amusing pathos in the pretensions of her fellow-countrymen (and women). Going to Maymyo - which she thinly diguises as 'Remyo' - and finding the hill station in the embryonic stages of town planning, she was sceptical to the point of scornfulness:

The Station is traversed crosswise by two rough tracks called by courtesy roads, and is surrounded by what is imposingly termed "The Circular Road". This road, but recently constructed, is six or seven miles long, and passes mostly outside the clearing, being consequently bordered in many places on both sides by thick jungle.

There is something infinitely pathetic to my mind about this poor new road, wandering aimlessly in the jungle, leading nowhere and used by no one. At regular distances there stand by the wayside tall posts bearing numbers. The lonely posts mark the situations of houses which it is hoped will, in the future, be built on the allotments which they represent. In theory, the circular road is lined with houses, for Remyo has a great future before it; but just at present, the future is travelling faster than the station, and consequently the poor road is allowed to run sadly into the jungle alone, its course known only to the dismal representatives of these future houses.

The only finished building near which this road passes is the railway station, a neat wooden erection, possessing all the requirements of a small wayside station, and lacking only one feature - a railway, for the railway, like the great future of Remyo, is late in arriving, and so the road and the railway station are left sitting sadly expectant in the jungle, waiting patiently for the arrival of that future ....

She did not confine her gentle scorn to the efforts of the imperialist male. Once she had done with the all-male Club House, she turned on the womenfolk:

At the foot of the Club House stands a tiny, one-roomed mat hut, the most unpretentious building I ever beheld, universally known by the imposing title of "The Ladies Club". Here two or more ladies of the station nightly assemble for an hour before dinner, to read the two months old magazines, to search vainly through the shelves of the "library" for a book they have not read more than three times, to discuss the iniquities of the native cook, and to pass votes of censure on the male sex for condemning them to such an insignificant building.

It has always been a sore point with the ladies of Remyo that their Club House only contains one room. They argue that if half the members wish to play whist, and the other half wished to talk, many inconveniences (to say the least) would arise. As there are but four lady members of the club, this argument does not appear to me to be convincing, but I do not pretend to understand the intricacies of club life.

I have sometimes been tempted to believe that the ladies would really be happier without a club; possessing one, they feel strongly the necessity of using it, and though they would doubtless prefer sometimes to sit comfortably at home, every evening sees them sally forth determinedly to their tiny hut. There they sit night after night till nearly dark, and then, not daring to disturb the lordly occupants of the big house, to demand protection, they steal home nervously along the jungle bordered road, trembling at every sound, but all the time talking and laughing cheerfully, in order to convince everybody (themselves in particular) that they are not at all afraid of meeting a panther or a tiger...

Given that the countryside was peaceful enough and the communications efficient enough for tourists to come by river, road and rail to see Thibaw's capital city only a dozen years after his deportation, young Beth Ellis was perhaps unwise to be so dismissive of British efforts to develop Maymyo. Perhaps she was surprised later in life to learn not only that members of the British royal family were visiting Mandalay, but also that Maymyo had become a lively and even glamorous resort to which the country's government would retire each year from the heat of the summer. But that would be in a new century.

A-htu-ma-shi Kyaung

Steamers of the Irrawaddy Flotilla Company

CHAPTER 9
Show and Shadow
Upper Burma, 1900 - 1914

> That beauty is not, as fond men misdeem,
> An outward show of things, that only seem.
> Edmund Spenser, An Hymn in Honour of Beauty

> The awful shadow of some unseen Power
> Floats though unseen among us ...
> Percy Bysshe Shelley, Hymn to Intellectual Beauty

As the new century came in, resistance to British rule continued but acts of violence were giving way to political activities under the aegis of newly-formed Buddhist societies; and as the troubles diminished, the Viceroy could afford to show more concern for the palace buildings. When visiting Mandalay back in 1886 the Viceroy of the time, Lord Dufferin, had been installed in its finest rooms, had held a levée on its eastern terrace and had consented to having the walled city named after him. In addition, the Upper Burma Club, as we have seen, was set up within the palace. In contrast, Dufferin's successor Lord Curzon decided in 1901 that a policy of preservation was needed. He recommended that 'traces of the recent occupation of the rooms in the Palace... should be removed', that the church should be dismantled as soon as possible and that the Upper Burma Club should be moved out of the palace proper - though he had no objection to its being re-housed in the summer-house where Thibaw had surrendered, which he thought 'unworthy of being preserved on its own account'. It had been in use for some years as the Mandalay Gymkhana Club bar. (The full text of Curzon's Minute is appended as a postscript in O'Connor, 1907.)

Western visitors' reactions to the palace buildings varied from the effusive to the scornful. One of the most scathing was Sir Frederick Treves, Sergeant-Surgeon to King Edward VII. The king owed his life to Treves' surgical skills, and it was Treves who cared for the pitiful 'Elephant Man'; but as he set out in 1903, boarding a ship in a freezing November fog that shrouded the Thames at Tilbury, the fog must have frozen his heart, for on arrival in Burma he found little to praise in its culture. Of the palace he was downright contemptuous:

> The King's throne is called the "Lion Throne", and the daïs of the Queen "the Throne of the Lily". They are designed to be imperial and impressive, but they would not impress any but a child of six. These seats

of the mighty are covered with gold leaf from balustrade to base, and are protuberant with carvings made with infinite labour, but little art. Inviting steps on either side lead up to the golden platform, so that the whole structure resembles nothing so much as the main entrance to a travelling circus... The whole spirit of the place is expressive of a feverish effort to be imposing, to attain to dignity by means of red paint, and to reach the solemnity of majesty through acres of gilt. The grandeur is puerile, the blazonry of kingship is that of the pantomime stage, and the poor attempt to be important is pitiable beyond words. It is pitiable because of its misdirected earnestness and its perversion of the possibilities of honest wood work. It is pitiable because...

(Treves, 1905)

... and so on. Opinion was not so divided about the town: Mandalay was for most of the year oppressively hot , dusty, flat and monotonous to look at, and much of it was a featureless grid of straight, rutted streets lined with the usual thatched, one-storey, wood-and-bamboo dwellings - still a perfect environment for fires. For many a tourist, then, the first impression of Mandalay was a terrible let-down. Burma was now attracting a steady stream of western artists, and the reactions of one minor painter of the day, first to the Shwe Dagon Pagoda and then to the town of Mandalay, illustrate the anticlimax most visitors felt:

I find it increasingly difficult to give any adequate idea of this marvellous building, which Edwin Arnold fitly describes as a "pyramid of fire". It is simply wonderful, and impossible of description. As, however, this, the greatest of all Burmese pagodas, is but a glorified example of the rest, I must make the almost impossible attempt to describe it. (...)

Viewed from a little distance, the Shwe Dagon is a graceful bell-shaped form rising above the trees which clothe the mount on which it is built, the apex being surmounted by a "ti" or umbrella, a graceful finial of wrought-iron overlaid with gold and studded with precious stones. From it depend little bells and cymbals which tinkle prettily as they swing in the breeze. The whole of this dome is gilt, a large portion being covered with plates of solid gold, and it may be imagined how glorious is the whole effect as it blazes under an Indian sun. A rather effective introduction of a single band of silver in one of its upper courses only adds to the richness of its appearance. (...)

The whole effect is one of golden splendour amidst which a throng, clad in all the most delicate tints of silk, move like scattered petals from a bouquet of roses.

(Kelly, 1905)

This fulsome prose (marred by that word 'Indian') conveys an enthusiasm that is markedly lacking when Kelly reaches Mandalay:

Never were my preconceived ideas so completely shattered as were my own with regard to Mandalay! I had expected to find a handsome city of Oriental character, instead of which it proved to be as mean as its river approach.

Climbing the high bund which protects the low-lying city from inundation, a drive of two miles or more, through streets lined with huts as poor as any I had seen in the country, brought me to the "fort", in the immediate neighbourhood of which is the only part of the city which can boast of any architectural pretension, though even here hovels lie between "pukha" built shops or the bungalows of residents. (...)

The city is well planned, however, and is laid out in rectangles. Four main thoroughfares, called A,B,C, and D Streets, run at right angles to the river; crossing these are others, which are numbered, though many have names also, such as 29th Fire Station Road, 84th Bazaar Street,etc., etc., a system which, though hardly picturesque, has its advantages, for such an address as "the corner of B and 22nd Streets" could not well be mistaken. Generally the streets are wide and shaded by trees, but are, as a rule, badly paved and very dusty. Each has its public fountain or well, at all times of the day thronged by a continual succession of figure groups, and at frequent intervals, rising from among the foliage which hides much of the poverty of the place, are handsome pagodas, kyaungs, or Chinese temples, which come upon one as a surprise, and please accordingly.

The commercial centre lies at the south-west corner of the fort, and appears to be prosperous, though the stucco buildings are as devoid of character as those of Alexandria or Port Said. For the rest, the town is simply an enlarged Burmese village, dilapidated but picturesque.

King Edward VII, on reading the book that his surgeon had dedicated to him, can hardly have been eager to see the palace of Mindon and Thibaw, but it did not discourage his son George. In 1905 the Prince of Wales and his wife Mary left their children in the King's care and embarked on HMS *Renown* for a tour of the Indian Empire. In their progress from Bombay to Calcutta there were dazzling processions, receptions and military reviews, and of course a special show had to be put on in the Province of Burma. Among the entertainments for their Royal Highnesses in Mandalay were boat races on the moat, on the north side of Fort Dufferin:

The two most interesting crews engaged were the Inthas, Shan tribesmen, who had journeyed all the way from Fort Stedman to compete. They paddle standing up in double rank, facing the bow, with the outer leg twined about the paddle and the outer hand on the head of it. The outer shoulder is swung forward for the stroke, the blade dipped well in advance of the body, the whole weight of which is used in driving the stroke through. It is a very taking style when the stroke is kept long, and all the gaily-dressed bodies with their tinsel plumes swing back right outboard together, and then bend forward with all their force against the straining blades, and perhaps over a longer course they would have worn down the Burmans. But they lost ground in trying to hold at the outset their quicker-

starting opponents, and could never afterwards get on terms. Also they had to row in borrowed canoes fitted with a hand-rail to which they were unaccustomed, and this was sufficient of itself to account for the failure of either boat to work its way through to the finals. They and their Shan supporters took their defeat depressingly to heart, the elder rowers, some of whom, keen old sportsmen, must have been past fifty, looking quite childishly woebegone, for they had set all their hopes on beating the Burmans, who are disposed to look down on them as a people of inferior attainments, and who even rather resented their inclusion in the regatta.

Before the rowing of the final heats the Prince and Princess embarked in a gorgeously gilded karaweik, which is a barge with a pyathat or pyramidal roof to it and weird wyverns at the bow and stern, and were thus towed round the course by canoes manned by white-robed white-filleted rowers, with singing and strange music, to which in the central canoe a Burmese girl danced.

(Battersby, 1906)

The entertainment, far from closing with the end of the tournament, reached its height with a tableau which Battersby (a journalist travelling with the royal party) calls 'pretty', but which might today be thought 'pretty-pretty':

... there was a pretty touch on the lake the same evening when, on the approach of the Prince's barge, great clusters of lotus blooms, pink and blue and white, seemed to rise from the water, from each of which floated as it came into view the sound of little cymbals and the thin reedy wail of the native clarinets and flutes, the central blossom opening as the music quickened, and a girl rising slowly from the heart of it like some entranced spirit of the flower.

Really it looked like that: and it is impossible, if you could expect a human shape to come out of a lotus, to conceive anything more appropriate than the affectedly fantastically decorative figure of a Burmese dancing-girl.

Perhaps the administration, dazzled by such spectacles and beguiled by the genuine gaiety of the Burmese on such occasions, assumed that the British presence was no longer resented. Perhaps their faith in their 'civilising mission', their view of themselves as benefactors in the development of the country, led them to underestimate the power of a new nationalism that was springing up. Improvements there certainly were in trade and transport. There were the beginnings of a phenomenal expansion in the production and export of rice, for example, and Sagaing was now served not only by the Irrawaddy Flotilla Company, whose steamers picked up cereals, cotton and other agricultural produce, but also by the Mu Valley State Railway. Rail passengers from Mandalay could now take a ferry from the Amarapura shore to Sagaing and then continue by rail as far north as Myitkyina. However, it was also true that the rice boom was leading not only to monoculture at the expense of other traditional crops but also to land-grabbing and malpractices in moneylending; and in the name of development, railways had been driven through the walled cities of both Amarapura and Mandalay, those of Sagaing meeting a different fate:

Of the once royal capital few secular traces now remain. But the old walled enclosure, an irregular square, can still be easily traced, and its walls will remain to bear testimony to its past for many centuries to come. Raised high above the intermediate hollows, they have now been converted into excellent high-roads, along which the wayfarers pass, and smart new people drive in painted gigs.

(O'Connor, 1907)

The new nationalism had appeared in Buddhist groups formed in Mandalay and elsewhere, and in 1906 came the founding of the Young Men's Buddhist Association, modelled upon the YMCA and destined in a few years to become an influential forum for Burmese attempts to gain self-determination. For a while the YMBA would avoid political contention and the land would remain calm. The Japanese had thrown a shadow across the horizon, however: by defeating the Russians so comprehensively, they had just demonstrated that not all European powers were invincible, and the message was not lost on the peoples of Burma and Southeast Asia.

⨿⨿⨿⨿⨿⨿⨿

Burma attracted large numbers not only of artists but also of Scots, the latter drawn as a rule by the country's development opportunities rather than by its picturesqueness. One evening in 1906 a man who was both a Scot and an artist arrived in a gharry at the entrance to the Mahamuni Pagoda (or Arakan Pagoda or Hpaya-Gyi):

The entrance was like that of other pagodas, two white griffins looking up at the sky, with busy modern life at their feet. There was a long approach of shallow steps between double rows of red pillars with much wood-carving overhead, and panels of poor fresco; but it was rather dark to see details, and the stall-holders from either side were departing, and we could see little but the flare of these ladies' cheroots. As we got up towards the centre of the temple, a light or two appeared, and worshippers came in from the shadowy outside. As the candle light increased it showed that we were under gilded Italian renaissance arches, and in the centre, where the four arcades met, were lofty elaborate ornate iron gates round a centre of great light.

Before the gates were curious umbrellas of pink and white silk, and pendant crystals and ornate vases of china and lacquer with peacocks' feathers in them; and a golden chest and huge silver bowl (full of flower petals) were in shadow to one side. More and more candles and hanging glass lamps from green-coloured beams were lit, and gradually worship-

*pers collected and knelt before the great gates facing the strong light with
the blue evening shadows behind them. They brought with them strange
tokens in shapes like marriage cakes but in brilliant colours, gold, emer-
ald, pink, and vermilion; these they placed on the pavement in front of
them. There were dark-robed people, men and women from somewhere
towards China, some of them old and tottering, and Chinese, Burmese,
Shans, Kachins, Karens, and people of Asia that I could not place, all
kneeling, sitting, and bowing in the warm glow of light that comes from
the great golden Buddha behind the gates. Amongst them were golden
and red lacquered boxes and bowls and a melée of effects and things, that
suggested a curiosity shop, yet withal a* bigness *in the golden arches and
a simplicity of worship that was simply grand. Ghost of Rembrandt! -
could you but have seen this and depicted it in your most reverent and
inspired moment!*

(Murdoch, 1908)

The scene was inspiring but it was too dark to do any painting, so
sketches had to suffice for the time being. Besides, he was not sufficiently
at ease: he felt that his 'long standing Western figure...in topee and flan-
nels with a sketch book, scribbling' stood out like a sore thumb:

*I fear an Occidental must look uncouth in such an Oriental setting;
you feel you ought at least not to stand up in a place like that; I mean for
aesthetic reasons - you overbalance the composition. (...)*
*We came out and caught a tram-car home, i.e. to the "Java" - an
electric car made in London - Ye gods - the short circuit of ideas!*

(Murdoch's surprise at the rapid spread of technology was perhaps
understandable: the very first tramway in the world had been constructed
in England only twenty years earlier, with the first tram running in 1885
between Blackpool and Fleetwood.) Throughout his stay, Murdoch persisted in his attempts to capture the spirit of the Mahamuni Hpaya in colour,
despite some delightful distractions:

*24th January. - This morning I have to try to paint the groups in the
Arrakan Pagoda, but in the bright daylight it is difficult to take one's attention from these Phrynes, who come down to bathe beside our steamer
- Phrynes, as to figure I mean. One of the two nearest has a little white
jacket and a tight hunting green cloth skirt and black velvet sandals; her
movements are deliberate, almost languid, and she is fairly tall, very well
proportioned, and when her white jacket comes off, the colour of her shoulders is very pretty in contrast to the jet black hair and undergarment of
blue. This garment,with its white band tight across her bust, remains on
when the green kirtle drops to her feet. Her friend is dressed in the same
way in different colours. They walk in and swim a few strokes - if you may
call it swimming - with other women already in the water. Then they wash
themselves very carefully with soap, and when the first comes out in her*

*blue tight garment, she slips the green kirtle over her head and the blue
dress drops off underneath it. There is no drying - the sun does that, and
they are hardy.*

Towards the end of his stay Murdoch admitted artistic defeat. 'I de-
spair', he wrote, 'of making anything ... of the Arrakan Pagoda'.

ᕦᕤᕦᕤᕦᕤᕥᕤᕥᕤᕥᕤ

Another who found the Burmese beauties distracting was a member of
the Indian Education Service who arrived in Mandalay in readiness for a
visit from the Viceroy. He was particularly impressed with Ze-gyo market, the largest bazaar in Burma, probably because it was so different from
an Indian bazaar; but while describing it his mind's eye wandered:

*Nowhere in Burma will you realise better what Burmese people are
like. You will be struck by the extreme cleanliness of everything, and the
absence of smells, even in the meat market. There you will notice how
quiet everybody is. A little bargaining, of course, goes on, but never nois-
ily, and you rarely hear a dispute. You are never asked to buy anything.
You may go anywhere and look at anything; no one will worry you; and
wherever you turn, your eyes will be charmed by the neat figures, the
smiles and the bright dresses of the Burmese women. But I am anticipating. This delightful topic I am saving for a future page....*
(Fraser, 1912)

On that later page Fraser effuses, and even asserts that Burma is the
place where 'the female of our species is perfect'!

Along with delight and beauty, Fraser saw suffering and ugliness. There
were two leprosaria in Mandalay, the one established by the Catholic
Church and the other under Protestant administration. Fraser went to the
former, where twenty-two nuns cared for about three hundred lepers,
including some of European extraction:

*Visitors are welcomed, and, as all languages are represented among
the nuns, all visitors find themselves at home. All stages of leprosy may be
witnessed in their development, from the first fatal spots to that strange
culmination when life clings to a wretch who has neither limbs nor features nor anything human in his form.*

The Buddhist knows that one's life here and now is the outcome of
one's previous existence, is determined according to one's *kan* or fate, and
is therefore not something that others should interfere with. Fraser was
aware of this but nevertheless thought it a pity that the Burmese had neither founded nor supported such institutions themselves:

*If they are going to take anything from the "materialistic" West, let it
be something of this kind, which Buddha himself need not have censured.*

Did I not hear ... among other deeds of the Buddha, recited, how he came and stayed a pestilence?

Leprosy was not the only disease that struck fear into the inhabitants, whether British or Burmese. Two years previously, on his first public arrival in Mandalay as Lieutenant-Governor of Burma, Sir Herbert Thirkell White had begun his address with the *good* news: Zegyo was perhaps 'the finest bazaar in the East' and the electric tramway, 'the first of its kind in Burma', was admirable; the project for 'providing the town with electric light' was commendable and the Mandalay canal system was now in full working order. Then came the *bad* news:

I cannot refrain from reference to the dark shadow which lies over the land and which is never absent from my mind, the possibility of the appearance of Plague. I am thankful, indeed, that so far this disease has not appeared in Mandalay. I have no wish to excite alarm. As I have said elsewhere, I have a good hope that conditions of life in Burmese towns and villages are such as to render it not impossible to prevent Plague from taking firm hold of the Province...

('A Loyal Burman', ed., 1910)

Nonetheless, the double negative betrays his pessimism: plague did indeed break out there soon afterwards. The epidemic was contained towards the end of that first decade of the century, but the disease would regularly recur well into the forties.

***

The traditional education carried out in the monasteries had achieved a high degree of literacy but was not geared to the needs of the modern state. In 1908 the President of the YMBA, U May Oung, observed in a speech that the system of education introduced by the British was a 'not unmixed blessing'; he feared that the 'tide of foreign civilization and learning steadily creeping over the land' would swamp the culture of the Burmans and even sweep away 'their very existence as a distinct nationality'. The concern with cultural identity was foremost, but political agitation would follow.

In their continuing ignorance of the Burmese way of life - in some cases despite their knowledge of it - many British visitors and even residents gave offence by breaking the cultural rules. We have seen how disrespectful it was to ride a horse into an important person's compound or a monastery, or to fail to remove one's shoes before entering the precincts of a pagoda; but using an umbrella could also be deeply offensive. By tradition, white umbrellas had been used only by the kings and the Buddhist fraternity, the golden ones by the princes and the most senior ministers; for the king there had been nine white ones, and for the heir apparent eight golden ones; the king's representatives might use *one* white umbrella; and so on. In Thibaw's day, punishments for breaking the rules had been severe:

> *Innocent, unwitting Englishmen got themselves into serious trouble in Mandalay by going about carrying silk umbrellas with white covers. The offence was treason and merited death. None actually underwent the supreme penalty, but there were a few who had vivid denunciations for the stocks.*

(Shway Yoe, 1882)

In the public mind, the rules continued to apply. To wander into a pagoda under the shade of a white or gold-coloured parasol was like strolling into Westminster Abbey wearing a mitre or into Buckingham Palace holding an orb and sceptre, yet people did so. When one visitor (yet another British artist) went to see the Eindawya Pagoda in Mandalay on Christmas morning, 1909, he found a warning:

> *Outside the gate of the Aindaw Pagoda, where some Burmans were playing a gambling game, a notice in five languages-English, Burmese, Hindostani, Hindi and Chinese, announced, "Riding, shoe and umbrella-wearing disallowed."*

(Fisher, 1911)

Some British residents still insisted, just as Cox had done more than a century earlier, that such prohibitions were merely tricks designed to demean the British. Although this was clearly not the case, it was true that the zeal with which the rules were enforced tended to vary with the fluctuations of the political temperature; and 'The Shoe Question' would persist until Burma gained full independence.

There was resentment of the Indian immigrant population too, though for different reasons. Ever since the opening of the Suez Canal in 1869 the British had invested heavily in their eastern territories. When the Burmans had proved reluctant to take part in the consequent exploitation of their country's resources, Indians - some as seasonal workers, others as settlers - had been imported for the purpose. Those who stayed set themselves up as merchants, or obtained administrative posts, or (if they were Chettyars, a southern Indian caste of moneylenders) exploited the naive Burman farmers by imposing exorbitant terms and then dispossessing any defaulters of their own land. The southern Indian complexion being so dark, a certain amount of racial prejudice also contributed to the problem, and the British insistence on treating Burma as an Indian province did not help matters. Bitterness against the Indian population became intense and remained so. Yet it was India that was beginning to show Burma the way to independence.

✼✼✼✼✼✼

In Ahmedabad at 8 a.m. on 13 September 1908 a prisoner was taken out of his cell. Just beyond the prison wall a train was waiting. Escorted by eight Moslem constables and their British officer, the Hindu prisoner was taken to Bombay harbour where a launch took him, under a new guard, to the troopship *Harding*, whose captain was the only person on board who knew where the vessel would be heading. The *Harding* steamed southwards and round the subcontinent, sailing for nine days before entering Rangoon harbour. Here, under Police escort, the prisoner was put on a train which drew up at 8 a.m. the following morning in Mandalay station. It was only a few minutes' trip from the station to his new prison in Fort Dufferin where, with remarkable equanimity, he settled down to writing a book and studying Pali, German and French.

He was Bal Gangadhar Tilak, a name not well-known in the West; but from the lengths to which the British authorities had gone in order to isolate him, we can judge how important he was to his fellow-countrymen. Ever since 1897, when a warrant had been signed for his arrest in Bombay, he had been a thorn in the flesh of the Raj. On that occasion he had been unjustly sentenced to eighteen months' hard labour for writing and publishing articles critical of the British administration and championing the cause of *swaraj* - self-rule. He continued to argue this cause fearlessly and became known as 'Lokamanya' - beloved of the people. After his release from Mandalay prison, he gave a Press interview; but by now it was 8 June 1914 and he was fifty-eight. Here are three short extracts:

"The Mandalay Jail is built in the north-west corner of the Mandalay Fort. I was never taken out of this building except on one occasion when cholera broke out in the Jail; then, for ten weeks I was removed to Mikattala (Meikhtila)." "Once the Lieutenant-Governor of Burma, on a visit to the Jail, came to see me and made enquiries about me. If any other official visitor or Englishman happened to pay a visit to the Jail, the Superintendent never brought him to me."

And on his release after six years:

"I was put into a motor-car and taken to the station. In the mail train which left at two o'clock a compartment was reserved for us. At the approach to a station all the windows were shuttered."

(Quoted by Tahmankar, 1956)

Shipped from Rangoon to Madras, taken on to Poona and released outside his home, Lokamanya Tilak lived for only six more years. On his death the leadership role passed to Mahatma Gandhi, but not before his ideas had fuelled Burmese calls for self-rule.

∽∽∽∽∽∽∽

From his first-floor cell, which he said was "like a wooden cage", Lokamanya Tilak would not have been able to see the walled city; but by now there was little worth looking at. Well before his incarceration its character had been altered, and by the time of his release it had changed completely:

> *Within the city walls, all round the palace, the space was closely packed with Burmese houses. Here were the dwellings of Ministers and other high officers, each surrounded by an ample compound (win) where lived a whole village of relations and retainers. Here also were the humbler dwellings of minor officials, soldiers, and the miscellaneous rabble collected about an Eastern Court.*
>
> *Now all is changed. The Palace remains a melancholy memento of Burmese sovereignty. The halls are tenantless, and the footstep of the infrequent visitor rings hollow on its floors. A fragment of the teak stockade is preserved. The rest is replaced by a neat post and rail fence. All the native houses have disappeared. The space within the walls is occupied by barracks, mess-houses, dwellings, polo-ground, and the like.*

(White, 1913)

Behind the city, up on the Shan plateau, the little outpost that Beth Ellis had found so pathetically ridiculous was now a flourishing hill station. The pleasant town was 'conspicuously un-oriental, more like a corner of Surrey than of Burma', thought White, and there was even a Frenchman who enthused about the place:

> *Maymyo is now the regular Burma hill-station. The Lieutenant-Governor and the heads of departments spend the summer here. A considerable town has been formed and excellent roads have been cut through the jungle. A reservoir for the drinking-water of the station has been constructed in the neighbouring hills. Shops of all kinds have been established, and all necessaries are easily obtainable. There are Japanese jinrickshas and tikka-gharis, or hackney cabs, and Maymyo is reached from Mandalay in four hours by rail, leaving the main line at Myohaung junction, a short distance south of Mandalay. The change from the plains to Maymyo is a very pleasant experience. There is a delightful freshness in the air, and all around one sees trees of great variety - teak, pine, ash, bamboos, besides many others. Lilies, carnations, roses, peonies, zinnias, petunias, phlox, and marguerites flower all the year through, and marvellous orchids burst into blossom on all sides during the rains. Creepers festoon the biggest trees in great profusion, and deck them with brilliant blossom. The heat is never too great nor the cold too severe. It is a real paradise.*

(Dautremer, 1913)

In that upland paradise, the European garrison and the regiment of Gurkhas had little to do but shine on parade and provide a band to play outside the now splendidly-appointed club-house. When the clouds began to darken the Burmese skies the British administrators and their families would return to the plains, leaving the rain to unfold a profusion of orchids. Meanwhile, the dark clouds gathering across Europe were casting a long shadow back home.

Royal barges on Mandalay moat

A modern karaweik

`The Centre of the Universe` 1886

A corner of the Palace, 1886

CHAPTER 10
The Guns Boom Far
Burma, 1914 - 1938

> *Strong gongs groaning as the guns boom far.*
>
> G.K.Chesterton, *Lepanto*

With hundreds of thousands of young men already dead - machine-gunned, mortared, shelled or gassed in a stalemate of trench warfare at Neuve-Chapelle, Ypres and Loos, or drowned or cut down in the Gallipoli campaign, that brainchild of Winston Churchill's in which more than half the Allied invaders perished - life in Burma went on unchanged. As the second city of the province, Mandalay was an important military as well as civil centre, and there was now the Police Training School that the Lieutenant-Governor had opened in 1909, when the plague outbreak was being brought under control. There was a large floating population of British servicemen and others who were not blind to the charms of young Burmese ladies; and while the topic of shocked conversation in Britain was the appalling 'legitimate' death-toll, in Mandalay it was the high 'illegitimate' birth-rate.

Perhaps because of a wartime bereavement, a young Englishwoman arrived alone in Mandalay towards the end of 1915, to work at St. Mary's School for Eurasian Girls. Mrs. Morris, whose parents had innocently named her Doris, noted in her diary that even the Civil Surgeon had 'five or six Burmese children', and added 'Really one wonders whether there are any moral men here apart from the clergy'. The school stood inside Fort Dufferin, which she found 'almost like a park':

> *It has a good many advantages over the rest of the town. There is Artesian water, so that one can drink unboiled water fairly safely, & it does not get so clouded with dust as the town outside. (...) When we were entering the Fort the sun was setting and the sky and the water were a gorgeous deep orange colour. It is very beautiful to look along the moat to the mountains in the distance...*

(Morris, 1915/16)

After tea one day Doris and a lady colleague went down to the river by tram just to see the sunset:

> *The trams have 2 classes. English people always go first class, but coming back we came 2nd as it seemed so silly, when there was an empty front seat in the 2nd cl., to pay double. The trams have one storey, with a*

shade over it, like the ones there used to be in Bradford.

A British woman who travelled second class was clearly not considered a *pukka memsahib* by her compatriots, and Mrs Morris later remarks, 'The snobbishness of Mandalay is appalling'. She seems to have been very conscientious in her work, and some of her comments will sound very familiar to teachers today. Plus ça change:

These children are difficult to teach. They are obviously used to looking bored in lessons and not listening & it requires a great deal of energy to make them attend. (...) I have to take 35 lessons a week & have not time to prepare them properly, so it makes things more difficult still.

Distant though it was, the Great War did impinge a little on the life of British expatriates in Burma. When in April 1916 the usual migration took place, from the steamy delta and sweltering plains to the coolness of the hill station that was once Pyin-u-lwin, there was a noticeable reluctance to take one's leave in Blighty. The staff of St. Mary's School booked a partly furnished house in Maymyo for the summer period but, says Doris,

we were fortunate to secure it as Maymyo is absolutely packed. So few English people are going home this year because of the submarines, that they all flock there.

In the fresh air of Maymyo it was good to take an early two-hour walk in the jungle and return to a breakfast of porridge, fish and salad, stewed beef and tomatoes, curry and rice, and then fruit and coffee; but within a month Doris had grown tired of the inane gossip and tinselly social life of her compatriots:

Sometimes I don't know how I shall endure another month here. I almost think Mandalay is preferable. At any rate there is work there to fill up one's thoughts.

Nonetheless she was sufficiently fond of gossip to record in her diary a fortnight later, perhaps with a trace of envy in her disapproval:

Miss Cook calls Miss Jackson Jones 'rapid', you can't exactly call her fast. I think she will be somewhere about 50 & she wears very short skirts and dresses rather youthfully.

Doris would also have disapproved of Private Bert Rendall. He had joined the Somerset Light Infantry expecting to be sent to the Western Front and, once aboard the *Ionian Trooper*, had asked the ordinary seamen where the ship was bound. Nobody knew and the ship was under blackout at sea because of the submarines, but it soon became clear that the vessel had left the Channel and was ploughing through the Bay of

Biscay, heading for warmer waters. In Rangoon the transfer from troop-ship to river steamer was immediate, and soon his Company was stationed in Alaunghpaya's old capital Shwebo.

In Shwebo, it was more or less a country place. It was here that a bit of the Song of Mandalay comes into it now. I was going down to Shwebo Bazaar which was a long lane of bodge-up huts which sold everything. Every week I bought a few postcards of Burma to send home. We had to dress to go out of the barracks and my friend had gone on ahead. I went off down the road and glanced at a little girl wearing a pair of slippers, no heels, dragging her feet just like the Burmese do, she was aged roughly 18. Without any hesitation she said, "You, young British soldier?" I said, "Yes" and that wound up, "Come ye back ye British soldier, come ye back to Mandalay." I won't tell you what happened, we'll leave it there. But I was very late down at the bazaar when I met my pal.

(Mills, 1988)

In the final weeks of 1916 the great guns were still pounding away on the Western Front but, as an acquaintance said to Doris Morris, "Manda-lay English people care about nothing but pleasure & are indifferent to the war". The pageantry of Empire went on, and the only heavy artillery heard by Doris and her companion was a series of salutes at a Durbar held in the Palace on 6 December.

...we could just see the throne. It is made of silver gilt & was used for King Edward & the Prince of Wales & has been sent here from Simla. The Palace itself is beautiful with its gold pillars and red roofs. As we were at the back we could see all the troops lined up outside. Then the Shan chiefs - the Sawbwas - drove up one by one, some were in carriages with bril-liant yellow sunshades over them & bright coloured seats for the driver. So many shots were fired from the battery as each one of importance en-tered the Palace. Their dresses were magnificent. Some had on these long coats with several capes on the shoulders, & queer kinds of gold head-dress like a large flat plate with a cup on it & then a spike on the cup. Some of the head-dresses were all crusted with jewels, & the material of their garments was wonderful. Green & gold shot cloth & all sorts of brilliant colours decorated with gold. After the chiefs the General came in, then the Lieutenant Governor, & finally, after the Royal umbrellas had lined up, the Viceroy....

(Morris, 1915/16)

❦❦❦❦❦❦

Long before the annexation of Upper Burma the British had experi-enced the difficulties of introducing a new education system both logisti-cally and politically, especially in relation to the *sangha*. An attempt to involve the monasteries in a grant-aided system had failed not only be-cause a *hpongyi* was unable to perform the duties of a full-time teacher without neglecting his duties as a monk, but also because Buddhist practice forbade his *hsayadaw* to handle money; besides, the cultural gap between the world-view of the *sangha* and that contained in the syllabuses could not be bridged overnight - and perhaps, given that the curricular content was so alien, no such bridging ought to be attempted. The new system had already given rise to that familiar phenomenon, educational elitism - and of course its corollary, high wastage. In villages across the country, lay primary schools increased in number as the monastery schools dwindled, but it was impossible for most pupils to progress from these Burmese-language rural primary schools to the middle schools because these were urban, were run by Christian missions and were conducted for some or even all of the time in English. The massive pupil drop-out rate represented a huge waste of human resources. A man who had served in Burma for twenty-seven years as magistrate and revenue officer put it this way:

> *The Education Department in Burma has not attempted to equip with knowledge the most intelligent of the people. What it has done is to equip, or attempt to equip, with knowledge the children of a tiny group of people who happened to have money or to live in Rangoon. As a result we have a handful of Burmans who are both educated and intelligent, a great many who are educated but not intelligent, and a great many more who are intelligent but not educated. (...) It is impossible... that eight million people should not contain many times the number of intelligent individuals as are contained in a hundred thousand. Public money which is now wasted could be spent on them to good purpose.*

(Brown, 1926)

Nevertheless the British-style system was beginning, as in India, to produce an elite that was both politically aware and vocal in English. Gandhi had returned to India from South Africa and had joined the Indian National Congress, and the persistent demands for political advancement there led the British Government to announce in August 1917 a planned 'gradual development of self-governing institutions' that would lead to 'responsible self-government'. The Montagu-Chelmsford Committee, sent out to report on how this intention could be put into effect, showed no intention of visiting Burma or of including it in their proposals despite the fact that Burma was still officially a province of India. The YMBA sent a delegation, but to no avail: the Committee decided that a system called 'dyarchy' would be introduced under which some of the Ministries would be in the hands of a largely elected Legislative Council, while others would remain 'reserved' by the Viceroy, and that this system would apply to the whole of British India except Burma. The Burmese (and many of their British administrators) were dismayed that a measure of self-rule awarded to the *kala* should be denied to the Burman; and objections to the wearing of shoes in pagoda precincts grew ever more heated.

In London, with the Great War over at last, those servicemen fortunate enough to survive were being demobilised. Among them was a would-be poet who before the war had served in Burma as a civilian and would soon be going back there. Since his own country, Ireland, had just demanded a free parliament, perhaps he was more sympathetic to Burmese aspirations than most Englishmen of his day. In February 1920 he arrived in Mandalay as senior magistrate, a post in which his feeling for the proprieties of Burmese tradition stood him in good stead. When Thibaw's court was dispersed in 1885, ladies with the title of princess were given small pensions and, however reduced their circumstances, they were still known as princesses; and so were their daughters. One such daughter brought a complaint before the magistrate, Maurice Collis:

> *Living in one of the simple wooden houses of a side street near the moat, in sight of the red royal walls inside which her mother had once resided, she was treated by her neighbours with a little more than ordinary consideration. When, therefore, a small shopkeeper shouted filthy language at her in the presence of passers-by, because one of her hens had entered his compound, she was more humiliated than a mere commoner would have been. The usual penalty... was a fine of ten rupees, about thirty shillings. I imposed, however, one of thirty rupees and ordered that it be paid in compensation to the complainant, a discretion which the law permitted. In making this order I remarked that, though everyone was talking about democracy, there remained distinctions and that for a princess to be publicly abused was more hurtful to her than it would be, say, for a bazaar girl.*
>
> (Collis, 1953)

This decision delighted the local population and the princess presented the embarrassed magistrate with roses the very next morning, prostrating herself in the process. But such gratitude was only skin deep, and the underlying resentment of British rule had been rekindled by the repercussions following the appalling Amritsar massacre of 13 April, 1919, which had destroyed Indian faith in the dyarchy reform scheme and led the Congress Party to adopt Gandhi's policy of non-cooperation. Even at this stage and even with his experience, Collis was insensitive about the wearing of shoes in Burmese pagodas:

> *In the Mandalay of March 1920 the shoe question, as it came to be called, had not yet reached this stage of definition. I had barely heard of it, and though the notice 'foot wearing prohibited' was already up outside the Arakan Pagoda, I did not think it would be enforced against me.*

Not wishing to embarrass him, his Burmese companions assured him that there would be no objection to his keeping his shoes on, and he entered the long colonnade.

> *Almost at once I had the uncomfortable feeling that the stallholders*

had taken note of my shoes and were disturbed at the sight of them. About halfway up a young man appeared from the side and blocked the way, saying something about my shoes. He was clearly irritated and ready to flare up into a temper.

'The Shoe Question'

The label 'The Shoe Question' was coined by the British, but they were not the first to experience the cultural conflict that it referred to.

In 1271 when Kublai Khan sent envoys to Pagán to demand the traditional payment of tribute, King Narathihapaté kept them waiting an inordinately long time, granted them no audience and in the end sent them home with one of his own envoys and an expression of diplomatic friendship. Two years later there arrived in Pagán, with three aides and a sizeable retinue, a senior ambassadorial figure bearing a letter from the great Emperor himself. In this document Kublai Khan quite reasonably pointed out that, since he had received the Burmese envoy with the usual courtesies, it was in the interests of the Burmese to reciprocate and form an alliance with his powerful empire, so as not to be the inevitable losers in the event of war. Narathihapaté had the embassy and all their retinue executed. The records say only that this was because the envoys had behaved disrespectfully; but in the Court of Ava there was a traditional account, noted by Burney in 1830, which stated that the visitors had on too many occasions refused to take off their footwear. If there was truth in that tradition, it would be no great exaggeration to say that the sacking of the glorious city of Pagán a few years later, when the Emperor sent his grandson south in command of a powerful army, was a direct result of a refusal to remove one's shoes.

The European merchants arriving in subsequent centuries were of course subject to the same etiquette, but seldom even mention having to remove their shoes. It was only when perceptions of *power* were involved that outsiders saw the practice as objectionable; those who simply wanted to make money accepted the 'unshoeing' as part of the bargaining process. The envoys of The East India Company, seeing themselves not as 'company reps' but as the agents of a great power, in fact as British Ambassadors in all but name, resented the requirement to 'unshoe' or 'discalce'. Even the knowledgeable Burney objected to the practice, seeing it as 'a means of exalting their king'; but then *all* monarchies seem to have had conventions serving the same function. If he feared that even the King of England would have been kept waiting and required to take his footwear off before entering the palace he was probably right, for procrastination and unshoeing were clearly part of a Court power-game.

All Burmese persons of whatever rank would enter the precincts of a holy place barefoot; and although this requirement was quite naturally extended to foreign visitors, people were generally tolerant of those who broke the rule except - once again - when power relationships were involved. It was an Arakanese monk called U Ottama who was largely responsible for elevating the requirement to 'unshoe' into the political sphere. Impressed by the advances he had seen during two stays in Japan, he returned to Burma in 1915 and set up the All Burma Buddhist Association, from which sprang the more politically-active YMBA. As Collis (1953) mentions, by 1920 there were 'foot wearing prohibited' notices outside pagodas. An Englishman visiting at the end of 1922 explains the British reaction to 'the new rule':

The visitor's first thought is "Well, why not? A foreigner is expected to re-move his hat in an English place of worship; ... what objection can there be, then, to complying with the demand of the pongyis ....?" The answer is that the demand is made with the direct intention of humiliating the Englishman. Its motive is political and not religious. For years past English visitors have been welcome at pagodas and kyaungs, and no such compliance with custom was either asked or expected. The new regulation .. shows the direction of the politi-cal wind, and no self-respecting Englishman will consent to obey it, since in obeying he is doing exactly what the pongyis want him to do - namely lowering himself in the eyes of the majority of the native population.

(Edmonds, 1924)

Edmonds was in Prome at the time, and wanted very much to see its 'par-ticularly fine pagoda'. "But," he says, "out of deference to the feelings and opin-ions of the British community, I was obliged to content myself with looking at the outside."

Today this all seems very petty, but it is remarkable how vigorously and how long the British community in Burma continued to resist making this harmless cultural concession. Winston Churchill's Minister of Information in the second World War was Duff Cooper, later created Earl Of Norwich. In his memoirs he quotes from a letter written by his wife Diana about their short stay in Rangoon. She was having tea with some of the Governor's closest associates, and the topic of conversation was the Shwe Dagon pagoda.

To my surprise no one had ever been inside. "Footwear," was the explana-tion; "you have to enter barefoot - an Englishman can't do that - people do everything there - full of lepers - the stink of the place" - out rolled the excuses. I said one's feet were washable, one did much worse with one's hands, leprosy isn't caught that way, (...) ... they looked exaggeratedly shocked. When the con-versation was over we drove in closed cars to have a look round.... and in a flash I had my shoes and stockings off and was following the votaries into the great dark doorway. It was one of the most repaying sights I have ever seen.

(Norwich, 1953)

Diana spent a whole hour inside the precinct and came out to find that one of the Governor's aides 'still looked nauseated' and later, at 'a dreadful dinner-party', the matter was 'talked about with bated horror':

My reasoning was that if they had put on the "no footwear" order to keep the British out, and the British stayed out, then the Burmese won. I'm glad I did not know all this political significance at the Pagoda gate, for I might then have hesitated to go in. I hope I would not have faltered as I'm sure it's all part of the Raj "tone" here, which is most shocking.

Diana's letter was written in late 1941, just before the first Japanese air-raid on Rangoon.

It was only when the young man (having learned who Collis was) had given way, and when Collis' companions were at their devotions, that the senior magistrate began to understand:

I alone remained standing, a conspicuous figure with my shoes on. It suddenly struck me that I was committing a rudeness, and I wished I had not come. The people showed no incivility but were cool and distant. I grew more uncomfortable and felt like an outsider, or worse, like an oppressor who was taking advantage of his office.

Collis had come to realise his position as an imperialist. By the end of 1920 a policy of resistance was finding expression in Burma too: the YMBA had developed into the more politically active General Council of Burmese Associations; the Act upgrading Rangoon College to university status was objected to because its stated aims and syllabuses were not sufficiently Burmese in character; and a student strike spread to the schools.

For the administrators and for the already overworked officers and men of the Indian Imperial Police serving in Burma the upsurge of political protest brought further headaches. The British felt the necessity to 'stick together', and one traveller arriving in Rangoon at this time observed that their club life served this purpose:

The club is not alone a place of enjoyment, it is a symbol of racial solidarity. It justifies your pride in being English without any ulterior implication; it is the non-committal half-way house between indifference and friendship.
There are various clubs in Rangoon with memberships nicely graded (in principle) according to social acceptability, but the largest and most generally popular is the Gymkhana Club, known all over Burma as the Gym, which, founded as a sporting club, is now equally notable for its dances and its bar. Its large buildings and playing-grounds, situated on the borders of the town, wake into life each evening about dusk and are shrouded again by half-past nine. But during these few hours Rangoon society, especially on the three nights a week when the Club's own band plays in the Club's own ballroom, is to be found there in force.
(Curle, 1923)

Curle uses the word 'English' loosely here, for he goes on to say 'Rangoon society is essentially Scottish'. A growing proportion of the population was Indian and Curle quotes a local saying 'God made the Burman, but the British soldier made the Eurasian', for the city had a huge population of Anglo-Indian civil servants and was rapidly losing its Burmese character. To savour that character to the full, one had to go to the Shwe Dagon Pagoda where, although there was much to see by day, the best time was the evening:

The time to leave is in the dusk, when the converging roads bring in the Burmans from the city, when the yellow-robed poongyis with their parchment umbrellas are making sedately for the monasteries, and when the gold and gold-leaf of the Shwe Dagon take on a lemon tint in the twilight. Then may you feel the poor present times to be obliterated and Rangoon itself but a lost name. These are the pilgrims from afar come with gifts and prayers; they do not wish to linger in the empty plains about the river, but would worship and be gone.

At all hours of night and day the footsteps of the pious resound upon the platform of the Shwe Dagon, while the protecting nats, those singular spirits superimposed upon Buddhism from heathen times, keep it forever in their charge. As dark falls the five tiers of electric globes hung around the plinth awake, and like a great tropic beast, mythical and argus-eyed, the Pagoda gleams and winks. One could never forget that sight, and especially if seen upon the night of Tazaungdaing, the Festival of Lights, which falls in November in a triumphant vindication of the spirit of Buddhism. The zayats and the tazaungs are lit up then, candles burn in their myriads, and a huge crowd, ever reinforced, slowly encircles the platform, tight-packed and cheerful, to the ringing of bells and the carrying of religious insignia. Above it all, remote, unmoved, sweeps the shining Pagoda with an intense majesty of repose.....

⌘⌘⌘⌘⌘⌘

At sunset on 26 October 1921 the battle-cruiser *Renown* moved out of Portsmouth harbour. Against the advice of many who understood only too well the political situation in India, Edward Prince of Wales was setting out on a tour that would last eight months and cover more than 40,000 miles, and during which he would visit every British possession from Gibraltar to Borneo and more besides. One of the staff accompanying him was a twenty-two-year-old Lieutenant who was in love with a vivacious young lady he had left behind. As predicted, the royal party encountered non-cooperation and even hostility in India, causing the Prince to write to the King:'I must tell you at once that I'm very depressed about my work in British India as I don't feel that I'm doing a scrap of good; in fact I can say that I know I am not.' (The Duke of Windsor, 1951) Fate was kinder to the lovesick young officer, for within a few weeks the woman he missed had joined him in Delhi, and on St. Valentine's Day 1922 the couple became engaged.

Using the troopship *Dufferin* for the Calcutta-Rangoon-Madras leg of the voyage the Prince continued his tour, receiving a warmer welcome in Burma and spending two days in Mandalay where, as usual, the entertainment was lavish. There was a carnival parade of all the minority groups of Upper Burma:

Six bearers, four of them sons of chiefs, held golden umbrellas over him as he walked to a covered pavilion... The chiefs did homage with much noise and then began as strange a procession as the most feverish imagination could conceive. Out of the darkness appeared weird and monstrous animals, pirouetting forward to the rhythm of great gongs. There were fat dragons thirty feet long, and thin dragons twenty feet high; specimens of an unknown breed of emu with ten-foot necks; tigers with flaming jaws...

(Phillips, 1922)

There was the usual regatta on the moat, in which this time Burman women paddling in orthodox style were beaten by Intha women rowing with their legs; there were the usual bullock-cart races; and soon it was time to move on... and on. It was not until 12 April 1922 that the *Renown* slid into Yokohama harbour, where the young Lieutenant was allowed to look over the latest Japanese battleship, the *Mutsu*. He was sufficiently impressed by what he saw to write in his unofficial diary at the end of the tour, 'As regards Japan from the point of view of a world power, my visit has been an eye-opener to me...'

Although the couple's engagement was supposed to be a secret, everyone in England seemed to know that Lieutenant The Lord Louis Mountbatten, MVO, RN, was going to marry Edwina Ashley; and less than a month after the *Renown* had docked they were married in Westminster.

᚛᚛᚛᚛᚛

The Irishman Collis, who had suddenly felt like an oppressor, was to become known not for his poems but for his very readable books about Burma. Now, in 1922, another young would-be poet was on his way to Burma. At the age of eleven he had written a jingoistic verse which was published in a local newspaper, and two years later another appeared in *The Henley and South Oxfordshire Standard*. Now nineteen, he had passed the necessary examinations for joining the Indian Imperial Police, had expressed a preference for Burma, and had been sent to the Provincial Police Training School in Mandalay. Here his experiences, or perhaps those of his comrades, did provide him with inspiration for one amusing little verse:

Romance

When I was young and had no sense
In far-off Mandalay
I lost my heart to a Burmese girl
As lovely as the day.
Her skin was gold, her hair was jet,
Her teeth were ivory;
I said "For twenty silver pieces,
Maiden, sleep with me."

She looked at me, so pure, so sad,
The loveliest thing alive,

And in her lisping, virgin voice,
Stood out for twenty-five.

(Quoted in Crick, 1980)

We shall meet this young man again soon. As with Collis, it would not be as a poet but for the quality of his prose that he would become well-known. In fact, Burma seemed now to be attracting not artists but young poets who turned to prose. An Oxford graduate who in 1916 had come down with a first in English and seen his first book of verse published in the same year was by 1925 an established novelist and was eastward-bound on a voyage from India to California, during which he became aware of how tenuous Britain's hold was upon her eastern empire. Aldous Huxley took the time to go up the Irrawaddy to Bhamo, where he enthused about the beauty of the Chinese architecture and of the crockery that was on sale at ridiculously low prices; but of Burmese culture he was contemptuous, as can be seen in his description of Shwe Dagon:

The precincts of the Shwe Dagon pagoda contain the world's finest specimens of what I may call the merry-go-round style of architecture and decoration. The huge bell-shaped spire, gilded from top to bottom and shining, towards the sun, with intolerable high lights, stands in the midst; and round it are grouped the hundreds of subsidiary shrines, elaborately fretted, glittering like Aladdin's cave at the panto-mime with a gaudy mosaic of coloured glass, gilded and painted, or dark, with the natural colour of the teakwood pinnacles and gables, against the golden shining of the pagoda. It seems a sacred Fun Fair, a Luna Park dedicated to the greater glory of Gautama - but more fantastic, more wildly amusing than any Bank Holiday invention. Our memories, after a first visit, were of something so curiously improbable, so deliriously and comically dream-like, that we felt constrained to return the following day to make quite sure that we had really seen it.

(Huxley, 1926)

Under the Montagu-Chelmsford reform the country's first elections had been held in 1922, but by now dyarchy was a present that no-one wanted. There was a parliament in Rangoon, but even a British civil servant of that time knew that the local government reforms were utterly inappropriate:

The system of local government we introduced was the result of a thousand years' experience in a totally different society. None of the classes which provide the real stiffening on our local bodies in England had any counterpart in Burma, and the whole thing was an alien make-believe with its formal committee-meetings, type-script agenda, resolutions, amendments and counter-amendments.

(Harvey, 1946)

British officials might blame the politicians or dismiss 'the Burman' as lazy, indisciplined and lacking in initiative, but the source of the unease lay deeper. An English holidaymaker was surely right when he suggested that the unrest was the result of nothing less than the clash of two diametrically opposed philosophies:

No-one doubts that the officials are zealous, earnest men. They are not to blame. The departmental administration is not to blame. It is the system itself which is at fault - the attempt to apply Western methods to an Eastern people. (...) It is this worship of money for its own sake - the cornerstone of modern civilisation! - which is ruining Burma, making a criminal class, and destroying the happiness of a once contented people. The Burman, it seems, must, like the foreigner, make money his god or go to the wall. Can one wonder, therefore, that a large section of the Burman population wishes to drive the foreigner out of the country?

(Edmonds, 1924)

The land problem was now acute, the Indian moneylenders having tightened their stranglehold on the Burmese farmers. A report on Mandalay district in the 1922 season (Searle, 1924) had shown that 85 percent of the farmers there were in debt, barely managing to keep body and soul together; most were not qualified to receive such financial assistance as was available because they had not managed to retain a fifty percent equity on their land. Seasonal agricultural labour was also now in the hands of Indians, as was much of the industrial work, and there was also a growing population of urban Chinese. Foreigners of one sort or another now comprised two thirds of Rangoon's population, and there was a fear that the whole land might quite literally pass into foreign ownership.

In its attempts to find some sort of charismatic leader Burman resistance produced two sorts of would-be saviour: monastic and monarchic. One of the monastic kind was a patriot who had resided for a time in India and had picked up ideas from the Indian National Congress. Dressed as a hpongyi and calling himself U Ottama he went round the country advocating sedition and urging monks to follow his example. He was twice arrested and imprisoned before eventually being jailed for life, but not before he had caused the Police considerable embarrassment - his followers had to be arrested even if they wore the robe - and had become something of a martyr. 'Saviour-kings' appeared one after another, usually in rural communities where ancient beliefs died hard. The Police sought one such 'king' in the Shwebo area who was believed to have the power of metamorphosis and even the more sophisticated nationalists might sometimes be expected to act as 'saviours'. U Chit Hlaing, head of an association and destined to become the Speaker of a future Senate, went upriver to preside at a meeting just south of Sagaing and discovered that

he was obliged against his will to parade in the guise of a saviour king. On landing from the steamer at a point some distance from Kinyua,

*he was met by 500 of the Association's members, who insisted on his mount-
ing a caparisoned elephant. Behind him on the elephant's haunches knelt
a man dressed as a royal attendant and who held a golden umbrella over
him. Beside the elephant marched farmers dressed as soldiers of the old
régime and an escort of mounted men. The main body of the members
followed on foot. On arrival at Kinyua, U Chit Hlaing was welcomed by
two thousand people in a pavilion which had some resemblance to the
palace of Mandalay.*

(Collis, 1953)

Knowing that there were detectives in the crowd, the speaker disclaimed
any royal pretensions and tried to get his audience to listen to his political
ideas, but before long almost every listener drifted away. 'People who
believe in magic', observed Collis, 'find an ordinary political address in-
sufferably boring.'

<hr />

The recruit we last saw at the Police Training School in Mandalay was
now in Moulmein, where Kipling had fallen in love at first sight with a
Burmese girl. The young officer's first three postings had been to small
delta towns, his fourth to Insein just north of Rangoon, and now in 1926
he was Assistant Superintendent in Burma's third largest town. Eric Blair's
little poem had simply told a tale of punctured romance, but by now he
was far more deeply disillusioned, having decided that British imperialism was evil. He felt, far more keenly than Collis, that he was an oppressor, and had come to hate his job.

*I was young and ill-educated and I had had to think out my problems
in the utter silence that is imposed on every Englishman in the East. I did
not even know that the British Empire is dying, still less did I know that it
is a great deal better than the younger empires that are going to supplant
it. All I knew was that I was stuck between my hatred of the empire I
served and my rage against the evil-spirited little beasts who tried to make
my job impossible.*

(Orwell, 1936)

The constant expression of anti-British feeling 'in an aimless, petty
kind of way' wore him down:

*No one had the guts to raise a riot, but if a European woman went
through the bazaars somebody would probably spit betel juice over her
dress. As a police officer I was an obvious target and was baited whenever it seemed safe to do so. When a nimble Burman tripped me up on the
football field and the referee (another Burman) looked the other way, the
crowd yelled with hideous laughter. This happened more than once. In the
end the sneering yellow faces of young men that met me everywhere, the
insults hooted after me when I was at a safe distance, got badly on my*

nerves. The young Buddhist priests were the worst of all. There were several thousands of them in the town and none of them seemed to have anything to do except stand on street corners and jeer at Europeans.

Blair took home leave in 1927, resigned and never returned to Burma; but his hatred of his job spurred him to write two vivid essays about his experiences there, and his contempt of the British administrators and their inane and racist club life provided the material for his first novel, *Burmese Days.*

Writers had been arriving all the time in spite of the troubles. In 1923 a famous English author had gone upriver to Mandalay ready to proceed on horseback through the Shan States to Siam on a journey that would take him on to Cambodia and Annam. The result was a book published in 1930 that the author called 'an exercise in style', a style that he had exercised most lavishly upon Mandalay's moated city:

In the broad water of the moat the rosy wall and the thick foliage of the trees and the Burmese in their bright clothes are sharply reflected. The water is still, but not stagnant, and peace rests upon it like a swan with a golden crown. Its colours, in the early morning and towards sunset, have the soft fatigued tenderness of pastel; they have the translucency without the stubborn definiteness, of oils. It is as though light were a prestidigitator and in play laid on colours that he had just crated and were about with a careless hand to wash them out again. You hold your breath for you cannot believe that such an effect can be anything but evanescent. You watch it with the same expectancy with which you read a poem in some complicated metre when your ear awaits the long delayed rhyme that will fulfil the harmony. But at sunset, when the clouds in the west are red and splendid so that the wall, the trees and the moat are drenched in radiance; and at night under the full moon when the white gateways drip with silver and the belvederes above them are shot with silhouetted glimpses of the sky, the assault on your senses is shattering. You try to guard yourself by saying it is not real. This is not a beauty that steals upon you unawares, that flatters and soothes your bruised spirit, this is not a beauty that you can hold in your hand and call your own and put in its place among familiar beauties that you know; it is a beauty that batters you and stuns you and leaves you breathless, there is no calmness in it nor control, it is like a fire that on a sudden consumes you and you are left shaken and bare and yet by a strange miracle alive.

Towards the end this reads like a description of lovemaking rather than of a moat, the climactic prose itself being enough to batter and stun and leave you breathless, and it comes as a surprise to learn that its author is Somerset Maugham (Maugham, 1930).

⁂

Shortly before Maugham's arrival in Burma one saviour-king called

Bandaha had moved down from Shwebo, the ancient source of kings, in an attempt to raise a rebellion. He had carried his own throne with him, dispensing magical medicines and urging his followers to avail themselves of the bullet-proof tattoos that were on offer. Now in 1930 we find another medicine-man from Shwebo claiming blood royal; bent on achieving national independence, he astutely moved down to Tharrawaddy, a disaffected district north of Rangoon where resistance to Poll Tax payment was perhaps greater than elsewhere. He called himself Saya San. Shortly after a serious rebellion had broken out in the area, a newly-recruited Forest Assistant was passing through the same district by train to take up his post:

An armoured train went before us, for there was war in the land. At the call of Saya San, the King of Dragons, the Only Golden Crow*, the braves of Tharrawaddy had risen against the British, and throughout the length and breadth of Lower Burma the flame of rebellion was alight.

We came to a bridge that the rebels had attempted to dynamite the night before.....

(Warren, 1937)

The revolt was to last two years, but the rebels were no match for trained Indian Army units. Saya San's typical follower was a rice farmer, brave but ignorant; armed with a long knife *(dah)* and perhaps a spear, he was protected only by his *Galon* tattoo, by an amulet or two and by guardian spirits *(nats)*. The organiser was as likely as not a politicised monk, and every one of Saya San's adherents had to swear a binding oath which included the following:

Oh come and witness our oath, O Bramah and all the great Nats of this world and of the world above.... Now at this time we are banded together to drive out all unbelievers. Oh hear us and bear witness. Till we are free from the rule of the English we promise to harm no member of the Galon brotherhood.... Grant to us liberty, and to the Galon King dominion over this land.

Many of the poor peasants who took the oath ran confidently towards the rifle muzzles, but the Galon King's hilltop palace, a simple wooden building was soon taken, Saya San himself managing to escape. Groups in various parts of the country were now rebelling in sympathy and attracting some followers who were merely dacoits. Forest Department houses, scattered widely among the teak forests, were a favourite target but our recruit was not one of the casualties. He went to Mandalay some time later for the purpose of taking an examination, and visited the palace with an elderly Burmese gentleman. If we assume that this companion was sixty-five, he would have been eighteen when the bullock-cart carrying Thibaw

---

* *This was the mythical bird, the* Galon, *not a crow.*

and his queen rumbled and squealed through Mandalay town to the riverside and the sun set on the Court of Ava. He shared a moment of nostalgia
with the forestry officer Warren:

> *Here is the watch-tower and, still hanging, the great gong, upon which
> was struck the passing of the hours. It commands a view over Mandalay,
> and far down the nearby Irrawaddy. Here, night and day, a sentinel stood
> scaring off with stones from a sling any birds of ill-omen which might seek
> to rest upon the palace, and keeping ceaseless watch and ward over the
> Royal Town ....*
>
> *Before I left the palace my Burmese companion and I ascended the
> watch-tower and gazed over the palace, and at the* pyathat *raising its
> seven curly roofs, one upon the other, up to the brilliant sky. Said he:
> "Well can I remember when King Theebaw yet reigned in splendour here",
> and then he was very silent. Perhaps into his mind came the Burmese
> proverb: "Pyit pyan pyet pyan loka dan", which being translated into
> Latin is: "Sic transit omnia gloria mundi".*

༼ᨠᨠᨠᨠᨠᨠ༽

Just before the rebellion, race riots had flared up in Rangoon and in
the space of three days some 120 Indians had been killed and 900 wounded.
Directed against Chinese as well as Indian workers, the fighting had quickly
been quelled, but Burman xenophobia continued to simmer and a great
deal of political activity was going on. In 1930 a student group formed the
Do-Bama ('We Burmans') Society, whose members called themselves
Thakin, a term which meant 'Master' rather than 'Mister' and which had
hitherto been used when addressing the British; and the following year
the All Burma Youth League (ABYL) was formed. At this time Maung
Nu, a young Burman recently graduated, was working in the delta as superintendent of a national (i.e. Burmese-language) school where his friend
Maung Thant was headmaster. Each of these friends was destined , in the
wake of tragic circumstances, to hold high office - Maung Nu to be premier following the assassination of Aung San, and Maung Thant to be
Secretary-General of the United Nations after the death of Dag Hammar-
skjöld. (Maung Nu had wanted to make his name writing plays in English
and had sent one of his scripts to George Bernard Shaw but received no
reply; on joining the ABYL he became more and more involved in political affairs.)

Saya San was captured and imprisoned. Boldly defended in the court-
room by a certain Dr. Ba Maw, he was nevertheless convicted and executed. As the unrest continued in Burma, a new Constitution was being
drafted in London at the Burma Round Table Conference. At least one
Burmese participant brought back a variety of political tracts, for the
Thakins were using their knowledge of English to help the imbibe any
ideas that might further their own aspirations: they studied pamphlets issued by Sinn Fein in Eire, British socialist writings, the works of Sun Yat-
sen, those of Marx, Lenin and Stalin, and even *Mein Kampf*. The Do-

Bama anthem ('our land, our earth, our Burman race') was reminiscent of *Ein Volk, Ein Reich, Ein Führer,* which might suggest that what was envisaged by the young patriots, who had never experienced democracy in action, was not so much a democratic Burma as a nation under strong central rule by a surrogate king figure.

When Maung Nu went back to university to study law in 1934 he was sufficiently politicised to be a member of an important group of students which included Aung San - who later steered Burma to independence - and which now secured control of the Rangoon University Students' Union. In 1935 the Government of Burma Act promised a new Constitution that would come into effect in 1937 and the Thakins consolidated by merging the Do-Bama Society and the ABYL to form the more heavyweight *Dobama Asiayone.* In 1936 Maung Nu (now Thakin Nu) was expelled from Rangoon University for criticising the Principal and inciting the students to go on strike, and Aung San met the same fate for printing in the student journal a scurrilous attack on a university official. The student body promptly voted for a walk-out and camped at the Shwe Dagon Pagoda on a three-month strike, and in that same year the elections were held. Two members of the Thakin movement were elected to the legislature, and on 1 April Dr. Ba Maw (he who had unsuccessfully defended Saya San) became the first Premier of a Burma at long last severed from India.

∽∽∽∾∾∾

In the cool season of 1937/8 there arrived in Burma a mildly eccentric British Major who was happy that in so many parts of the world 'harmless lunatics are treated with special consideration'. He had already travelled down the Mississippi and the Nile, and now it was the turn of the Irrawaddy. His harmless lunacy lay merely in his preferred mode of transport: the canoe. He planned to go upstream by steamer as far as Katha and on to Myitkyina by rail, build a canoe and then set off downriver with the help of a local lad. The country's newly-detached status was not evident as he set out upriver on board the steamer *Java.*

> *I met a disappointment at the outset. I had hoped for Burmese crews, the chance to learn a little Burmese, possibly even to borrow a youngster as a companion. Instead I found that the whole crew was Chittagonian, Moslem Indian: the chief reason seems to be that they are cheap and will put up with living conditions that a Burman would not accept. Even the steward and cooks and waiters were Indian, and the sweepers: these lived right aft, in one of two fowl-houses on stilts (ducks occupied the other). Their "home" was decorated with pictures of Hindu gods and naked women: they made music there, the skinny boy playing a typewriter-keyed one-string zither, the man a little drum.*
>
> *The food was good, and very Scottish (the Irrawaddy Flotilla Company is registered in Scotland) with Dundee marmalade and Crawford's biscuits and porridge daily: most of the officers were also Scottish.*

(Raven-Hart, 1939)

Having built his canoe in Myitkyina, the Major paddled off down-stream with a Kachin lad as companion and translator, bypassed the 'grubby mess' of the Mandalay shore and went on to Chouk before returning by steamer to see Mandalay at leisure. Raven-Hart did not suffer British fools gladly, but managed not to explode when he was buttonholed at one club:

Didn't I think that perhaps to go about as I did, treating my compan-ion as a friend more than a servant, and doing things for myself, and paddling myself, and so on - wasn't it perhaps conceivably tending to lower British prestige? And that is so important out here, you know: once we lose our prestige ...

I was polite, and passed it off with something about harmless lunatics like canoers being tolerated as exceptions. I wanted to explode, and say that if British "prestige" depended on that sort of thing ...well, then the sooner British "prestige" was "lowered" the better.

Under his bluff exterior, Major Raven-Hart was sensitive and broad-minded. In Mandalay he admired the Palace - even its roofs of corrugated iron - adding two afterthoughts, each in parentheses:

I doubt if I should have had the courage to say I like it, or gilt mirrors and bits of coloured glass, before visiting Mandalay: that Palace gives a thorough and salutary shaking-up to one's accepted ideas of art.

And if there are moments when it seems a little cheap, remember that in 1857 when it was built we were admiring the Crystal Palace and pre-paring to admire the Albert Memorial.

His views make a refreshing change from the 'club mentality' that he and many other visitors had encountered. Before going to Mandalay he had read Symes' account - especially the details of the processions - and in the palace he had visited the little museum to see the preserved cos-tumes of the Burman courtiers so that he could people the empty build-ings in his imagination; like many a Burman, Raven-Hart felt a sense of loss:

My own great regret is that we did not retain the Monarchy at the annexation, under supervision, so that the Palace would be a living thing to-day instead of an empty shell, and Burmese art and music and litera-ture would flourish in its shadow. It seems to have been a near thing: Geary, writing a year later, says that even the candidate had been chosen, a young Prince of fourteen: he might well be ruling now at sixty-six, a living link with the great past of the Burmese Empire.

The Burmese Empire may have had a great past; but to a Burman king monarchy under supervision would have been a contradiction in terms. Besides, it was upon British imperialism that the sun was now beginning to set. George Orwell had said that the empire he hated was dying, and perhaps the good Major had considered how fragile were the defences of the far-flung British Empire; but neither could have foreseen where, how soon and how swiftly the first blow would be struck.

The Watch-tower, Mandalay

The Burma Road

After the battle in Arakan

CHAPTER 11
They Come
Burma, 1938 - 1945

> *Hang out our banners on the outward walls;*
> *The cry is still, 'They come'; our castle's strength*
> *Will laugh a siege to scorn.*
>
> William Shakespeare , *Macbeth, Act 5, Scene 3.*

It had been rapid industrialisation that had enabled the Japanese to defeat first the Chinese and then the Russians in the period 1894-1905. Fearing the increased might of the new Soviet Union, they had in 1931 again invaded the mainland in order to establish their own militarist state of Manchukuo on Manchurian territory, and had later entered into an Anti-Comintern Pact with Nazi Germany. In 1937 they had proceeded to occupy important areas of China proper. This expansionism was for the purpose of establishing an economic empire, the Greater East Asia Co-Prosperity Sphere, an empire to supplant those of the western powers in the region, who would be too preoccupied with problems nearer home to interfere.

In 1938 Chinese forces, isolated inland, managed by an immense effort to complete the 700-mile Burma Road, spanning in the process that fifty-mile corridor through whose canyons four of the world's greatest rivers tumble, and so creating a vital supply line linking Burma's Lashio railhead to the city of Kunming in Yunnan. In that same year the Japanese made their first political overtures to the Burmese Prime Minister, Dr. Ba Maw. In November the British steamer *Stanhall* unloaded in Rangoon 6,000 tons of Russian arms and ammunition bound for Chiang Kai-shek's forces in China, and within a month five more ships with similar cargoes arrived. As trains laden with munitions rattled northwards through Mandalay to Lashio there were Burmese protests that such transhipments could involve Burma in the Sino-Japanese war, and in Tokyo the *Japan Chronicle* had already expressed alarm that this route was being used to supply their enemies. When further consignments arrived, many were henceforth sent less obtrusively by steamers that chugged past Mandalay to Bhamó.

The year 1938 happened to be 1300 in the Burmese era and was considered a highly auspicious one; this belief added excitement to a situation that was already tense, and civil unrest mounted. In Rangoon there were more anti-Moslem riots: 192 Indians were killed, almost 900 were injured, hundreds of houses were looted and the violence spread to other towns. The Thakin Party organised strikes, and in one fracas a student died from a truncheon blow. Maung Aung Gyaw thus became the Thakins' first martyr, and more were created when in Mandalay the following February seventeen people died as police opened fire on demonstrators. As the Second World War approached, Dr. Ba Maw's party was joining forces with others, including a Thakin group headed by Aung San and the respected nationalist veteran Kodaw Hmaing. Although it might have seemed to the British that an age had passed since the Court of Ava held sway, Kodaw Hmaing could remember how as a boy of ten he had watched the sad procession making its way to the Mandalay shore as Thibaw and his queen were sent into exile. Now he was looking forward to the ousting of the British.

No sooner had war been declared in Europe than a Burma-Japan society was formed in Tokyo. Posing as a journalist in Rangoon, a Japanese agent called Colonel Minami (alias Suzuki Keiji) had been winning the confidence of the Thakins. On the understanding that the collaboration of a Burmese army would lead to independence, he had already arranged with Aung San that selected Burmans would be sent to Japan for military training. For a long time the Burmans had tacitly acknowledged the technological superiority of the Europeans; but now the Japanese were not only equal to the *kalabyu* in this respect, they were also Asian and apparently sympathetic to Burmese aspirations. Those who pointed out the tyranny and cruelty meted out by the Japanese in China were contending with rose-tinted folk-memories of absolute Burman monarchy and with the current attractiveness of such powerful role-models as Stalin and Hitler. The Freedom Bloc, an alliance of Dr. Ba Maw's party with the Thakins, was publicly opposed to any involvement in the 'European War'; the Burma Revolutionary Party, a secret organisation also formed at this time, was in embryo the Socialist Party of the post-war era.

Separated now from India, Burma had been looking forward to direct negotiations with Britain. It was hoped that 'Dominion Status' would be granted as a step towards complete independence, but when no such undertaking was made Burmese patience began to wear thin. It seemed that only an armed struggle would achieve results, and that such resistance might as well aim at total independence rather than self-government within the British Empire. One series of open-air political meetings in Mandalay in June 1940 well illustrates the nature of the nationalist fervour of the time. An old legend about a mystic, a certain Bo Bo Aung, had recently resurfaced and been made the subject of a popular song. Once upon a time, the story went, Bo Bo Aung had appeared at the king's Amarapura palace and the king had felt threatened by his strange powers. He decided to have the mystic killed but Bo Bo Aung, divining this, went to the king's chamber and on the wall drew a single circle (the Burmese letter corresponding to *W* in English). The king, he said, would have to erase the letter before he could dare to kill him. When the king tried to rub out the circle, two more instantly appeared; and each time he tried, the letters simply doubled in number. This legend had rekindled the old desire for an invincible saviour-king who would multiply Burmese glory a hundredfold, and on the first night of the Mandalay meetings Dr. Ba Maw had only to tell the throng not to worry about being unarmed because Bo Bo Aung would provide, and the crowd roared in excitement. The next morning worshippers at the Arakan Pagoda

> *saw in the wind-blown light of the candle-flames faint circles glowing on the soft and uneven gold of the great Buddha image. What some saw at first all began to see in time, and the number of circles began to grow. The story went quickly round that Bo Bo Aung's O's had appeared at the most sacred pagoda in the town. The conference was at once called Bo Bo Aung's Conference.*

(Ba Maw, 1968)

Aung San was making an open bid for leadership and in 1940 attended a session of the Indian National Congress, at which he was presented to Mahatma Gandhi and to Nehru. On his return he found that many nationalist agitators were being arrested: Thakin Nu was sent to Mandalay Jail and Ba Maw was imprisoned when the Freedom Bloc called the oilfield workers out on strike. A warrant had been issued for his own arrest, but he took up the Japanese vice-consul's suggestion and slipped out of Rangoon on board a ship bound for Amoy, where the Japanese Army could arrange for him to be transferred to Tokyo. On 8 August, the day the Battle of Britain began, he and a fellow Thakin were on board a Norwegian freighter, disguised as Chinese labourers but heading down the Rangoon River with only the battle for Burma in mind. Suzuki later flew to Taipei to arrange for their onward journey to Tokyo. The Japanese High Command was sure that an isolated and beleaguered Britain would be unable effectively to defend both her own shores and her eastern possessions; and if they ever believed the carefully nurtured myth about the impregnability of 'Fortress Singapore' they were not fooled for long. For the moment, though, they needed to cut off the lines of supply to China, and while Aung San was in Tokyo the *Minami Kikan* (Southern Agency) was formed. This was a joint Japanese Army/Navy venture whose main aim was to cut the Burma supply route to Chungking. (France was soon to fall victim to Hitler's forces , whereupon the Japanese were able to occupy French Indo-China and thus seal some of the supply routes. Japanese diplomatic pressure at this time was such that even Churchill capitulated by temporarily closing the Burma Road.) The *Kikan* was also, it was said, charged with the task of helping Burma to gain independence.

In March 1941 Aung San reappeared in Rangoon after spending some months in Tokyo's War Office. He now contacted the Burma Revolutionary Party to arrange the secret recruitment of volunteers for military training. Thirty young men (including Aung San) were smuggled out to Japan; in May, after a little preliminary instruction, they were transferred to the island of Hainan for further training, the language of communication being broken English. Six months later they returned to Thailand to recruit expatriate Burmans for service in the new Burma Independence Army (BIA). In December, while this recruitment was going on, Japan attacked the major naval base of Pearl Harbor without bothering to declare war, thus provoking the United States to enter the conflict.

With BIA recruitment in Bangkok going well, the thirty original comrades now met to perform a traditional symbolic blood-brotherhood ceremony known as *thwe thauk*. Apart from the mercurial Aung San those present included the military father-figure Colonel Minami (Suzuki) and Shu Maung, who until recently had been a postal clerk. The assembled comrades each cut a finger so that a little blood fell into a silver bowl, whereupon the blood was topped up with strong liquor and each drank his share while joining in a chorus - an oath of unity in the fight against the British enemy. Each assumed the title *Bo* (a rank of military command) and a charismatic *nom de guerre*. Suzuki was now Bo Mogyo ('Captain Thunderbolt'), Aung San became Bo Teza ('Captain Fire') and Shu Maung graduated to Bo Ne Win ('Captain Brilliant Sun') - a name that he maintained for the rest of his life. It was agreed that the Thakin Party's flag should now be the BIA's colours: a peacock on a field of equal yellow, green and red horizontal bands.

On 23 December 1941 the Japanese launched their first air raid on Rangoon, and the bombing continued for a month. On the last day of the year both Suzuki and Aung San addressed BIA recruits at the Thailand-Burma border. By the middle of January 1942 all their units were either at or already across the Thailand-Burma border. The Burmese armies of yesteryear had attacked Siam by marching down to the lowlands of Moulmein and crossing a convenient pass. On 20 January two Japanese Divisions used the same route in the opposite direction to push into Burma, and the speed of their progress was a measure of British unpreparedness in London and Rangoon. For the BIA this was the fourth Anglo-Burmese war, the one in which they - with the help of their Japanese friends - would see every inch of so-called British territory returned to rightful ownership; and for the next three years the only 'travellers' in Burma would be the advancing and retreating combatants and the bewildered refugees.

⚬⚬⚬⚬⚬⚬⚬⚬

James Lunt had joined the Burma Rifles in 1939. Now twenty-five, he was stationed in Moulmein and when the invasion came was in hospital with dysentery. On his release he was horrified to find that his wife had not been evacuated. It was necessary to use a ferry to cross the Salween and then to go on from Martaban to Rangoon by train.

Fortunately there were still trains running from Martaban to Rangoon, although the ferries were uncooperative. Accordingly I hired two sam-pans at about 4 pm on 22 January, paid an exorbitant price to two un-

Thibaw leaves Mandalay:
A Burmese view

The Shwe Dagon: Pyramid of Fire

*willing boatmen, and set out across the three-mile-wide river. My wife, I
and the two dachshunds occupied one* sampan; *Maung Shwe, our servant, with two suitcases, the other. The journey seemed to take hours. On
one occasion we ran aground on a sandbank, the other half occupied by
a dead elephant, twice the size of a captive balloon and stinking. On
another, a couple of Japanese naval 'Zeros' came sweeping down the
river, shooting up whatever came into their sights. It made sense to me to
take to the water while the planes howled overhead, but I climbed back
aboard, wet and dripping, to see my wife sitting calmly in the prow, the
two dachshunds still attached to her by their leads.*

(Lunt, 1986)

Less than a week after Mrs. Lunt caught the 'Rangoon Mail' the Japanese army was in Moulmein and more and more people were leaving the
southern towns and the capital itself - the Indians heading for Bengal, the
Karens, Burmans and others seeking relatives or friends in the countryside. With only a miniature air force in place at this time there were only
six bombers available for an attack on Moulmein, and there was little the
RAF could do to delay the Japanese advance. When a reconnaissance
pilot sighted an enemy column of about three hundred vehicles approaching the Sittang River, the fighter planes defending Rangoon joined a small
newly-arrived force of Blenheims in attacking this target, but could not
avert disaster. The Japanese were heading for the Sittang Bridge, half a
kilometre in length, across which ran the railway linking Moulmein to
Rangoon. Having begun a withdrawal across it but with most of his troops
still engaged on the far side, General Smyth had to decide whether to
leave the way open to Rangoon or to blow up the bridge, which was
under heavy fire. At 5.30 on the morning of 23 February the bridge was
blown up and Smyth's Division, having lost many men and most of its
arms and transport, was no longer an effective fighting unit. Some of the
stranded troops managed to get across the river by boat, and others swam.
One of the latter was Bill Crowther, a Medical Sergeant serving with the
2nd. Duke of Wellington's Regiment:

*On the morning of February 23, 1942, I found myself behind a ma-
chine-gun and Bandsman Les Williams feeding the belt through. While
our ammunition lasted I suppose we were enjoying ourselves ... When
our ammunition ran out I started to dismantle the gun, throwing the breech
block into the river. I said, 'Follow it, Les.' To which he replied: 'Not me.
I've to take my chances with the Japs. I can't swim.' I offered to take him
but he wouldn't have it. So I shook hands with him, wished him the best,
and dived in. (...) How long I spent in that river I don't know - helping
chaps to anything that floated. Some time during it a bullet, practically
spent, entered my right leg. I bled a lot, but it didn't hurt. I was put in
hospital...*

Thirty years were to pass before - in a chance encounter - Mr. Crowther again saw his comrade Les, who was captured and spent the rest of the war as a prisoner in Burma.

At the end of February General Wavell's request for further assistance was met when Chinese forces crossed from Yunnan into Burma. It was becoming clear that Rangoon, already a ghost city, could not be held. On 1 March the Governor, Sir Reginald Dorman-Smith, left the capital and drove up to Maymyo, and four days later General Alexander arrived as the new Commander-in-Chief. Alexander ordered the demolition of all useful plant, the burning of supplies and the withdrawal of the garrison, hoping to regroup his forces in the upper Irrawaddy valley. The Irrawaddy Flotilla Company's fleet was already being transferred upstream, laden with as many supplies as possible; except for three steamers that had been ordered to go downriver and along the Arakan coast to Akyab (Sittwe), the whole fleet was soon trapped upriver by the Japanese advance. By midday on 8 March the Japanese had set up their headquarters in Rangoon, and in the next few weeks massive troop reinforcements arrived. Upriver the oilfields of Yenangyaung were defended until mid-April, there being no other source of fuel, but these too were then destroyed.

Meanwhile, thousands of refugees - many of them Indians and most of them having travelled on foot for all or much of the way - had been streaming daily into Mandalay. Exhausted and racked with cholera, they trudged along the roadside, enveloped time and again in the vast blinding clouds of dust raised by overladen vehicles heading north. Here many of them were encamped, and everywhere the stench was sickening. Mrs. Gwenllyan Coward had always hated Mandalay but, as her husband was a railway officer stationed there, and as no arrangement had been made for 'railway wives', she was still there when the Chinese Fifth Army arrived at the station.

"They were a rabble in arms wearing poor cotton uniforms. Their colonel was dressed exactly the same as the men, but the discipline was extremely strict. When someone reported the theft of some tools from an engine shed, he paraded his men and had their kit examined. When the culprit was found, an officer cut off his ear with his sword and said, 'In future this man will be known for what he is.' Another refugee train arrived which had been sabotaged by dacoits and the occupants robbed. The Chinese hunted them down and crucified them against the walls of a pagoda as a warning to others."

(Draper, 1987)

On Good Friday, 3 April, three dozen Japanese bombers flew in relays over Mandalay and carpet-bombed the defenceless and overcrowded town. There was not even an air-raid warning because, as Mrs. Coward remembered long after, the system was complicated and the staff unreliable.

"There were various colours to indicate the degree of danger. The sirens were to be sounded when the telephone exchange received the yellow and the Anglo-Indian girls manning the switchboard were to remain at their posts until they received the red, which meant enemy bombers were approaching. Then everyone should go to the shelters, but the girls downed their receivers and left on receipt of the yellow."

The unopposed raid lasted three hours, and when the aircraft finally disappeared the old palace building that had housed the Upper Burma Club was a heap of burning teak, bodies floated in the moat where the bomb-blasts had hurled them, limbs lay strewn across the streets, the station - where hundreds of refugees had gathered - was a shambles, and people were still being burned alive in the spreading fires. It was thought that perhaps three thousand had been killed and more than five thousand wounded. In the next few days of intense heat there were two more raids; Thakin Nu, incarcerated in Mandalay Jail, noticed that the pall of smoke was by now too thick for the sunshine to penetrate, but that in spite of the terrific noise and destruction ' the Burmans in the jail who placed so much faith in the Japanese went on laughing, and clapping their hands, and waving a welcome with their shirts.' (Thakin Nu, 1954)

⟨⟨⟨⟨⟨⟩⟩⟩⟩⟩

Even as late as March, with the Japanese land forces surging northward towards the Burma Road, up in Maymyo there were still strawberries and cream for tea, and whisky at the Club. Then, just after Generalissimo and Madame Chiang Kai-shek had arrived there, the first air-raid shattered any lingering illusions. Though the remaining British personnel were joined by others hoping to get on a flight to India, the shady roads were now almost deserted. As the whisky ran out, the anxiety grew. Some could not believe that their comfortable way of life was about to end; others took sensible precautions.

Laurence Dawson, managing director of an agricultural loan bank in Lower Burma, had brought with him to Maymyo a fortune in gold and jewels, security upon which cultivators had borrowed money from his Bank. He was much concerned about the safety of his treasure; and as he was due to fly to India shortly he could take with him no more than he could carry. The gold and jewels must be left behind.

Dawson one day found an acquaintance digging a hole in his garden. On inquiry he was told by the digger that he was burying his plate and silver until he could recover it after the war. "Let me use the hole, too," begged Dawson. "I'll have it lined with bricks and properly cemented over." His acquaintance agreed, and the work was done. After the other's valuables had gone into the cache it was sealed up and the ground above it smoothed over. But Dawson's friend had not seen the Bank's treasure placed in the hole. In fact it had gone into the bare earth beneath the brick flooring provided by the banker.

After the war a search showed the cavity to be empty. Dawson's friend lost all his belongings; but the floor was unbroken, and Dawson's Bank duly recovered its valuable securities.

(Foucar, 1956)

On 25 April Governor Dorman-Smith was working in a Maymyo bungalow when the American Consul-General, rushing in to say goodbye, informed him that the Japanese had bypassed Maymyo and had cut the Burma Road near Lashio, a hundred miles to the north-east. Pausing only to burn his papers and snatch a bite to eat, Dorman-Smith hastened by car down the winding hill road, through the still smouldering ashes of Mandalay, through Amarapura, across the Ava bridge into Sagaing and, next morning, on to Shwebo — perhaps, as he did so, mentally travelling back through Burma's history to the founding of its last dynasty. From Shwebo he took a northbound train to Myitkyina, 250 miles up the line.

Meanwhile, on the very day when the Governor left Maymyo, General Alexander had learned that the Chinese 5th Army would not be able to hold out much longer. Deciding that his forces should fall back across the Irrawaddy, Alexander unwittingly left the Governor stranded in Myitkyina.

It was now clear that Burma would have to be abandoned. John Morton, the eleventh manager of the Irrawaddy Flotilla Company, had not only the very important task of helping in the withdrawal of troops, casualties and supplies but also the doleful duty of scuppering his fleet. On 28 April he wrote in his diary:

Mandalay was evacuated yesterday, the I.F. being the last to go. The Army is retreating up the Chindwin. Our men won't be many days at Monywa and I expect them to retire up river and so through to Manipur. Macnaughtan has been at Semeikon (below Mandalay) ferrying the Army across the Irrawaddy. I have a guarantee from General Slim that he and the crews of the steamers there will be taken safely to Monywa.

We are being chased out even quicker now than was expected and I have orders for more sinkings here at Kyaukmyaung. There are over two hundred of our fleet sunk at Mandalay. Imagine how I felt drilling holes in their bottoms with a Bren gun.

(Quoted in McCrae and Prentice, 1978)

Just downstream from Mandalay stood the only bridge across the Irrawaddy, and over it Lt. Gen. Slim was now withdrawing the British forces under his command. Built in 1935, the Ava Bridge had not been designed for heavy military use but Slim had no other choice; and after the withdrawal the bridge had to be 'blown' in order to slow down the Japanese advance.

A Stuart tank weighs some thirteen tons, and a notice warned us that the roadway running across the bridge on brackets each side of the rail-

way had a maximum capacity of six tons. I asked who had built the bridge and was shown a tablet with the name of a well-known British engineering firm. My experience has been that any permanent bridge built by British engineers will almost certainly have a safety factor of one hundred per cent, and I ordered the tanks to cross, one by one. (...) At last even the Chinese C-in-C agreed that all his men were over, and so 63 Brigade was withdrawn across the bridge. With a resounding thump it was blown at 23.59 hours on the 30th April, and its centre spans fell neatly into the river - a sad sight, and a signal that we had lost Burma.

(Slim, 1956)

Allied troops having been withdrawn from Mandalay, the Japanese marched into the city accompanied by BIA troops. Meanwhile up in Myitkyina Governor Dorman-Smith received an order from Winston Churchill to leave his post and, as Mandalay fell, he was among the refugees airlifted out to India. Dr. Ba Maw, who had escaped from Mogok Jail and established contact with the Japanese, was shocked to find Mandalay in ruins. His phrase 'nearly gone', however, may be an exaggeration:

A good part of the city had been wantonly bombed and burnt and sacked. The old Burmese palace with its priceless treasures and memories was nearly gone, most of the landmarks had similarly disappeared, and whole areas within the city were now a mass of charred posts and ruins.

(Ba Maw, 1968)

Not all of the Allied troops were withdrawing to India, however. Chiang Kai-shek had, on paper only, accepted the US General Stilwell as commander of Chinese forces in Burma despite having already appointed his own General Tu Lü Ming in that capacity. The consequent misunderstandings and misgivings did nothing to sweeten a man already known as 'Vinegar Joe Stilwell', commander also of the US army and air forces in the China-Burma theatre. Just before the Ava bridge was blown, Lashio had fallen and now there were Allied troops retreating towards China. At this stage US air power played a valuable role. The American Volunteer Group (AVG), a mercenary force under Major General Claire Chennault, were known as 'The Flying Tigers'; they flew on reconnaissance missions, helped to destroy abandoned supplies and communications before the enemy could reach them and also engaged in combat missions. Furthermore, now that the Burma Road was cut the Allied forces in China might never have recovered from this defeat without the high-altitude airlift of supplies from Assam to Chungking by the India-China Wing of the Tenth Air Force. Flying 'over the hump' was fraught with difficulties and dangers: in a single Himalayan storm later in the war nine planes were lost, thirty-one crew members being listed as killed or missing.

With the Chinese army broken, the occupation of Burma was virtually complete by the end of April. Freed from British administration and Indian exploitation, the Burmese public now had to contend not only with the often arrogant and racist behaviour of their liberators but also with the depredations of the BIA, which had been renamed the Burma National Army. Some BNA units were so violent that villagers and townsfolk would actually ask the local Japanese officer to step in, and such incidents caused some friction between the two forces.

In June 1942 the Imperial General Headquarters in Tokyo issued an order for the construction of a Burma-Thailand railway. A labour corps of 'young and able Burmans' was to be set up:

> 1. *Corps members shall not be treated as common laborers as in the past. The term* coolie *shall be strictly prohibited.*
> 2. *They shall not work in the same area as existing labor groups.*
>
> (Trager, 1971)

Presumably these existing groups were Allied prisoners of war to whom such provisions did not apply. Nevertheless, Burmese men working on the notorious 'Death Railway' were as harshly treated as if they were 'coolies', Burmese women were raped, monks abused, pagodas desecrated; and everywhere the Japanese practice of face-slapping was detested. Not only was there as yet no whiff of independence in the air, there were actually signs that a new imperialism was being established. In February 1943 the Military Administration announced that a number of Japanese language schools were to be set up: a hundred teachers were to be brought from Japan, the textbook illustrations would show 'the natural beauty of Japan and the superiority of Japanese culture' and two of the major curricular aims would be to enable Burmese students

> *to understand correctly Japanese culture and its national character, and to spread the ideas of the Greater East Asia Co-Prosperity Sphere in order to obtain better cooperation with the Japanese forces.*

In November, Dr. Ba Maw - along with delegates from Manchukuo, occupied China, the Philippines and Thailand - was summoned to Tokyo for a pep-talk in the course of which Prime Minister Tojo warned his own countrymen against adopting 'a superior and haughty attitude' towards the peoples of occupied countries. 'Of course,' he continued,

> *'we intuitively feel that we Japanese are superior. However, just because we are superior we are inviting eventual troubles if we should hold the attitude of looking down on others. Even if they are inferior to us, we must treat them with love and understanding.'*
>
> (Christian, 1945)

No doubt many a Japanese infantryman privately dissociated himself from this sort of overweening conceit and wished he were back home,

In the Ganges River flowing from the Himalayas
The sons of Japan are fishing for crocodiles.
In London Town swept clear of fog
The carp* are flying high.
The Tower of London and the Eiffel Tower
Are look-out towers for the Japanese police.
Berlin today and Moscow tomorrow,
Then snowy Siberia in the Emperor's hands.
In the city of Chicago, free from gangs,
Our grandsons raise monuments to the loyal dead.
When making water from the Great Wall of China,
A rainbow appears on the Gobi Desert.
If I should die, I shall gather the devils
At the River Styx and have a wrestling match.

The Burmese were becoming increasingly disillusioned by their new masters, who were not only stripping the country of useful equipment and commandeering livestock, but also leaving basic commodities undistributed. As tons of rice lay rotting on riverbanks and railway sidings down in the delta, many people in the districts of Mandalay and Sagaing were nearing starvation; and the cooking-oil produced in these areas was not reaching the delta. For the Burmese farmers the failure to export the 1942 rice harvest was serious; they were not to know how disastrous it was for the population of Bengal the following year, when a million and a half people died of starvation as a direct result. The Japanese did at length allow a declaration of 'independence' to take place in August 1943, Ba Maw calling himself *Adipadi* - a Pali word meaning 'chief', or as some saw it, 'fuhrer'. It is possible that Ba Maw saw himself as a potential 'saviour-king', for at the ceremony Court music was played and he was addressed in royal terms; when his consort received visitors, she was seated on a dais in the old Court manner; and when Ba Maw and his associates had devised a national flag (wide yellow and green horizontal stripes with a red rising sun in one corner) they echoed the traditional means of making a bid for the throne by having the prototype banner brought down from Mandalay to Rangoon along with some 'soil of victory' from Alaunghpaya's old capital, Shwebo. However, these procedures may simply have been intended as symbols of national sovereignty rather than as claims to personal power. The group also planned a consecration ceremony in which they would sign the flag in their own blood before raising it on a holy site; but the Japanese military authorities knew that the whole 'independence' process was a meaningless charade, and they refused to allow this ceremony to take place.

Tokyo's propaganda nevertheless proclaimed Burma's independence as well as Japan's impregnability against the expected counter-offensive. Here is Yasua Yamada, in a 'News on Parade' radio programme broadcast

---

* *Symbol of Japanese festival*

on 9 September:

> *The entire people of Burma have now come to realise that they are liberated from the British yoke, and have achieved complete independence through the assistance of their Asiatic neighbour, Japan.*
>
> *Anglo-American forces may meet in the near future some surprising reception committees ... on the borderline of India and Burma.*

The young naval Lieutenant who twenty years earlier had been so impressed by Japan's latest battleship was now Supreme Commander, Southeast Asia Command. In the same month, in a programme directed at the United States, it was Yamada's voice that issued the following warning:

> *The appointment of Lord Mountbatten may mean that the Allied forces in East Asia at last are mustering their strength to start something. Japan knows that very well. (...) She is more firmly entrenched in Burma now than she ever was. Her new ally, Burma, can furnish large numbers of fighting men with amazing zeal of oriental patriotism. Such being the spontaneous national psychology of the people, it is no exaggeration to say that every Burmese is now ready to fight against any and all invaders ....*

A British ground offensive was indeed being prepared in India, but the Japanese now had enemies closer to hand. The so-called declaration of independence had done nothing to mollify the Thakins, who by the end of the year were so antagonistic towards their 'liberators' that they were running a small but efficient resistance movement. By now, too, the first expedition of Orde Wingate's Chindits had provided the Allies with a great psychological boost by harrying and sabotaging the enemy deep inside Japanese-held territory. Later, the 5307th Provisional Regiment, an American 'long range penetration' group known as Merrill's Marauders, would be undertaking similar forays on the China-Burma front.

As Supreme Commander, Mountbatten considered that his priorities were to re-establish an India-China land link and to redouble the airlifted supplies to China 'over the hump'. In Assam, the British had already begun work on the Ledo Road and by February 1943 had reached the Burma border. After six months of rains, US Army engineers took over, carving the truck route through forest-covered slopes, swampy jungle and passes as high as 4,000 feet. The Ledo Road, one of Merrill's marauding men recalled long after the war had ended,

> *was well designed to separate the men from the supermen, as one toiling marcher put it. The construction of the road has been called the greatest engineering feat in the annals of the United States Army. From what we saw of it, we would not dispute the claim. (...) What we saw of the Ledo Road was a great, broad, raw gash through the forest dipping, rising, cutting back, going on days without end.....*

(Ogburn, 1960)

Just before the year ended, the leading bulldozer emerged on to the plain of Shingbwiyang. Behind it came more than fifty truckloads of Chinese troops ready for battle. Almost a year was to pass before the road reached Myitkyina, with its important railhead and nearby airfields, and not until January 1945 did the first convoy of trucks reach the Chinese border. Meanwhile, early in 1944, in an attempt both to disrupt the airlift and prevent or at least delay the expected invasion from India, the Japanese launched a determined offensive on the Indian border - the 'surprising reception committeee', perhaps, that Tokyo's radio propagandist had mentioned. There followed a three-month battle, the climax of which was the epic thirteen-day siege of Kohima in April. Here, in spite of being surrounded, heroic troops of the British Fourteenth Army were enabled to continue fighting when RAF planes dropped food and ammunition by parachute; and when the enemy gained possession of the water-supply, the planes even came in at low level to drop car inner-tubes filled with water. Lacking such support the equally heroic Japanese at last broke and fell back in exhaustion, having lost at least 53,000 men and many of their guns and vehicles.

It was the turning-point. Stilwell's Chinese Army took Myitkyina, the British crossed the Chindwin and the Japanese fell back to the Irrawaddy. Lieutenant-General Slim decided on a two-pronged thrust: his 19th 'Dagger' Division would cross the Irrawaddy north of Mandalay, leading the Japanese to expect an attack to come from that direction, while the rest of his forces would cross downstream and head straight for Meikhtila, an important communications and supply centre south of Mandalay. The northern prong was in the hands of Major-General 'Pete' Rees. When he took the ancient capital Shwebo in January 1945, the Ledo Road was at the point of completion. Crossing the Irrawaddy, Rees struck sharply south with a rapid advance column - aptly named 'Stiletto' - and sent a brigade to take Maymyo. Mandalay was of no great strategic importance, but for Rees it had prestige value; and the Japanese High command seems to have thought likewise for, as at Kohima, orders were given to fight to the last man. The Division holding the city was capable of nothing more than delaying the British advance; knowing the futility of it all, the new commander, Major-General Yamamoto Seiei nevertheless accepted the order and wrote a poem to distribute among his men in the hope that they would take courage from it.

Kimi ga tame	For their sovereign
Waga tsuwamono yo	Our warriors will fall
Tomo ni chire	Defending to the end
Tsutome hataseri	This town of Mandalay.
Mandaré no sato.	*(Allen, 1984)*

Held by Seiei's resolute troops, Mandalay Hill presented a formidable obstacle. From pre-war experience Lt.Col. Hamish Mackay knew the lie of the land, was sure that his Gurkhas could take the hill, and asked to be given the task. Rees consented and on that same night, the night of 10/11 March, Mackay's battalion attacked. At dawn the summit was taken. Lt.Col. John Masters, later to become a famous novelist, takes up the story:

We stood, so to speak, on top of Mandalay. We also stood, at much closer range, on top of a good many Japanese. The temples, cellars, and mysterious chambers covering Mandalay Hill were made of reinforced concrete. The 4th Gurkhas had taken the summit, and no Japanese was alive and visible; but scores of them were alive, invisible, in the subterranean chambers.

A gruesome campaign of extermination began, among the temples of one of the most sacred places of the Buddhist faith. Sikh machine-gunners sat all day on the flat roofs, their guns aimed down the hill on either side of the covered stairway. Every now and then a Japanese put out his head and fired a quick upward shot. A Sikh got a bullet through the brain five yards from me. Our engineers brought up beehive charges, blew holes through the concrete, poured in petrol, and fired a Verey light down the holes. Sullen explosions rocked the buildings and Japanese rolled out into the open, on fire, but firing. Our machine-gunners pressed their thumbpieces. The Japanese fell, burning. We blew in huge steel doors with PIATs (bazookas), rolled in kegs of petrol or oil, and set them on fire with tracer bullets. Our infantry fought into the tunnels behind a hail of grenades, and licking sheets of fire from the flame-throwers. Grimly, under the stench of burning bodies and the growing pall of decay, past the equally repellent Buddhist statuary (showing famine, pestilence, men eaten alive by vultures) the battalions fought their way down the ridge to the southern foot - to face the moat and the thirty-foot-thick walls of Fort Dufferin.

(Masters, 1961)

After three days of street fighting the town had been cleared, but still Seiei held the Fort. He would surely have admitted that some of the credit for his determined stand should go to King Mindon's engineers and labourers for, as Mountbatten's own official report admitted, the walls were almost indestructible:

On the 16th, Hurricanes and Thunderbolts (P-47), carrying 500-lb. bombs, made three attacks on the walls of the Fort; one of these strikes damaged the north wall, but did not breach it; even medium artillery fire at 500 yards range failed to break through the massive walls and their earth embankments.

(Mountbatten, 1951)

When a breach was at last made the infantry were driven back by heavy fire, and not until the 19th. was a real breakthrough made, when

three Mitchells (B-25), carrying 2,000-lb. bombs, made an experimental attack on the wall, using skip-bombing technique - and succeeded in blow-

ing a 15-foot hole. When, on the morning of the 20th, two squadrons of Thunderbolts successfully attacked the north wall and our troops entered the Fort, it was found that the enemy had decided to abandon it and had moved out under cover of darkness.

Seiei's men were obviously well-informed about the Fort, for they had escaped from the south side through a drain under the moat; but virtually all escapees and stragglers were captured in the next few days. Of Mindon's palace buildings almost nothing remained. Some damage had been inflicted by the Japanese air raids of 1942, and Seiei may have caused some in the act of destroying supplies; but it seems likely that most occurred during the Allied bombardment

One of the British officers killed during the battle for Mandalay was Captain the Marquis of Dufferin and Ava, who was serving with the Royal Horse Guards as a member of a Field Broadcasting Unit. His name, along with those of others who had no known grave, was later inscribed on a memorial in the Commonwealth War Graves cemetery near Mingaladon airport, Rangoon.

The Fourteenth Army now struck southwards in a bid to take Rangoon before the monsoon arrived. In the capital, Aung San's BNA units were preparing to march northwards out of the city as if in support of the Japanese, who were unaware that months earlier the BNA had secretly arranged to join forces with other political groups to form a national resistance group. Once out of Rangoon, units would take to the jungle and become a guerrilla force, the Anti-Fascist Organisation (AFO), an alliance coordinated by Aung San himself. One of the most important of its components was a Karen group. Largely because of a long-standing Christian tradition established by Judson and other Baptist missionaries, the Karen favoured the British and distrusted the Burmans; and they hated the Japanese. It was Karen resistance which was at this time engaging the Japanese in fierce jungle combat and thus helping to clear the way for the advancing Allies; and it was among the Karen that the British had long before established one of their underground intelligence organisations, known in Southeast Asia as Force 136. When the Japanese had sent out punitive expeditions against the Karen, Major Hugh Seagrim, head of this branch of Force 136, had surrendered in order to save them from further torture and execution. A few months earlier he and seven Karen had been tried and sentenced to death. Seagrim had stepped forward and said,

'Do not punish these Karens. It is only because of me that all these Karens have got into trouble. This war is between the Japanese and the British, not between the Japanese and the Karens. I beg you to release all these Karens here.'

(Morrison, 1947)

Nevertheless both Seagrim and his Karen friends had been executed in great secrecy in a corner of Kemmendine cemetery in Rangoon.

On 16 March 1945 a Defence Council of Japanese and Burmese officers met, and plans were made for Aung San's BNA to march out of Rangoon, ostensibly for the battlefront. The next day there was a military review of combat units, but their departure was postponed by the Japanese. Under Allied air attacks the impatient Burmese units became more uneasy. On 23 March some officer cadets marched out of thir Mingaladon quarters and did not return. Reports arrived that up in Mandalay and in Pegu, Burmese units had already made contact with the British army. Then, on 27 March, after attending a meeting of Japanese and Burmese officers at Shwedaung, Aung San disappeared and BNA units took up arms in earnest. Though he had yet to make personal contact with the British, he had been promised safe conduct by agents of Force 136. On 3 May, just before the monsoon broke, the advancing Allies entered Rangoon to find that the enemy had left some time before; and on the 15th Aung San met Slim to discuss his position and the future of Burma, making it clear that he was in charge of the Burmese nationalist movement and that he would be satisfied by nothing less than his country's independence.

Dr Ba Maw

CHAPTER 12
Free At Once
Burma, 1945 - 1948

> ... to walk into history is to be free at once,
> to be at large among people.
> > Elizabeth Bowen, *The House in Paris*, Part 2, Ch.8

> *'I will not die, even if they kill me.'*
> > Giovanni Guareschi, *The Little World of Don Camillo*

Although the whole country was virtually in Allied hands a fortnight after Aung San met Slim, remnants of Japanese units continued fighting week after week. Unaware of what was happening at home, some continued after the incineration of Hiroshima and Nagasaki and even after the Japanese Government's surrender on 14 August. Terence O'Brien was an Australian who had gone to Britain to enlist in the Royal Air Force and had later joined Wingate's venture, landing behind enemy lines with a Gurkha unit. He was now commanding an RAF group based at Jessore, near Calcutta. From here, Dakotas flew on missions to Burma and Thailand, and even as far as Indo-China and Malaya. With the Japanese continuing to fight in the southern hills the Karen could not afford to lay down their arms, and O'Brien was still dropping supplies to Force 136, some of whose men were trying to get the killing to stop. One of these, O'Brien recalls, was a man called Lewes.

I was dropping supplies to him three weeks after the surrender when, so he told me later, he heard sounds of fierce action in the distance. He waited until we had finished the drop, waved the usual goodbye, then went off to investigate the noisy action. A mile away he came to a wide valley where there was a huge area of paddy field with a wooded knoll in the centre. His Karen guerrillas were all firing at the knoll and their fire was being returned by a party of Japanese trapped there. 'It was such a silly business,' he said. 'The war was over. I had to stop them.'

He put up a white flag, approached the hill, and a Japanese lieutenant came out of the trees to meet him. They had no language in common but Lewes managed to make him understand they should await an interpreter, and he sent off one of the Karens to the village to fetch an Italian nun who spoke Japanese. The two of them waited in the paddy field, the Japanese accepting a cigarette, until she arrived. When she did, and told the lieutenant there had been a general surrender, he refused to believe such a story.

They were manifestly lying. The Japanese Imperial Army would never surrender. Lewes was trying to capture his group by deceit. So he went back to the knoll, and presently the shooting started again. Next morning when Lewes checked the knoll the Japanese had gone, leaving just one dead man under the trees.

(O'Brien, 1987)

Only a day or two after Aung San's meeting with Slim, the British government had issued a policy statement the terms of which were not acceptable to Burmese politicians impatient to see their country made whole and freed of imperialists. Its terms not only delayed the handover of power but also laid down that the administration of the Shan States and other hill areas would remain in the hands of the Governor. Now that Burma had been 'liberated' - the Burmans would have said 're-occupied' - British military matters gave way to a welter of Burmese political activity. The BNA, it had been agreed, would now be the Patriotic Burmese Forces, and in a victory parade the Anti-Fascist Organisation flag flew alongside the Union Jack. (Senior British officials may not have been aware that the label 'fascist' was often applied to the British as well as to the Japanese at this time.) At the end of June 1945 enlistment had begun for a regular Burmese army, in which Aung San was offered the rank of Brigadier; this he turned down, preferring to build up his own power-base in the form of the People's Volunteer Organisation (PVO), a network which was soon represented in every district and town. In August the AFO was renamed the Anti-Fascist People's Freedom League (AFPFL), whose representative Aung San demanded an end to military rule, the formation of a Cabinet, freedom to hold elections, and total independence. Within two months civil rule was restored and negotiations were under way for the formation of an Executive Council.

U Saw, the former Prime Minister whom the British had interned in Uganda because of his Japanese contacts, was now released. On arrival in Rangoon in January 1946, he set about challenging Aung San's bid for leadership, trying to outdo him in the concessions demanded from the British and acquiring arms for a private army of his own. The political scene was becoming more and more complex and confusing. Within the AFPFL, the Communist supporters split into two factions: a breakaway group called the 'Red Flags', who now formed a Communist Party, and a remaining group called the 'White Flags' who preferred to work towards a Communist state inside the existing arrangement. Another component group, the hitherto secret Revolutionary Party, became an open Socialist Party within the league. In an orchestrated war of nerves, there were demonstrations, processions, harangues, rumours. In June during a mass demonstration four people were killed and in the same month Governor Dorman-Smith resigned for reasons of health. In July the 'Red Flags' began a violent anti-government campaign and a Karen delegation went to London to lobby for 'Home Rule' for their people.

By now the demobilisation of British military personnel had begun.

Among the senior officers of HQ Burma Command due to sail home on the *Carthage* were the Deputy Assistant Adjutant General (DAAG) who was being replaced by one 'Tony' Younger. There was an Officers' Mess farewell party in their honour on 22 July.

After the buffet there was a song session to the accompaniment of flute and borrowed piano. Came a deathly hush, and the flute started solemnly playing 'Rule Britannia'. It was immediately indicated to the quietened guests that the Governor and Aung San were about to make their appearance. And so they did. The Governor, tall and dignified in a dinner jacket, entered, accompanied by a small and slight Aung San, in a red longyi with white shirt and white headkerchief. They got a tremendous cheer, particularly when it was perceived that the dignified Governor was Tony Younger and the somewhat cringing Aung San the departing DAAG. (...) The junior officers of Command HQ had a pretty shrewd idea that Aung San was destined to lead Burma.

(McEnery, 1990)

On 5 September Sir Hubert Rance arrived as the new Governor, and within a week the Police were on strike, to be joined by the postal, railway and oilfield workforces and students at school and university. Before the end of the month Rance had come to terms and formed a new Council so dominated by the AFPFL that Aung San was virtually Premier, and the strike was called off. Towards the end of the year Britain's new Prime Minister Clement Attlee invited a Burmese delegation to England to discuss the advance towards independence. Among those arriving with him in London on 9 January 1947 was the ambitious U Saw.

While these talks were going on the British novelist Compton Mackenzie was, at the invitation of the Indian Government, touring and reporting upon those battlefields where Indian troops had fought during the war. He had already followed the invasion route down from Kohima and Imphal and was now in the old capital, Shwebo. Here, he was lucky enough to see part of a traditional marionette show, or *yoke-the-pweh*, which evidently enthralled him:

The back cloth was painted in four panels - a throne room with a vermilion rug, a house and garden, a moat with a red wall and mountain in the distance, and a woodland lake.

The performance began with the entrance of a marionette dressed in rose du Barri who offered bananas to the nat *or spirit who presides over the play. Then a monkey did a dance while two parakeets flew round him all the time. A hermit followed this with a lively dance for his age, the only evidence of which was a stick held over his head. The hermit vanished. A white horse pranced about the stage. Then a golden throne was brought on and put against the throne-room panel, after which the Queen, with white face and silver dress, entered and sat on the step of the throne to hear the reports of three ministers and a provincial governor. The han-*

dling of these puppets was astonishing. They were utterly alive; their painted faces seemed to change expression to suit the dialogue.....

(Mackenzie, 1948)

Meanwhile, Aung San was getting what he wanted. The Attlee-Aung San Agreement signed on 27 January recognised his Cabinet as an interim Government, made provision for elections within four months and for the incorporation of the hill areas into Burma, and also promised to nominate Burma for full membership of the United Nations. On hearing this news U Saw repudiated the Agreement, perhaps hoping to outdo Aung San, though it is difficult to see what further concessions he could have gained. On the very day of the signing Mackenzie was driven in a jeep from Shwebo to Mandalay, via Sagaing, along rutted and corrugated roads.

About ten miles this side of Sagaing the road was transformed into Western avenue and we spun along without a bump. Before reaching Sagaing itself we stopped to turn aside and look at the great Pagoda which is different in design from any other. Legend says that the Queen who built it was approached to find out what design she wanted. Pulling open her dress she asked what better design than her own breast. Certainly the pagoda is exactly the shape of a woman's breast. (...) The precincts of the Pagoda are covered with temples, pagodas and shrines, many of them badly knocked about. In one a magnificent gilded Buddha surveys with sublime indifference the scrabble of names and crude drawings made by British and Indian troops.

Mandalay was battle-scarred but bustling, and Mackenzie noted that 6,000 Japanese prisoners were held there, 'none of whom had heard a word from Japan since the surrender'. The Arakan Pagoda had escaped damage, and so had 'Father Lafont's very ornate Gothic church, St.Joseph's, with as many saints in niches as at Chartres'. Of the old palace, however, nothing was left 'except the steps up and the two old guns on either side'. On Mandalay Hill, Mackenzie was shown the great concrete roof beneath which Seiei's troops had been cornered and overcome by the Second Royal Berkshire Regiment. This hall was now the audience room of the famous *hsayadaw* U Khanti, now eighty but still able to climb the hill two or three times a day. The venerable old man met Mackenzie's group, shook hands with everyone, ordered coffee for all, blessed them and then sat back as they sipped from their cups. Staying that night in Maymyo, Mackenzie was then driven down to Meikhtila, through 'a country rather like pictures of Mexico with several varieties of cactus and small dry shrubs'. There, a 360-mile Dakota flight awaited him: he was going to Myitkyina to see the Ledo Road, fourteen miles out of the town on a very bumpy road.

At last we came to the head of the famous road built through the jungle by 10,000 labourers, mostly Indians. It much resembled the other end of it at Ledo nearly 300 miles away. We drove along for about a mile... (...) The immense expenditure of time, toil and money on this road was a complete waste. It was finished in time for two or three convoys to pass down it with supplies for China, and that was the end of its utility. It will now revert to jungle....

Aung San had by now returned from London with an agreement that provided for early independence - "within a year", Aung San was promising. But his Burma consisted not only of the Burman heartland, the territory with which this book has been mainly concerned, but also of the surrounding hill areas inhabited by sizeable minority groups who had enjoyed a measure of autonomy under British rule; and some of these (the Karen, Arakanese, Shan and others) had shown no desire to become part of an independent Burma run by Burmans.

ᖇᖇᖇᖇᕽᕽᕽᕽ

On 4 February Mackenzie and his escorts left Meikhtila for Pagán. They passed through Kyaukpadaung, now a firmly Communist area, through a forest of rusty derricks in the Chauk oilfields and on to Pagán, which far surpassed Mackenzie's expectations:

The area of Pagan can hardly be less than four square miles, and this is covered in every direction the eye looks with huge pagodas, fragments of pagodas, and many temples as well. One dome at least is larger than the dome of St. Paul's and the architectural influence of India is everywhere apparent. The greatest number are now rose-red brick, the plaster (if they ever were plastered) having worn away in the course of over 800 years, but the dryness of the climate in this part of Burma has preserved the brick in the same way as I imagine Petra, the "rose-red city half as old as time", has been preserved. It would be rash after such a brief glimpse as mine, to claim peculiar beauty for any single one of what are reputed to number 5,000 pagodas in some form or other, but the Nagayon Temple in which General Crowther had his headquarters is certainly one of the most beautiful. (...) Not all the pagodas are rose-red brick. Some are white as wedding-cakes. One at least is covered with gold leaf. Others are plastered with stucco now a mellow grey. These abandoned pagodas and the abandoned derricks of the Chauk oilfields provide a strange, indeed a startling contrast.

A week later, up on the Shan plateau in Panglong, there was a meeting at which Aung San and some AFPFL members met representatives of the hill peoples in order to establish the relationship of these groups to 'Burma Proper'. The Chin, Kachin and Shan were fully represented; the Karen, because of their distrust of the Burmans, sent only observers. Three days later Aung San returned from Panglong. The representatives of the hill peoples had promised to cooperate with his interim government in return for various concessions and undertakings, including a measure of autonomy. The Karen held aloof, believing that their sterling services in the Allied cause would be rewarded by the British with the creation of an independent Karen state. The agreement signed on 12 February was fragile, but was nonetheless another remarkable achievement for Aung San.

Mackenzie meanwhile had taken a Dakota to Mingaladon airfield and in Rangoon that evening had taken part in a Brains Trust organised by The British Council. (The one question that had made the Burmese audience really sit up was "What is love?") On then to Thaton and Moulmein where, as the Panglong representatives were preparing to sign the Agreement, Mackenzie sat by the old Moulmein Pagoda puzzling over Kipling's poem.

I cannot find any satisfactory explanation of Kipling's mistake about the aspect of the Moulmein Pagoda. If one makes it the Burma girl who is looking eastward to the sea, it is still a geographical impossibility, and in any case the girl who was hoping a British soldier would come back to her would be gazing into the west. Presumably the road to Mandalay is the road of a troopship across the Bay of Bengal. I believe "eastward" was a misprint for "westward" and that having changed currency Kipling decided not to correct it in a later edition.

Mackenzie, about to leave Burma, had no doubt that the days of the British Empire were numbered; but in Moulmein he found what he thought might be a symbol of hope after all the scenes of death and destruction he had visited.

On a sidewalk near the quay at Moulmein there is a statue of Queen Victoria sitting under a stone canopy illuminated by a solitary electric lamp. This was erected in 1897 to commemorate the Diamond Jubilee. The Queen has her back to the quay and now surveys, sceptre and orb in hand, the ruins of bombed Government offices on the other side of the road. There is not a chip to be seen in statue, throne or canopy, and I would hazard a guess that the very bulb above her crown has survived the Japanese occupation. It was asking too much of the fancy not to attach to this statue a symbolic significance. In exactly fifty years the decline and fall of the British Empire has been consummated. Queen Victoria in Moulmein eyes the ruins. The great Commonwealth we optimists hope to see emerge from the ashes, if peace be granted to the world for another fifty years, will have little in common with the British Empire. Nevertheless, the foundation of that Commonwealth will be that old British Empire, and I found in that solitary lamp alight over the head of Queen Victoria an omen of its vitality in the future. This was sentimental self-indulgence, no doubt, but I venture to think that most people would have succumbed to it in the atmosphere of Moulmein.

෴෴෴෴

It was now necessary to hold elections for a constituent assembly. Although these were boycotted by the Communist and Karen organisations, they took place in an orderly manner and as expected the AFPFL won the vast majority of the seats allocated to 'Burma Proper', a proportionate number of seats having been reserved for the peoples in the 'Frontier Areas'. The Assembly duly met and Thakin Nu, who had intended to devote himself to literary pursuits henceforth, was not only persuaded by Aung San to re-enter the political arena but was then elected President of the Assembly. Work now began on the drafting of a new Constitution. For a week or so everything went well, and then tragedy struck. At 10.40 a.m. on 19 July 1947, four gunmen entered the Secretariat and machine-gunned those present at a Cabinet meeting, killing Aung San and six others. Within minutes Governor Rance had been informed. Learning that the Secretary of the Council and two others had survived unharmed, the Governor invited the two members Aung Zan Wai and Pyawbwe U Mya to come and see him at Government House; and having sent an armed escort for them he got ready a bottle of brandy and some glasses. The Governor himself takes up the story.

The two Councillors described the assault. U Mya said he was sitting to the left of the Chairman, almost at the end of the table. When the assassins entered, Aung San stood up and received the first burst of fire — U Shwe Baw, the Secretary of the Council, was sitting at the left of the table and made a dash for the side door which was locked on the inside. Shwe Baw unlocked the door, promptly fainted and fell, whereupon Pyawbwe U Mya who was close behind fell over the recumbent body. The double fall undoubtedly saved both men's lives. Aung Zan Wai, who was very short in stature and of slight build, took cover behind one of the thick legs of the table and was unscathed except for an almost indiscernible bullet graze on his shin. They thought that U Ba Gyan, who was slightly wounded, took similar cover. The incident was all over in a few seconds and they did not recognise the murderers, but both thought that at least two persons were involved. Both assassins fired, firstly at Aung San and then to the right of him and then to the left. Both Councillors were obviously very shaken and the brandy was most useful.

(Rance, in Tinker 1984)

Rance had also invited Thakin Nu, who since he was not a member of the Executive Council had not been at the ill-fated meeting. On arrival he was asked to take Aung San's place and, though it was clear that no-one could adequately replace the implacable patriot who had steered his country to the brink of independence, he agreed to stand in. Aung San's wide Burman following experienced a huge sense of loss, and it was hardly surprising that some began to blame the British authorities for failing to take sufficient precautions; but the sad truth was that Burman dissension and pride were largely to blame. Some weeks earlier two hundred Bren guns had been issued to a Police party led by a Burman officer. A little later a British officer reported a suspicion that there was an arms cache in the lake by U Saw's house, but the authorities placed no credence in this at the time. A fortnight later still, a party of Police to whom some Bren ammunition had been issued were found to be impostors, and it was now realised that the requisition documents for both the guns and the ammunition were forgeries. Four days before the assassination Aung San informed the Governor, whereupon Rance mentioned the rumour that U Saw had an arms cache. He suggested that the lake should be dragged but neither Aung San nor Thakin Nu took any action. Furthermore, the entrance to the council Chamber had been guarded by two armed British NCOs whenever the council was in session, but these had recently been removed because their presence offended Burmese pride. In their place stood one inexperienced Burman policeman.

A week after the assassination the ambitious U Saw and his henchmen were caught and imprisoned, but with much still to be done there was no time for recriminations and lengthy legal processes. (Not until well after Independence were the accused tried under Burmese law and executed. It was determined that the assassins' bullets had been fired from one Sten and three Thompson sub-machine guns, not from the stolen Bren guns.) Ten days after the tragedy the Assembly met again and agreed that Sao Shwe Thaik should take U Nu's place as President now that the latter was Premier. Within another two months a new Constitution had been drafted which U Nu described as 'Leftist' in that each citizen would benefit according to need and there would be no distinction between the governed and the governing classes. In mid-October the Union of Burma was formally recognised as an independent republic in a treaty signed in London by Clement Attlee and U Nu, and this was endorsed by the British parliament on 10 December. There were areas of Burma that by now were out of government control - where the 'White Flags', 'Red Flags', Arakanese separatists and others held sway - but the timetable was paramount. Though Aung San was dead, everything possible was being done to fulfil the promise he had made of independence within a year, and already his portrait could be seen in shops, offices and homes over much of the country. He had left fatherless three children, one of them called Suu Kyi, a little girl aged two. Forty years later she would, in very different circumstances, be taking up her father's struggle for a free Burma.

As the day grew nearer when the Union Jack would be hauled down in Rangoon, in John Company's old capital Calcutta arrangements were being made to dismantle a huge ornate wooden structure. Taken apart, it would consist of about four hundred and fifty pieces. These would be packed into sixty cases and sent off to Burma. They would not arrive until the beginning of February, unfortunately, but the workmen dismantling it would travel with the cases and carefully rebuild the structure in Rangoon.

∽∽∽∽∾∾∾∾

On 3 January 1948, HMS *Birmingham* lay at anchor on the Rangoon River holding an 'open day' and awaiting the moment of Independence. The Thakins had wanted this to fall on the sixth day of the month, but the astrologers had determined that the auspicious moment would be at precisely 04.20 on 4 January. The colourful, excited crowds left the ship, the hours of darkness passed and at the specified time the guns of HMS *Birmingham* fired a salvo to mark the end of British rule. This was the signal for the last rites to take place. The Governor, Sir Hubert Rance, later described the ceremony.

> *At Government House a farewell military parade took place at 6.30 a.m. I inspected the troops and then joined Sao Shwe Thaik, Sawbwa of Yawnghwe, the first President of Burma, on the saluting platform. A special flagpole had been erected to take the National Standards. The Union Jack was lowered and the Union of Burma flag hoisted, while at the same time the Governor's Personal Standard, at the top of Government House, was lowered.*
>
> *We then drove through the crowded streets of Rangoon to the Docks, where my wife and I ... prepared to embark in HMS* Birmingham.
>
> *Our last act on Burmese soil was to shake hands and say goodbye to U Nu and his cabinet. It was a heart-rending experience for my wife and myself.*
>
> (Rance, in Tinker 1984)

The lifeline that swept down from the roof of the world past the old Burman capitals - Shwebo, Mandalay, Amarapura, Sagaing, Ava, and greatest of them all Pagán - now also flowed into the Twante Canal and entered the Rangoon River where stood the last and least Burman capital of all. While the new President of the new republic was on his way to address the waiting Parliament, the current was assisting HMS *Birmingham* on her way downstream as she carried the last British Governor out of Burmese waters.

These were not quite the final rituals, however. A few weeks later, the workmen who had travelled from Calcutta with their crates managed to complete the assembly of the wooden structure that was to be presented to the nation in two days' time. At 10 a.m. on 12 March all was ready in the ballroom of Government House. Standing on the stage in front of closed curtains was Lord Mountbatten.

> *"Behind me", said Mountbatten, "is the Mandalay Hlutdaw throne, which was last used by King Theebaw of Burma when he visited the Hlutdaw in Mandalay, and which is a replica of the famous Lion throne of King Theebaw, which used to stand in the great Hall of Audience in the Palace of Mandalay - now, alas, burnt to the ground. I also bring with me another object of historical interest: a silver mat which, according to tradition, was woven by Queen Supayalat for King Theebaw." Thereupon, with the assistance of most of his staff, he opened the curtains, and a huge wooden structure over thirty feet high, about the size of a two-storied house, was revealed.*
>
> (Campbell-Johnson, 1951)

In another part of the city, more than six months after the tragic event, the assassins' victims were still lying in State in their glass coffins. The Burmese, having endured the ravages of the Chinese from the north, the British from the west and the Japanese from the east, would now have to deal with the enemy within.

Bogyoke Aung San

U Nu   *Orde Wingate*

Great Moulmein Pagoda

BIBLIOGRAPHY OF WORKS QUOTED

Allen, L. 1984. *Burma: the longest war.* London : J.M. Dent.

'A Loyal Burman'. 1910. *Selections of speeches by His Honour Sir Herbert Thirkell White, etc.* Rangoon : British Burma Press.

Anon. 1886. *Far off: or, Asia described. Part 1.* London: Hatchard.

Badger, G.P. 1863. *The travels of Ludovico di Varthema.* London: Hakluyt Society.

Ba Maw. 1968. *Breakthrough in Burma.* New Haven & London: Yale Univ. Press.

Battersby, H.F.P. 1906. *India under royal eyes.* London: George Allen.

Brown, R.G. 1926. *Burma as I saw it, etc.* London: Methuen.

Browne, H.A. 1907. *Reminiscences of the Court of Mandalay:etc.* Woking: Oriental Institute.

Campbell-Johnson, A. 1951. *Mission with Mountbatten.* London: Robert Hale.

Carletti, F. (trans.H.Weinstock) 1964. *My voyage around the world.* New York: Random House.

Christian, J.L. 1945. *Burma.* London: Collins.

Colbeck, J.A. 1892. *Letters from Mandalay:etc.* Knaresborough : Lowe.

Collis, M. 1953. *Into hidden Burma.* London: Faber & Faber.

Cox, H. 1821. (1971 reprint) *Journal of a residence in the Burmhan Empire.* Farnborough: Gregg International.

Crawfurd, J. 1834. (2nd. edn.) *Journal of an Embassy from the Governor-General of India to the Court of Ava in the year 1827: etc.* London: Henry Colburn.

Crick, B. 1980. *George Orwell: a life.* London: Secker & Warburg.

Crosthwaite, Sir C. 1912. *The pacification of Burma.* London: Edward Arnold.

Curle, R. 1923. *Into the east: notes on Burma and Malaya.* London: Macmillan.

Dalrymple, A. 1793. *Oriental repository.* London: Chapman.

Dautremer, J. 1913. (trans. Sir J.G.Scott) *Burma under British rule.* London & Leipsic: T. Fisher Unwin.

Desai, W.S. 1939. *History of the British Residency in Burma,1820-1840.* Rangoon: Univ. of Rangoon.

Draper, A. 1987. *Dawns like thunder.* London: Leo Cooper.

Duroiselle, C. 1925. *Guide to the Mandalay Palace.* Rangoon: Government Printing.

Edmonds, P. 1924. *Peacocks and pagodas.* London: George Routledge.

Ellis, B. 1889. *An English girl's first impressions of Burmah.* Wigan: R. Platt, and London: Simpkin, Marshall, Hamilton, Kent.

Fisher, A.H. 1911. *Through India and Burmah with pen and brush.* London: T. Werner Laurie.

In a Burmese Monastery

The Ava Bridge

Foucar, E.C.V. 1956. *I lived in Burma.* London: Dennis Dobson.

Fraser, J.F. 1899. *Round the world on a wheel.* London: Macdonald.

Fraser, J.N. 1911. *In foreign lands: etc.* London: John Ouseley.

Frazer, J.G. 1922 (abridged, 1987). *The golden bough.* London: Macmillan.

Geary, G. 1886. *Burma after the conquest, etc.* Bombay: Thacker, and London: Sampson, Low, Marston, Searle & Revington.

Gouger, H. 1862. (2nd edn.) *A personal narrative of two years' imprisonment in Burmah.* London: John Murray.

Grant, J. n.d. 1879? *Cassell's illustrated history of India.* London, Paris & New York: Cassell, Petter, Galpin.

Hall, D.G.E. 1928. *Early English intercourse with Burma, 1587-1743.* London: Longmans, Green.

—— (ed.) 1955. *Michael Symes' journal of his second embassy to the Court of Ava in 1802.*
London: George Allen & Unwin.

—— 1974. *Henry Burney: a political biography.* London: Oxford Univ. Press.

Hamilton, A. 1727. (ed. Sir Wm.Foster,1930) *A new account of the East Indies, Vol.II.* London: The Argonaut Press.

Hart, Mrs.E. 1897. *Picturesque Burma past and present.* London: J.M.Dent.

Harvey, G.E. 1925. *History of Burma: etc.* London: Longmans, Green.

—— 1946. *British rule in Burma: 1824-1942.* London: Faber & Faber.

Huxley, A. 1926. *Jesting Pilate: the diary of a journey.* London: Chatto & Windus.

Kelly, R.T. 1905. *Burma.* London: A. & C. Black.

Lunt, J. 1986. *'A hell of a licking': the retreat from Burma, 1941-2.* London: Collins.

Mackenzie, C. 1948. *All over the place.* London: Chatto & Windus.

Major, R.H. 1857. *India in the fifteenth century.* London: Hakluyt Society.

Manrique, Padre F.S. 1649. *Itinerario de las Missiones,etc.Vol.II.* Rome: Francisco Caballo. Translated by Lt. Col.C.E. Luard, assisted by Father H. Hosten, S.J.,1927. Oxford: Hakluyt Society.

Marks, Dr. J.E. 1917. *Forty years in Burma.* London: Hutchinson.

Masters, J. 1961. *The road past Mandalay.* London: Michael Joseph.

Maugham, W.S. 1930. *The gentleman in the parlour.* London: Heinemann.

McCrae, A. and Prentice, A. 1978. *Irrawaddy Flotilla.* Paisley, Scotland: James Paton.

McEnery, J.H. 1990. *Epilogue in Burma: 1945-48.* Tunbridge Wells: Spellmount.

Military Proceedings, Burmah 1885-86 (2768). Military Department, Government of India.

Mills, C.P. 1988. *A strange war: etc.* Gloucester: Alan Sutton.

Mitton, G.E. 1936. *Scott of the Shan hills.* London: John Murray.

Morris, D. 1915/16. *Personal diary, India Office Records: Mss. Eur. c. 3991/2.*

Morrison, I. 1947. *Grandfather Longlegs.* London: Faber & Faber.

Mountbatten of Burma, The Earl. 1951. *Report to the Combined Chiefs of Staff by the Supreme Allied Commander South-East Asia: 1943-1945.* London: HMSO.

Murdoch, W.G.B. 1908. *From Edinburgh to India and Burmah.* London: George Routledge & Sons.

Norwich, Viscount. 1953. *Old men forget.* London: Rupert Hart-Davis.

O'Brien, T. 1987. *The moonlight war.* London: Collins.

O'Connor, V.C.S. 1907. *Mandalay and other cities of the past in Burma.* London: Hutchinson.

Ogburn, C. 1960. *The Marauders.* London: Hodder & Stoughton.

Orwell, G. 1936. 'Shooting an elephant'. *New Writing*, No. 2, London.

Parliamentary Blue Book, 1852. Papers relating to hostilities with Burmah. (C-1490)

——— 1886. *Correspondence relating to Burmah. (C-4614)*

Phillips, Sir P.(ed.) n.d. 1922? *The Prince of Wales' eastern book.* London: Hodder & Stoughton.

Purchas, S. (ed.) 1625, repr. 1905-7. *Hakluytus posthumus, or Purchas his pilgrimes.* Glasgow: Maclehose.

Raven-Hart, Maj. R. 1939. *Canoe to Mandalay.* London: Frederick Muller.

Sangermano, Father V. (trans. W.Tandy) 1893. *A description of the Burmese Empire.* Westminster: Archibald Constable.

Scott, J.G. 1886. *Burma as it was, as it is, and as it will be.* London: George Redway.

——— 1924. *Burma from the earliest times to the present day.* London: T. Fisher Unwin.

'Shway Yoe' (J.G.Scott) 1882. *The Burman: his life and notions.* London: Macmillan.

Sladen, Col. E.B. 1885a. *Diary. (India Office Records: Mss. Eur. E290/65)*

——— 1885b. *Report to H.M. Durand, dated 16 December. (India Office Records: L/MIL/17/19/32/1)*

Slim, Field-Marshal Sir W. 1956. *Defeat into victory.* London: Cassell.

Snodgrass, Maj. J.J. 1827. *Narrative of the Burmese War: etc.* London: John Murray.

Stewart, A.T.Q. 1972. *The pagoda war.* London: Faber & Faber.

Stilwell, J.W. (ed.T.H.White) 1949. *The Stilwell papers.* London: Macdonald.

Symes, Lt.Col. M. 1800. *An account of an embassy to the Kingdom of Ava in the year 1795: etc.* Edinburgh: Constable.

Tahmankar, D.V. 1956. *Lokamanya Tilak.* London: John Murray.

Tavernier, E.T. 1684. 'Collections of travels,&c.' In J. Pinkerton.1808-14. *A general collection of the best and most interesting Voyages and Travels in all parts of the world.* London: Longmans.

Thakin Nu. 1954. *Burma under the Japanese.* London: Macmillan.

Tinker, H. (ed.) 1983-84. *Burma: the struggle for independence, 1944-48.* London: HMSO.

Trager, F.N. (ed.) 1971. *Burma: Japanese military administration, selected documents, 1941-1945.* Philadelphia: Univ. of Pennsylvania Press.

Treves, Sir F. 1905. *The other side of the lantern.* London: Cassell.

Vibart, H.M. 1914. *The life of Sir Harry N.D. Prendergast: etc.* London: Eveleigh Nash.

Vincent, F. 1873. *The land of the white elephant: etc.* London: Sampson, Low, Marston, Low & Searle.

Warren, C.V. 1937. *Burmese interlude.* London: Skeffington.

White, G.S. 1885. *Letter to Jane White, 5 December. (India Office Records: Eur.F. 108)*

White, Sir H.T. 1913. *A civil servant in Burma.* London: Edward Arnold.

Winston, W.R. 1892. *Four years in Upper Burma.* London: C.H. Kelly.

Woodman, D. 1962. *The making of Burma.* London: The Cresset Press.

Yule, H. 1858. *A narrative of the mission sent by the Governor-General of India to the Court of Ava in 1855: etc.* London: Smith Elder.

OTHER WORKS CONSULTED

Bird, G.W. 1897. *Wanderings in Burma.* London: Simpkin, Marshall, Hamilton, Kent; and Bournemouth: F.J. Bright.
Bruce, G. 1973. *The Burma wars, 1824-1886.* London: Hart-Davis, MacGibbon.
Butwell, R. 1963. *U Nu of Burma.* Stanford, Cal.: Stanford Univ. Press.

Christian, J.L. 1945. *Burma and the Japanese invader.* Bombay: Thacker.
Collis, M. n.d. 1943? *The Burmese scene.* Bognor Regis and London: John Crowther.
—— 1956. *Last and first in Burma.* London: Faber & Faber.
—— 1970. *The journey up.* London: Faber & Faber.

Donnison, F.S.V. 1953. *Public administration in Burma.* London and New York: Royal Institute of International Affairs.

Fergusson, B. 1945. *Beyond the Chindwin.* London: Collins.
Ferrars, Max and Bertha, 1900. *Burma.* London: Sampson, Low, Marston & Co.
Fytche, Lt.Gen. A. 1878. *Burma past and present, etc.* London: Kegan Paul.

Hall, D.G.E. 1964. *A history of South-East Asia.* (2nd.edn.) London: Macmillan.
Harmer, E.G. n.d. 1900? *The story of Burma.* London: Horace Marshall.
Hunt, G. 1967. *The forgotten land.* London: Geoffrey Bles.

Koenig, W. 1972. *Over the hump: airlift to China.* London: Pan Books.

Lach, D.F. 1968. *Southeast Asia in the eyes of Europe: the sixteenth century.* Chicago: Univ. of Chicago Press.
Lebra, J. 1977. *Japanese-trained armies in Southeast Asia.* New York: Columbia Univ. Press.
Libermann, V.B. 1984. *Burmese administrative cycles.* Princeton, N.J: Princeton Univ. Press.
Luce, G.H. 1985. *Phases of pre-Pagan Burma.* Oxford: Oxford Univ. Press.
Lu Pe Win. 1960. *Historic sites and monuments of Mandalay and environs.* Rangoon: UBSCP.

Ma Mya Sein. 1944. *Burma.* London: Oxford Univ. Press.
Mason, F. 1860. *Burma, its people and natural productions: etc.* London: Trübner.
Morgan, G. 1971. *Ney Elias.* London: George Allen & Unwin.

Nisbet, J. 1901. *Burma under British rule - and before.* Westminster: Archibald Constable.

O'Connor, V.C.S. 1928 (2nd. edn.) *The silken east.* London: Hutchinson.

Parks, G.B. (ed.) 1927. *The book of Ser Marco Polo.* New York: Macmillan.

Phayre, Lt. Gen. Sir A. 1883. (repr. 1969) *History of Burma.* New York: Kelley.
Pointon, A.C. 1964. *The Bombay Burmah Trading Corporation Limited, 1863-1963.* Southampton: The Millbrook Press.

Searle, H.F. 1924. *Initial report on the second revision settlement in the Mandalay district.* Rangoon: Burma Settlement Department.
Stuart, J. 1910. (2nd. edn.) *Burma through the centuries.* London: Kegan Paul, Trench, Trubner.

Than Tun (ed.) 1983-90. *The royal orders of Burma, A.D. 1598-1885.* Kyoto: Center for Southeast Asian Studies, Kyoto University
Tinker, H. 1961. (3rd. edn.) *The Union of Burma.* London: Oxford Univ. Press/ Royal Institute for International Affairs.
―――― 1966. *South Asia: a short history.* London: Pall Mall Press.
Trager, H.G. 1966. *Burma through alien eyes.* Bombay: Asia Publishing House.
Trotman, Rev. F.E. 1917. *Burma: a short study of its people and religion.* Westminster: Society for the Propagation of the Gospel.

Wayland, F.1853. *A memoir of the life and labours of the Rev. Adoniram Judson, D.D.* London: James Nisbet.
Windsor, The Duke of. 1951. *A King's story.* New York: Putnam.

Ziegler, P. 1985. *Mountbatten: the official biography.* London: Guild Publishing.

INDEX

A

A-htu-ma-shi Kyaung: see Incomparable Pagoda.

Akyab (Sittwe): 154

Alaung-hpaya: birth and youth, 23; takes Pegú, 24; takes Lower Burma, attacks Ayuthaya, dies, 27.

Alexander, Lt-Gen Hon Sir Harold: 154, 156.

Alison, Roger: 18.

Alves, Capt. Walter: 27-28.

Amarapura: xv,xvi; founded by Bodaw-hpaya, 31; descr. of his palace,35-36; abandoned by Bagyidaw, 43.

America, United States of: 73, 81; enters WWII, 152.

American forces: 'The Flying Tigers' (American Volunteer Group) and Tenth Air Force, 157 ; 'Merrill's Marauders', 160 .

Anauk-hpet-lun, King: 12, 14.

Anáw-rahta, King: 20, 72.

Andaman islanders: xiii.

Angkor Wat: 33.

Animals: ants (*kha-chin-nee*), pythons, rhinoceros, 2 ; crocodiles, 7; rats , 11; tigers, wild elephants, rhinoceroses, 14-15; tamed elephants, 17, 51-52. See also White Elephants.

Arakan: xiv, xv; ~ Pagoda, see Mahamuni.

Arms: as gifts, 24, 26 ; Enfield rifle, 71; torpedoes in Mandalay, 89 ; sent through Burma to China, 149.

Assam: xiv, 42, 46, 47, 157, 160.

Attlee, Clement PM: 167 ; ~-Aung San Agreement, 168.

Aung San: as student, 145 ; as head of Thakin group, 150; attends Indian National Congress, goes to Japan for training, recruits army in Rangoon and Bangkok, 151 ; re-enters Burma, 152; contacts British Army, 164; as head of AFPFL, 166 ; goes to London, 167-8; is assassinated, 171 .

Aung San Suu Kyi: 172.

Austen, Jane: 55 ; Admiral Charles ~, 62 .

Ava city: established xv, xvi ; early visitors, 1, 3, 16, 17; capital in 1634, 14; destroyed by Binnya-dala,21; capital again, 43; descr. in 1826, 48-50, 52; in decay, 68-9 ; ~ Bridge, 156-7 .

Ayuthaya: 11, 27, 28, 33.

B

Ba-gyi-daw: becomes king, 42; character, 45, 51-2; becomes insane, 56, 59; deposed, 60.

Balbi, Gasparo: 5, 9.

Ba Maw, Dr: 144, 149-151, 157, 158, 159.

Bandula, Maha: 46, 49.

Bangkok: 55, 56, 152.

Baker, Capt. George: 23, 24.

Bassein River: 27.

Bayin-naung, King: 5, 8.

Colbeck, Rev. John: 87, 89.

Collis, Maurice: 133-4, 136, 140-141.

Cook, Thomas: 109, 130.

di Conti, Nicolo: 1-3, 14, 16.

Cooper, Duff (later Earl of Norwich), and Diana ~: 135.

Cox, Capt. Hiram: 37-43; death of: 39; 55, 67, 125.

Cox's Bazar: 39.

Crawfurd, John: 47-55; 60, 67, 76.

Crosthwaite, Charles: 107-8.

Culture-clash: Burmese view, 57; Christian views, 85; bribes, 13, 17, 20, 34; 'unshoeing' 26, 35, 45, 56, 64, 82 ; 'The Shoe Question', 133-6; umbrellas, 124-5; government, 139,40; Japanese culture, 158.

    See also Education.

Curzon, Lord: 117.

D

Dagon: 4, 23; see also Yangon, Rangoon.

Dalhousie, Lord, Governor-General: 60, 61, 62, 64, 66, 69.

Dalla: 6.

Danu-byu: 46, 49.

Diseases: cholera 54; smallpox, 90, 91; plague, 124; leprosy, 123-4 .

Dorman-Smith, Sir Reginald: 154, 156, 157, 166.

Dress: of Burmese women, 19, 110, 122 ;of Bodawhpaya, 36; of British officers, 76; of Mindon's Queen, 65-6 . See also Culture-clash.

Dufferin: Lord ~, 101, 117 ; Fort ~, 108, 119, 126, 129, 162 ; troopship HMS ~ ,137; Capt. the Marquis of ~ and Ava, 163.

Dyarchy: 132-3, 139.

E

Earthquakes: 28, 44, 67, 68, 111.

East India Company, English ~ ('John Company'):16, 23, 26, 47, 73, 134.

Education: 124, 131-2.

Edward: King ~ VII,117, 119; ~ Prince of Wales, 137.

F

Famines: Pegú, 11; Bengal, 159.

Fedrici, Cesare ('Caesar Fredericke'): 5, 11.

Ferry, M. Jules, French Premier: 94.

Fitch, Ralph: 3, 9-12.

Fleetwood, Edward: 17-18.

Forrest, Henry: 12, 14.

French, influence in Burma: 18, 20, 23, 39, 83, 94, 103; ~ Indo-China: 89, 93.

G

Gandhi, Mahatma: 126, 132, 133, 151.

George III, King: 34 ; George, Prince of Wales: 119-120. .

Godwin, Lt-Gen. Henry: 62.

L

Lambert, Cdre. George: 60-62.

Lane, Mr Charles: 56.

Laos: xiii, 3, 5, 89.

Lashio: 149, 156, 157.

Ledo Road: 160, 161, 168-9.

Leslie, James: 17.

Lester, Ensign Robert: 26.

Let-ma-yun prison: 46.

M

Macao: 6.

MacLeod, Capt. William: 60.

Maghs: 15.

Maha-muni image: 15, 35; capture of, 33 ; ~ Pagoda, 53, 121-3, 168; brass cannon, 33,36-7; Khmer bronzes, 33, 53.

Mali Kha, River: xiii.

Manchukuo: 149, 158.

Mandalay: city site chosen, 69; constructed, 71-3;taken by British force, 97; looted, 98; bombed by Japanese, 154; evacuated, 156; bombed by British and captured, 162-3; as seen by visitors, 104-6, 117, 118-9,142, 144, 146, 168; ~ Hill, 69, 90, 161-2, 168.

Manipur: 27, 28, 29,42, 47, 156.

Manrique, Sebastião: 14-15.

Margary, Augustus: 82, 88.

Marryat, Capt. Frederick: 46.

Martaban: xv, 5, 17, 152; Gulf of ~,xiii.

Massacres: in Pegú, 12; on Negrais, 27; by Naung-daw-gyi in Ava, 28; of kinsmen by Bodawhpaya, 29; by Thibaw,87-8; of prisoners by Thibaw, 94; Amritsar ~ , 133.

Masters, John: 162.

Maugham, W. Somerset: 142, 176.

Maung Maung, King: 29.

May, Col. James: 107.

May-myo: 107, 112, 113-5, 127,130,154,155-6, 161, 168.

Meik-htila: 126, 168, 169.

Mekkara Prince: 56-7.

Mekong River (Lancang Jiang): xiii, 82.

Minami, Col (Suzuki Keiji):150, 152; *Minami Kikan*, 151.

Mindon, King: takes throne 64; gives audience to Phayre's mission, 65-7; Court rebellion against, 77; introduces telegraphy, 80; holds Fifth Buddhist Synod, 80; approaches USA, 82; dies, 84.

Minhla: 96.

Mingun: xvi; pagoda, 'palace', *chinthe*, 38-9; bell, 111.

Minre-kyaw-din, King: 17.

Missionaries and ministers: xiv, 41, 85; W.R.Winston, 105-6; Dr Adoniram Judson, 46, 55,57, 60, 163;

Pinya: xv.

Political organisations in Burma: Young Men's Buddhist Association (YMBA), 121, 124, 132, 136,; All Burma Buddhist Ass'n, 134; Do-Bama Soc/ Asiayone, All Burma Youth League, Thakin Movement, 144-5; Thakin Party, 149-150; Burma Revolutionary Party, 151; Freedom Bloc, ; Anti-Fascist Organisation/ Anti-Fascist People's Freedom League (AFO/AFPFL), 163, 166, 167, 169; Communist Parties, 166, 172; Revolutionary/Socialist Party, People's Voluntary Organisation (PVO), 166.

Polo, Marco: 1, 4, 22.

Prendergast, Maj-Gen. Sir Harry,VC: 95-8; 101, 105, 113.

Pyé (Prome): xiv, xv, 23, 26, 64.

Pyin-u-lwin: see Maymyo.

R

Races of Burma: xiii-xiv.

Railways: Rangoon-Toungoo-Mandalay, 108,111,113 ; Mu Valley State ~, 120; to Maymyo, 127; 'Death ~', 158.

Ramu: 14, 46.

Rance, Maj-Gen Sir Hubert: arrives as Governor, 167; 171-2; leaves Burma, 173.

Rangoon: v, 10, 69, 77, 78, 83, 88, 90, 94, 95, 100, 101 103, 112, 113, 126, 131, 132, 135, 136, 137, 139, 140, 141, 143, 144, 145, 149, 150, 151, 152, 153, 154, 159, 163, 164, 166, 170, 172, 173. See also Yangon.

Rees, Maj-Gen 'Pete': 161.

Refugees: from Pegú to Siam, 11; from Arakan to Bengal, 34, 39, 41-2; from Burma in WWII, 152-5.

Rogers, Mr ('Yadza'): 40-1, 44, 46, 47, 85.

S

Sacrifices, foundation: 72-3, 75, 93.

Sagaing: xv, xvi, 27, 29, 37, 53, 67, 94, 96, 109, 120-1, 140, 156, 159, 168, 173.

Salween (Nu Jiang), River: xiii, xv, 82, 152.

Samuel, Thomas: 12.

Sangermano, Padre Vincentius: 10, 29-31.

di Santo Stefano, Hieronimo: 4.

Sao Shwe Thaik, President: 172-3. .

'Saviour kings': 140-1,143-4, 159.

Saw, U: 166-8, 171; captured and executed, 172 .

Scott, James George ("Shway Yoe"): 73, 90-93, 98, 99-100, 125.

Seiei, Maj-Gen Yamamoto: 161-3, 168.

Shan: xiv, xv, 14, 20, 23, 103, 107, 119, 122, 127, 131, 142, 166, 169.

Shaw, Mr R B, Resident in Mandalay: 83, 87-9.

Shin-saw-bu, Queen: 4.

Shoe Question and 'unshoeing': see Culture-clash.

Shu Maung ('Ne Win'): 152.

Tibao, Capt.: 14-15.
Tilak, Bal Gangadhar ('Lokamanya'): 125-6.
Tojo, Prime Minister of Japan: 158.
Tokyo: 149, 150, 151, official Burmese visit, 158, 159, 161.
Toungoo: xv, 5, 11, 94, 108.
Trade: 5, 7-9, 12, 16, 23-4, 27, 31, 34, 37, 46, 59, 77, 82, 90, 94-5, 120-1; saltpetre and lac,18, 20; rubies, 18; Manchester cottons, 43, 52.
Trams: 109, 122, 124, 129.
Tripitaka: 80.
Turkish 'ambassador': 83.

V

di Varthema, Ludovico: 5, 175.
Victoria, Queen: 73, 76, 78, 83, 92, 95; statue of, 170; 1872 Burmese mission to, 82 .

W

Wars, English: with France and Spain, 18, 20; in Afghanistan and S. Africa, 89, 90; with Burma: First ~, 46-7; Second ~ 61-4; Third ~,95-6. Indian Mutiny, 71. Russo-Japanese ~, 149. World Wars: First ~ , 129-132; Second ~, 151-166.
Wavell, Gen Sir Archibald: 153.
Wellesley, Marquis, Governor-General of Bengal: 40.
White, Col. George, VC: 96.
White, Sir H.T: 100, 105, 124, 127.
White elephants: 7-8, 10, 28, 73, 78, 99, 105.
Williams, Dr. Clement: 77.
Wingate, Maj-Gen Orde: 160, 165.
Wood, Ensign Thomas: 35.

Y

Yandabo: 51; Treaty of, 47, 55, 60.
Yangon: v, 23, 24, 27, 28, 29, 34, 37, 39, 40, 41, 43, 46, 59, 60, 61, 62,69. See also Dagon, Rangoon.
Yangtze (Jinsha Jiang), River: xiii.
Yenan-gyaung: 154.
Yule, Capt (Col) Henry: 64-7, 109.
Yunnan: xiii, xiv, 82, 149, 154. See also China.